Raising the standard for collaboration

Developing effective collaborative relationships through the implementation of BS 11000 to enhance business performance

Raising the standard for collaboration

Developing effective collaborative relationships through the implementation of BS 11000 to enhance business performance

By David E Hawkins

bsi.

First published in the UK in 2013

By
BSI Standards Limited
389 Chiswick High Road
London W4 4AL

©The British Standards Institution 2013

All rights reserved. Except as permitted under the Copyright, Designs and Patents Act 1988, no part of this publication may be reproduced, stored in a retrieval system or transmitted in any form or by any means – electronic, photocopying, recording or otherwise – without prior permission in writing from the publisher.

Whilst every care has been taken in developing and compiling this publication, BSI accepts no liability for any loss or damage caused, arising directly or indirectly in connection with reliance on its contents except to the extent that such liability may not be excluded in law.

While every effort has been made to trace all copyright holders, anyone claiming copyright should get in touch with the BSI at the above address.

BSI has no responsibility for the persistence or accuracy of URLs for external or third-party internet websites referred to in this book, and does not guarantee that any content on such websites is, or will remain, accurate or appropriate.

Typeset in Great Britain by Letterpart Limited

Printed in Great Britain by Berforts Group, www.berforts.co.uk

British Library Cataloguing in Publication Data

A catalogue record for this book is available from the British Library

ISBN 978-0-580-78737-9

Contents

About the author   vii
Acknowledgements   ix
Preface   x
Introduction   xii

PART 1: Why?   1
Chapter 1 – The importance of relationships   1
Chapter 2 – Collaboration   9
Chapter 3 – Relationship risk and opportunity   19
Chapter 4 – Culture   31
Chapter 5 – Creating trust   43
Chapter 6 – Collaborative leadership   57
Chapter 7 – Positioning relationships   69

PART 2: How?   81
Chapter 8 – Background and introduction to BS 11000   81
Chapter 9 – Awareness   95
Chapter 10 – Knowledge   103
Chapter 11 – Internal assessment   109
Chapter 12 – Partner selection   117
Chapter 13 – Working together   123
Chapter 14 – Value creation   133
Chapter 15 – Staying together   143
Chapter 16 – Exit strategy   151
Chapter 17 – Implementing collaborative certification programmes   159

PART 3: Where?   171
Chapter 18 – Customer engagement   171
Chapter 19 – Supply chain   181
Chapter 20 – Outsourcing   191
Chapter 21 – Collaborative contracting   203
Chapter 22 – Alliance modelling   219
Chapter 23 – Collaborative maturity   233
Chapter 24 – Mergers and acquisitions   245
Chapter 25 – SME collaborative clusters   255
Chapter 26 – Collaborating for sustainability   263
Chapter 27 – Third sector   277
Chapter 28 – Future of collaboration   283

Further information 286
Index 287

About the author

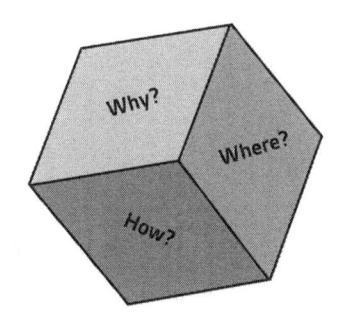

David E Hawkins FCIPS

David has an extensive career in projects and procurement within the construction industry. For over 40 years he has been associated with the development and implementation of major projects in many parts of the world, which has provided an insight into the many organizational and cultural challenges that projects can generate. Over the past decade he has been an active promoter of collaboration and partnering concepts, together with the development of extended enterprises through the building of alliances.

As a strategic thinker he has deployed these approaches to support from manufacturing to outsourcing programmes, capitalizing on the opportunities within project operations to exploit global sourcing. Building on these experiences he has helped a number of major organizations to implement change management programmes in different industrial arenas including chemical processing, oil and gas, power generation and mining and minerals processing.

He was the architect and author of the CRAFT collaborative methodology and technical author of the British Standards Institution (BSI) PAS 11000 framework, the world's first collaborative business relationship standard. He was the driving force behind the creation of BS 11000-1: 2010 *Collaborative business relationships – Part 1: A framework specification*, and chairman of the BSI committee who developed the standard. In 2009 he was acknowledged as one of the world's top 100 thought leaders on corporate social responsibility (CSR). As an established author he has several publications to his credit including:

About the author

- *Sun Tzu and the Project Battleground: Creating Project Strategy using the Art of War*, Palgrave Macmillan, 2004;
- *The Bending Moment: Energising Corporate Strategy*, Palgrave Macmillan, 2005;
- *Corporate Social Responsibility: Balancing Tomorrow's Sustainability with Today's Profitability*, Palgrave Macmillan, 2006.

Acknowledgements

The author would like to acknowledge and extend appreciation to those colleagues, employers, customers and suppliers who throughout his career have provided input to the learning experience and provided many challenges, which have contributed to the thinking behind this book. A special thanks to the Institute for Collaborative Working (ICW) (formerly PSL) Executive Network for providing a broad range of inputs to the development of CRAFT, which was the foundation for BS 11000-1: 2010. Thanks also to fellow committee members who brought their expertise and worked hard to develop the standard alongside the BSI standards team. And a special thanks to those organizations who provided case studies which add great practical insight to the value of the standard.

Preface

The benefits of a collaborative standard

There can be few executives or senior managers in the global business community who would not recognize the importance of relationships as a key ingredient for success, whether these relationships are with consumers, business customers, key suppliers, business partners or internally across large organizations. These relationships are a critical success factor but also a major source of risk, where the benefits and challenges of interdependency need to be recognized to underpin sustainable business. The concept of working in collaboration is recognized for its contribution to both the effectiveness and efficiency of these relationships.

If you ask any group of business people how efficient they believe their own organization is, the response is frequently: 'Lower than 70 per cent'. If you then consider two or more organizations working together, the potential to enhance performance is easy to see. Collaborative working sounds worthwhile, but the challenge is to harness and deploy this approach where it can add value to the business. The potential impacts (both positive and negative) of relationship management are significant, but often the topic is not regarded as a mainstream issue for market development or skills enhancement.

Collaborative working is not new, but to a large extent it has been organically implemented as an adjunct to traditional business models. Evidence from across all sectors of industry identifies the potential commercial benefits and efficiencies of collaborative working for companies large and small, ranging from £ billion cost savings to £100 K operational improvements by working in a more integrated way.

While the fundamentals of collaboration may be understood, the time is now right to more effectively harness the benefits and move these concepts from ad hoc approaches to mainstream business operations. The pressures of economic stress, increased competition and demand for greater efficiency present a significant challenge to organizations in both the public and private sectors. To accelerate engagement, a common language and structure through a recognizable standard provides the platform on which to build mutually beneficial relationships in a rapidly expanding and changing business environment; this can be introduced at every level of the trading spectrum from small to medium enterprises

Preface

(SMEs) to multinational corporations and governments. We are seeing the creation of new trading models whose success is largely dependent on the ability of diverse organizations to work together. This new economic age, using the connectivity of technology, also needs to embrace the critical impact of relationships to achieve its goals.

The next decade – and beyond – offers a complex and changing vista of relationship challenges as globalization and technology draw the business world closer, while increasing the risk of conflict on many levels. There is clearly a significant role for relationship management: it must focus on quality in maintaining performance of people and products, together with supporting the organizational change that will be necessary to deliver the new business models.

BS 11000-1: 2010 provides a platform to build capability in a changing world. In this dynamic environment, agility, flexibility and collaboration are key ingredients to maintain competitive advantage. Adopting a structured approach will accelerate engagement and effectiveness.

David E Hawkins

NOTE All tables, charts and models contained in this book, unless otherwise stated, are included courtesy of Midas Projects Limited and shall not be reproduced without prior written agreement.

Introduction

Aim of this book

The aim of this book is to introduce readers to a broader perspective of relationship management (collaborative working) and to encourage senior executives to consider how their organizations can better exploit its potential. The emergence of the national standard BS 11000-1: 2010, driven by both UK and multinational organizations, provides a foundation to take advantage of the benefits of working with external organizations to build alternative business models. Companies that combine resources and capabilities can develop new competitive and cost-effective value propositions, reducing operating costs and risk while enhancing market competitiveness.

The approach in this book is to investigate collaboration from three perspectives:

- **Why?** Looking at the benefits of a collaborative standard, opportunities and risks in the context of collaborative working and how this can support a business development strategy that positions relationships to maximum effect;
- **How?** Exploring the benefits, structure and implementation of BS 11000 to provide a robust framework for collaborative working to ensure a sustainable business;
- **Where?** To explore the potential applications of the approach in ensuring the creation of business value.

BS 11000 provides a platform to build capability in a changing world. This book has been created to help those seeking to enhance their collaborative capability and establish the foundations to meet the challenges of the 21st century. The intention of the book is to help readers to understand what makes some collaborations work and not others – up to 80 per cent of all collaborations fail because of unclear expectations and undefined business processes that did not create an effective environment for collaboration.

Who is this book aimed at?

This book should be of value in particular to those whose remit is to develop and manage stakeholder relationships either within large multinational organizations or external to those organizations. The job functions of marketing and procurement in particular should benefit from the subject matter but it should also be of interest to all those at director level in large organizations that require a more structured approach to relationship management.

About BS 11000: the benefits of a collaborative standard

Collaborative business relationships have been shown to deliver a wide range of benefits, which enhance competitiveness and performance while adding value to organizations of all sizes. The publication of BS 11000 is a landmark for business. It is the first national standard in the world to address collaborative business relationships. The structure of the framework is drawn from practical experience, which has been established over 21 years of involvement in relationship management. It does not represent a one-size solution, but rather provides a consistent framework that can be scaled and adapted to meet particular business needs. Collaboration between organizations may take many forms from loose tactical approaches through to longer-term alliances or joint ventures.

- **Better engagement**
- **Underpins effectiveness**
- **Stronger processes**
- **Improved risk management**
- **Neutral starting point**
- **Efficiency improvement**
- **Skills enhancement**
- **Sustainable relationships**

Surrounding items: Collaborative benchmark, Public and private sector, Pan industry, Consistent platform, Efficiency and effectiveness, Risk management, Resource development, Process and systems

Figure 0.1 – Impacts of BS1100

BS 11000 does not enforce a single rigid approach but focuses on providing a framework that can complement existing approaches, where these are already in place. It recognizes that every relationship has its own unique considerations while achieving a range of benefits as shown

Introduction

in Figure 0.1. For those organizations with well-established processes the framework provides a common language that can aid implementation and engagement. For those starting out on the journey, the framework creates a road map for development.

The adoption of any standard has to be balanced against the value that it can deliver to the organizations that choose to adopt it, whether this is for improving internal performance or to enhance confidence in the market. In this respect BS 11000 is no different from other internationally recognized standards such as ISO 9000. The BSI certification programme, launched in April 2009, establishes a measurable independent assessment for internal benchmarking of continuous improvement and people development, together with independently validated pan-industry recognition of an organization's collaborative capability in the marketplace. At a more detailed level some of the benefits already recognized by multinational organizations include:

- 20 per cent reduction in operating costs;
- improved risk management;
- 15 per cent savings through supply chain aggregation;
- improved delivery performance;
- enhanced investment.

The standard creates a robust framework for both the public and private sector, providing a neutral platform for effective mutually beneficial collaborative programmes. Its core value is commonality of language and application between delivery partners. This leads to improved integration and acts as a bridge between cultures to form partnerships by reducing confusion, providing confidence to participants and providing a foundation for innovation. As it was developed through pan-industry input it is not sector-specific; it provides a basis for broader adoption and engagement, a common foundation for developing repeatable models to enhance communication and engagement.

The standard is a basis for benchmarking the collaborative capability of organizations (both internally and externally) through BSI independent assessment, enhancing partner evaluation and selection together with establishing market differentiation. It creates a focus to promote customer confidence and more effective joint risk management, whether related to the challenges of specific programmes or to the relationship aspects of collaborative working. It reduces the likelihood of misunderstandings or a mismatch of objectives, constrains hidden agendas and reduces the probability of conflict.

The standard's structured approach facilitates integration of collaborative working within operational procedures, processes and systems. Thus it establishes more effective governance; it also speeds the development of

Introduction

a baseline to support resource development and training, which increases an organization's collaborative capability to enhance the skills and ability of personnel.

In short, BS 11000 is a framework that will promote better engagement and effectiveness through strengthened business processes, while improving risk management, enhancing dispute resolution and providing a basis for skills development. Most importantly of all, it improves the potential for sustainable relationships that deliver value.

> BS 11000 is the world's first collaborative business relationships standard, which has been developed from pan-industry best practice, recognizing the growing use of alternative business models such as outsourcing, alliances, partnerships and consortia. It can be deployed in any business context where successful performance depends on strong relationships and exploits the capabilities of two or more organizations working in an integrated manner.
>
> The standard is unique in that it has an eight-stage life cycle approach for strategic development, engagement and management of business relationships from concept through to disengagement. Its sector-neutral positioning provides a practical model. It identifies the key principles that organizations should adopt to effectively build more sustainable relationships that deliver performance, innovation and create value for the parties involved. Its core benefits include:
>
> - **efficiency improvement:** where organizations' business objectives rely on interdependent partners working together to achieve results, which in turn rests on their ability to jointly create a seamless delivery process;
> - **greater effectiveness:** by working together, organizations are able to share knowledge and experience to focus their resources on reducing waste and duplication of effort;
> - **improved engagement:** where customer requirements or market value propositions require the combined capabilities of one or more partners, their joint success relies on commitment to common objectives and thus speed of implementation;
> - **cost reduction:** where organizations are jointly engaged in developing and delivering objectives, the standard provides a practical approach to creating a shared environment that allows costs to be optimized or eliminated through rationalization;
> - **improved risk management:** where interdependent relationships are crucial in meeting business objectives there are significant risks. The structured approach to identifying and

> managing these relationships reduces the risk of failure while creating a focus for joint management of risks;
> - **enhanced performance:** by establishing an open and trust-based joint working environment based on a common framework, organizations are able to share capability, knowledge and experience to adopt innovative approaches that remove constraints on performance;
> - **foundation for skills development:** as organizations seek to build alternative business models such as outsourcing, alliances, partnerships and consortia there is a greater need to develop skills and competencies. The standard creates a stable platform to focus staff development programmes.
> - **improved systems and processes:** to exploit the benefits of collaborative working, the standard provides a structured basis for integrating the key elements of best practice into operational processes and systems. This provides the triggers and governance for more effective collaboration;
> - **consistency of approach:** deployment ensures that best practice is embedded in the organization. Thus effective operation is not solely dependent on individuals who may over time be replaced because of their career development;
> - **sustainable strategic relationships:** adoption of the standard provides a platform for the benefits of collaborative working relationships to be developed and sustained over time, which maximizes their value.

How to use this book

This book provides the reader with a route map to successful collaboration. As outlined at the start of this chapter, it is organized in three parts, each with a different perspective: why, how and where.

Part 1: Why? This part explains why relationships are important; outlines the growth of collaboration and its main characteristics; examines risk and relationships; discusses the impact of organizational culture; explains how trust in collaborative relationships is developed; describes the challenges of leadership in a collaborative setting; and discusses how relationships should be positioned for maximum benefit. Checklists at the end of each chapter in this part help you to identify your organization's readiness to move forward; they are drawn from BS 11000 checklists.

Part 2: How? This part provides a practical step-by-step route map to implementation of the standard. It introduces BS 11000, explains how to raise awareness of the business case and benefits of BS 11000; describes how to obtain the required organizational knowledge; discusses internal assessments of readiness to adopt the standard; advises on partner selection; discusses the practicalities of working together; and highlights the importance of an exit strategy. Key messages and checklists are provided at the end of each chapter in this part.

Part 3: Where? This part explores the various ways in which collaborative arrangements can add value, both now and in the future. It discusses customer engagement, supply chains, outsourcing, collaborative contracting, alliance modelling and collaborative maturity. Subsequent chapters in this part explore new scenarios for collaboration: mergers and acquisitions; SME collaborative clusters; collaborating for sustainability; and the third sector. This part concludes with a forward look to the future of collaboration.

PART 1: Why?

Chapter 1 – The importance of relationships

> This chapter explains the importance of relationships in business as a crucial aspect of sustainable success. Most people in the business community (both public and private sector) will appreciate that relationships are central to developing, performing and maintaining effective operations. It is the interaction of relationships between organizations that creates the dynamics of business.

Business relationships are often given lower priority than processes and systems, on the assumption that individuals already have the right characteristics for developing and sustaining good relationships. In many cases key relationships are linked to people and do not take account of the overarching culture of the company. But can organizations afford to have such a critical aspect of success left solely to individuals or should relationship management be embedded in their operations?

Operational performance is often separated from either customer or supply engagement, due to policies and processes. Front-line support will often be established and measured against service level performance rather than outcomes. This focus on contractual compliance in intercompany relationships creates a culture that is based on 'contracting for failure' where the foundation is to establish the boundaries for potential failure and litigation. And a focus on processes will inadvertently create negative compliance, where adherence to procedures overrides outcomes.

Effective risk management has always been a major consideration for business, where the development of value propositions is accompanied by appropriate risk mitigation. But it is rare for businesses to realize that relationships are perhaps one of the principal risks that they must manage. In the last decade or two there has been a significant shift towards alternative business models such as outsourcing, alliances, consortia, partnerships and joint ventures focused on developing integrated solutions. These complex business models encompass a high degree of interdependency where successful outcomes depend on the ability of organizations to work in an integrated way. The vulnerability of these ventures is frequently due to their failure to build effective relationships.

Customers today are seeking to divest themselves of non-core activities, or obtain more complex solutions, through outsourcing programmes that frequently have a direct interface with end-users or consumers. Supply chain performance and dependability have become an integral aspect of performance; third parties are now a critical aspect of building value propositions. Many organizations claim to be totally focused on customer satisfaction with supply chain management that is developed around building robust relationships. However, the challenge for these organizations is to evaluate how their approach to performance works in practice and the incentivization schemes they deploy to motivate their personnel, which may be less about building relationships and more about short-term gains. The problem is compounded when organizations work together: many organizations operate at less than 70 per cent efficiency and when working together with others their effectiveness is reduced further. Despite the advances of technology, it is still people that make an organization function; it is reasonable to assume that the relationships they form are a critical success factor that is important to all stakeholders.

Key corporate issues for relationship management

The following section highlights some of these aspects in more detail, with a view to challenging the reader to consider whether their organization has the appropriate corporate focus on its relationship management capability.

Strategy and leadership

Collaboration will make a business strategy vulnerable if the strength of relationships and organizational or cultural compatibility are not considered adequately, thus putting business propositions in danger of failure.

Risk management

Risk is most often categorized by financial, performance, safety and external events, whether natural or social/political. Yet the most likely risk for any business is the breakdown of relationships with customers, partners or suppliers.

Value creation

Effective relationships are crucial to unlocking the potential within the value chain. But organizations frequently ignore the hidden benefits of sharing process improvements, skills development, product enhancement and performance towards overall competitiveness.

Knowledge management

At the heart of most relationship issues is the concept of 'knowledge is power'. This is the main barrier to benefiting from the value of interaction between organizations; it is a failure to build up a level of trust to ensure that knowledge is exploited for mutual benefit.

People, behaviours and trust

The challenge in all business relationships is people and how they are managed, measured, incentivized and rewarded. Despite organizations investing in skills development programmes and cultural initiatives, the conflict of policies and process will drive individuals to adapt their level of commitment, enthusiasm and engagement.

Internal relationships

Internal boundaries and divisions may not only impede external relationships; they also have the capacity to undermine collective performance through incompatible agendas and performance criteria. The way in which individual elements of a business are measured will have a significant impact on how these elements work together as a whole. And as business ventures become more complex, so their internal capacity to harmonize cross-functional activities faces increased pressure and stress on overall performance.

Relationship management engagement areas

In helping organizations to integrate, these key principles are common across most types of business relationships. It is equally important to consider these impacts in a variety of trading, operational and business environments. In doing so it is hoped that the reader will start to consider where a more integrated collaborative approach (and perhaps the application of BS 11000) could bring additional value or security to their projected outcomes. These principles are addressed in greater detail in Part 3.

Customer engagement
The challenge is to be recognized as a preferred provider in the relevant

sector or service. As customers' needs become more complex, so the need for both horizontal and vertical relationships becomes a crucial element of success.

Supply chain optimization
It is common to find 50 per cent to 80 per cent of operational cost being channelled through the supply chain; with such a high cost, supplier development and integrity is a critical dimension in terms of competitiveness and performance.

Outsourcing
Outsourcing approaches have become an accepted aspect of business, which means that external organizations are moving inside operational boundaries or firewalls to become part of the overall delivery process. These providers' remote locations mean they are not physically absorbing the customer's ethos or culture and may be operating with different and conflicting values.

International relationships
Operating across national boundaries increases complexity; those who operate in a global market will be acutely aware of the challenges thrown up by cultural differences, whether national, regional or corporate. Differences in national traits are highlighted and it takes time to build effective relationships that really deliver.

SME collaborative clusters
For small to medium enterprises (SMEs), competition and an increasing focus on economies of scale has widened the gulf between the multinationals and the smaller local companies. Collaborative clusters of SMEs are forming, to enable them to compete with the larger companies. They are taking advantage of the opportunities and benefits that may be exploited through collaborative approaches to create competitive edge.

Corporate social responsibility
There can be few board meetings today that do not address their current corporate social responsibility (CSR) profile. There is a difficult balance between the corporate drivers of competitiveness, shareholder value and sustainability. The practical implications of ignoring sustainability issues, either directly or indirectly, together with the pressures of balancing the demands of regulators, customers, consumers and pressure groups, has become very complex. Today CSR embraces corporate governance, ethical trading, human rights, environmental impact, and regulation etc.

Partnerships, alliances, consortia and joint ventures
The blending of different business processes, cultures, incentive schemes and performance measurement across a chain of partners (or other alliances) can create potential conflict and lost efficiency. Relationships become a critical aspect of their potential for success.

Chapter 1 – The importance of relationships

Mergers and acquisitions

Mergers and acquisitions depend on operational fit and also on the ability of organizations to harness and optimize their combined capability. While mergers and acquisitions are arguably the quickest way to grow a company they can be risky, when considering the investment and rationalization cost. Anecdotal evidence suggests that 85 per cent of mergers and acquisitions are failures; an important aspect that is missing is analysis of the organizations' cultural compatibility in their approach to relationships to drive success.

Third sector

For many years the voluntary (third) sector has been providing services, whether for social outcomes or emergency relief. More recently governments have taken a more proactive approach in seeking to harness the skills and resources of voluntary organizations. Relationships between local government, industry partners and the voluntary organizations will need to be developed to avoid potential culture clash, because the motivations and principles of each can be very different.

Developing relationships

Relationships of any kind have a life cycle; to maximize the benefits it is important to consider the longer-term implications of our actions on the value-creating potential to deliver improved performance. This can be considered at three levels: the strategic intent, the engagement process and the ongoing management. Every relationship is different, whether vertical or horizontal; however, the key issues will be common to most. It is these key factors that BS 11000 captures and thus provides a common and consistent foundation for collaboration. Establishing the right platform on which to create a relationship is crucial; while there is clearly a need for a contract it is equally important to jointly set out an appropriate governance model that will support collaborative working. Table 1.1 highlights some of the positive and negative impacts on relationships.

Table 1.1 – Positive and negative impacts on relationships

Positive contributors to collaboration	Negative contributors to collaboration
Executive sponsorship Committed leadership Early stakeholder engagement Integrated planning Joint government structure Open book (if appropriate) Clarity of objectives	Poor behaviour management Lack of stakeholder commitment Lack of partnering skills Lack of management support Lack of strategic direction Poor upfront planning

PART 1: Why?

Relationship management plan Good communication at all levels Joint ownership of success Behavioural charter Joint risk management Effective information sharing Early integration of processes Joint skills development Joint change management Appropriate performance measurement Integrated continuous improvement Effective dispute management Joint exit strategy	Poor partner evaluation Failure to address cultural differences Lack of shared goals Poorly defined measurement Lack of benefit analysis High focus on risk transfer Hidden agendas Poor communication Ineffective dispute resolution Lack of exit strategy Negative approach to contract Lack of innovation

Most relationships are multidimensional. They need to be recognized for the value they bring and the potential risk that emerges from failing relationships. More importantly, as alternative business models are developed it is essential that they are built on a structure that places the relationships above the individual and embeds relationship management in the organizational policies, procedures and systems. It is therefore important to consider what will drive the success of relationships and what may undermine them.

Evaluating relationship management initiatives

Given this background, it is perhaps surprising that the critical issue of relationships is often left to the capabilities of individuals, rather than adopted as a corporate ethos that embeds the appropriate characteristics. These observations prompt a key question: if relationships are important, should organizations be making greater strides to develop their profile, structure their policies and processes, and develop the skills of their people to drive more sustainable business models? Effective relationships will not simply happen because we want them to; they need to be managed appropriately to ensure they are a factor for success and not a cause of failure.

Conclusion

Relationships are important, so it is unrealistic to assume that such a critical aspect can be left to chance. It is also important to understand that while organizations can try to project a particular ethos, they are made up of people and thus partially dependent on their people. So relationships cannot be left to luck, nor can organizations rely on indirect activity to develop the appropriate behaviours to support that ethos. Far

Chapter 1 – The importance of relationships

from being a side issue, relationships are a fundamental aspect of business processes and a key factor in driving business success. Organizations should understand the importance of relationships and strive to embed both structure and leadership to exploit the potential benefits.

PART 1: Why?

Checklist

The following checklist may help to raise awareness of relationship issues. Identify the key issues that are appropriate to your business operations to create a focus from your perspective as you move forward to the next chapters. Your response will help you to consider the next steps for developing a structured approach for your organization.

Table 1.2 – Initial relationship checklist

Initial relationship checklist	Priority		
Issue	High	Medium	Low
Strategy and leadership			
Risk management			
Value creation			
Knowledge management			
People, behaviours and trust			
Internal relationships			
Customer engagement			
Supply chain optimization			
Outsourcing			
International relationships			
SME collaborative clusters			
CSR and sustainability			
Partnerships, alliances and joint ventures			
Mergers and acquisitions			
Third sector			

Chapter 2 – Collaboration

> Collaboration is not new. However, building on the principle that relationships in business are a crucial aspect of performance and success, organizations need to consider the catalysts required to develop, promote, implement and maintain effective collaborative practice. At the same time, they will need to explore and evaluate the interdependence between operational practices and the behaviours that underpin performance and outcomes. In this chapter the aim is to provide some background thinking on the broader subject of collaboration.

Many people think of collaboration and partnering as 'soft and fluffy' but have perhaps not understood the potential benefits or real challenges. Some believe it is simply a question of changing behaviours, while others promote the view that driving operational process changes will enforce the right behaviours. The reality is that to exploit the full potential you must have an environment that fosters and supports its effective adoption and thus creates the right behaviours.

Terms like 'corporate culture', 'ethos' and even the 'DNA' of an organization are heard frequently. It might be reasonable to assume that the operating style of an organization is something that is a result of nature, not nurture. It should be noted that real-life biological DNA evolves slowly over time and is a relatively static framework. The culture of an organization ('the way we do things round here'), on the other hand, is more likely to be a product of its management structure and national identity, while the ethos (the company values) is far more likely to be driven by those in authority through governance. An organization can vary based on how it is managed, all of which influences the people that it employs to meet its objectives. So the debate continues: is it nature and absorption or process and governance that formulate the collaborative profile and capability of an organization to influence the behaviours of its personnel?

There are many books and papers on the subject of partnering and collaboration, which may be useful for those who seek to broaden their understanding. Each reference source helps to focus on one or more aspects and benefits. This was a key aspect of the research paper *Vision*

PART 1: Why?

2010 published by PSL[1] in 1999, which focused on future supply or value chains and supported the view that future competitive edge would be driven by harnessing the most powerful value network.

The growth of collaborative working

The concepts of collaboration, partnering and alliances have been around for a long time. However, depending on who you speak to across various sectors of industry, you may easily be convinced that collaborative working and partnering is either well established and delivering results or, alternatively, a concept of executive management or marketing department's imagination. In reality neither is wholly true, though we should recognize that there have been many examples of good practice and future practice, which deliver significant value.

Collaborative working is not simply about cutting cost, though clearly that is a business imperative. It offers enhanced capability to build new value propositions beyond the capabilities of an individual organization. It is apparent from many studies that alliances and partnering can be related to corporate value and performance, but the vast majority are regarded as having failed – anecdotal evidence suggests more than 80 per cent. Various surveys also suggest that organizations that have effective alliances demonstrate higher returns on capital investment and share value. This may be true in part, but perhaps better reflects those alliances with a unique selling point that drives revenue.

Research work resulting in the publication of *Future Connections* looking at business in 2020[2] identified the trend towards greater reliance on alliances, partnership and collaborative networks. Subsequent work focused on the lack of skills development to manage in this arena and the wide variety of approaches offered to help organizations build these collaborations. The obvious outcome was the need to create a degree of uniformity through the development of a standard framework, which could address the key principles, accelerate engagement and provide a structure for skills development.

---

[1] PSL (Partnership Sourcing Limited): Now known as the Institute of Collaborative Working: www.instituteforcollaborativeworking.com
[2] www.ucisa.ac.uk/~/media/groups/ssg/PAS11000/future_connections2020%20pdf

Chapter 2 – Collaboration

Network Rail – case study

The rail industry has been challenged to deliver greater value for money. The Rail Value for Money review (*Realising the Potential of GB Rail*) led by Sir Roy McNulty, published in May 2011, identified greater collaboration between organizations within the industry (among other things) as being one of the means of achieving this. In addition to embarking upon a programme to work more collaboratively with our customers, one of Network Rail's other strategic objectives is to implement a partnering approach with our supply chain to improve levels of performance, introduce greater levels of innovation and deliver cost efficiencies. Working more collaboratively with our partners will enable us to align objectives in pursuit of these goals.

Delivering significant and growing capital works programmes in a safer, quicker and more efficient manner is a key corporate objective and is an imperative, given the challenge laid out to the industry to deliver better value for money for the fare-paying passenger and the taxpayer. The successful delivery of these programmes depends on the critical link between outcomes and the means of delivery. Knowledge and experience are essential, but it is through collaborative working that sound, cost-efficient solutions will be found. Working together with our suppliers, from the early stages, will enable us to overcome uncertainties and risks.

We identified the adoption of BS 11000 as a means of enabling greater collaboration with our supply chain. In addition to supporting the goals of greater efficiency outlined above, other identified objectives included enabling the cultural and behavioural change associated with more collaborative working and delivering a more consistent means of engaging with our supply base.

Perhaps the single biggest benefit of working to BS 11000 that we have found is the requirement for greater structure and process in the management of the relationship; this is something that can be described as 'having different conversations' from those that would normally be the case for traditional contract management. The requirement to focus on continual improvement and demonstrating value through the collaboration, rather than only meeting the project outputs, has helped to create a focus on the effectiveness of the relationship for our project teams and its overall contribution to success.

> One of the major benefits to date has been the sharing of information and knowledge with key partner organizations who have responded positively to our policy to adopt BS 11000 as they embark upon their own journeys to certification. This knowledge-sharing process has already facilitated the sharing of best practice collaborative working from other industry sectors. Such learning represents a key driver in our own continual improvement drive as we respond to the ongoing value for money challenge in the rail industry.
>
> Neill Carruthers
> Head of Contracting Strategy, Investment Projects

Leadership and objectives

The role of leadership is crucial in managing partnering, alliance or collaborative programmes where marketing, sales, operational performance and delivery processes cross organizational boundaries. The potential power of cross-organizational collaboration is paramount, but more importantly there is the need for clear and concise objectives. Developing an effective team focus is a challenge in most business environments; but where the traditional command-and-control structure is replaced by cross-functional operations, the coordination and direction of activities is even more complex and one where motivation and influence are vital to success. It is frequently, however, the single most common point of failure. Where complex relationships are driven and sustained by senior individuals on either side of these relationships they are particularly vulnerable when faced with a departure on either side. Making the shift from a traditional 'master and servant' relationship to co-creators often demands both organizational and personal realignment of thinking and fostering internal collaboration to maintain the focus on objectives and outcomes.

The conflicts of behaviours and policy

The historical approach to many of these interface challenges has been to focus predominantly on the behaviours of people, to build and maintain those relationships that are both critical and fundamental to business success. The challenge many will have experienced is that investment in cultural, behavioural development and training initiatives is often diluted or wasted when business processes effectively mandate 'business as usual'. If the potential benefits of collaboration approaches are to be realized it is impractical to rely on individuals and informal absorption to achieve collaborative working behaviours. Organizations need the policies, processes and systems to support robust and sustainable relationships that are less reliant solely on charismatic champions.

Chapter 2 – Collaboration

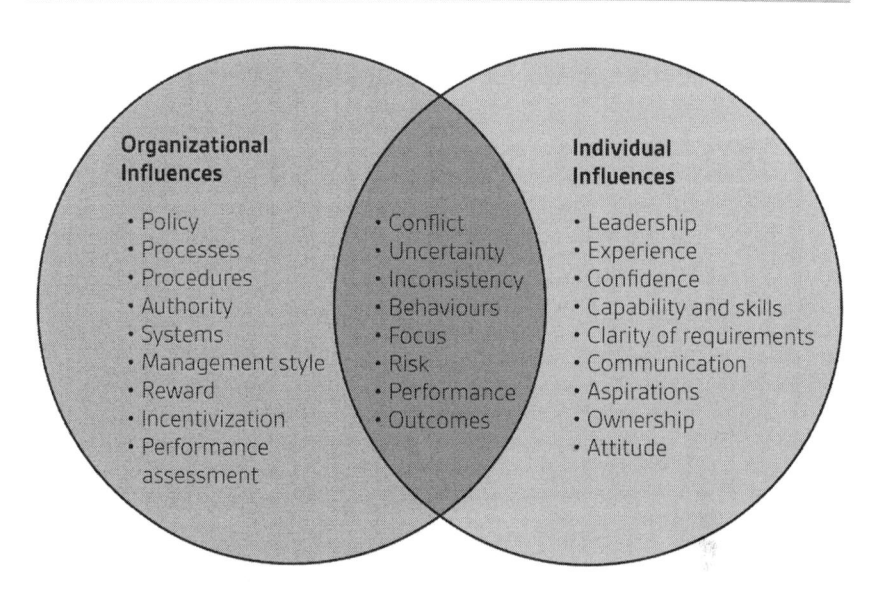

Organizational Influences
- Policy
- Processes
- Procedures
- Authority
- Systems
- Management style
- Reward
- Incentivization
- Performance assessment

Individual Influences
- Leadership
- Experience
- Confidence
- Capability and skills
- Clarity of requirements
- Communication
- Aspirations
- Ownership
- Attitude

Intersection:
- Conflict
- Uncertainty
- Inconsistency
- Behaviours
- Focus
- Risk
- Performance
- Outcomes

Figure 2.1 – Organizational versus individual influences

The potential conflict between the demands of the organization and the pressures on individuals as highlighted in Figure 2.1 can foster an environment that creates uncertainty and thus drives poor behaviours and focus, leading to increased risk and poor performance.

Alliances' and partnerships' relationships can involve both vertical and horizontal collaborations. Meeting or creating market demand is the essence of business success, and the right solution or value proposition at the right time defines winners and losers. However, providing the right solution at the right time is not enough for business success. A common problem emerges when the euphoria of a business 'win' dissipates and people have to get down to delivering outcomes and meeting internal policies, processes and performance measures.

Picking the right partners

What also becomes clear is that organizations, whether developing and marketing a collaborative approach or seeking to find suitable collaborative partners, will need to look beyond traditional evaluation criteria and assess the following:

Attributes   In terms of how their business operates and its policies
Ability   In terms of their experience and/or capability to work collaboratively
Attitude   In terms of an embedded culture and ethos of collaboration

Collaboration draws its strength from the ability to work in an open and honest way to build trust between both the organizations and the individuals involved. Trust is frequently seen as a prerequisite for collaboration; however, trust cannot be contracted – it must be developed and nurtured over time. To put this in perspective, consider for example that while you may build up trust with individuals working for an organization it is more difficult to adopt the same empathy with their organization.

An example might be a government department with influences that are difficult to predict or control. The premise is that you can rely on some individuals and can build up a high degree of confidence and trust; however, you recognize that their influence and authority have boundaries beyond which they cannot control aspects of your relationship. On the other hand, consider those organizations that have such a reputation for customer service that you would be willing to trust any representative of that organization. It is easy to see which of these options presents the most attractive prospective collaborative partner and which ideally reflects the profile of your own organization. It is not difficult to assess which offers the most sustainable relationship, whether you are selling your organization or looking to find a suitable partner.

Integration of culture

The task of creating an integration culture (e.g. a culture that accepts integration) is driven by policies that the organization deploys, both in terms of operational effectiveness and throughout the selection, development and management of the people that represent the public face of the organization. If collaboration is to be adopted as a repeatable business model then it cannot be solely dependent on behavioural training, team building or individual skills focusing on the 'soft' issues. Collaboration must be embedded in the governance and processes of the organization, reinforced in every aspect of the business through policy, process and systems. In the highly unusual case of the John Lewis chain of retail stores, all their people are partners in the business and its principles were embedded in its articles of incorporation by its founder. Few businesses will have this benefit, but it is easy to recognize the potential benefits of replicating these driving principles.

Chapter 2 – Collaboration

How people are managed, targeted, measured, incentivized and rewarded has a major influence on how they interface with others, whether internally or externally. If there is a conflict between the collaborative principles being promoted and how individual performance is evaluated, it is easy to guess which will have the dominant impact. Similarly, if the processes by which they have to operate are robustly structured and enforced but the business objectives do not clearly reflect a collaborative approach, most employees will quickly revert to more traditional 'business as usual' approaches and take the low risk option. So, despite organizations investing in skills development programmes and cultural initiatives, the conflict will force people to adapt their level of commitment, enthusiasm and engagement in line with Maslow's Hierarchy[3] or 'what's in it for me'.

Conclusion

The challenge is how an organization can embed and sustain a collaborative approach, given the volatility of the market, the transient nature of its people, variability of skills and experience and the historical focus of exploiting trading relationships. It was this dilemma that was instrumental in the creation of the world's first national standard, BS 11000, which would provide a consistent model around which organizations could build more sustainable relationships. There is plenty of evidence that collaboration (in whatever form) can enhance performance. The risk is that if collaboration is adopted as a bolt-on to existing business processes or the principles of collaboration are acquired through informal absorption, it is likely to be deemed a failure – or worse, be counterproductive in the longer term. The introduction of BS 5750 / ISO 9000 has demonstrated what can be achieved in terms of quality and operational performance, so it is logical that if we are to be more dependent on collaboration then the adoption of a standard will enhance operational consistency and performance. BS 11000 offers organizations the opportunity to adopt a recognized model for building their collaborative approaches. It also enables them to benchmark themselves against industry good practice, providing the foundation for developing sustainable relationships to deliver value-based performance.

---

[3] Maslow's hierarchy of needs: theory in psychology, proposed by Abraham Maslow in his 1943 paper *A Theory of Human Motivation*.

PART 1: Why?

Checklist

Table 2.1 may be helpful in challenging your thinking by scoring your organization's inclination to collaborate.

Table 2.1 – Scoring your organization's inclination to collaborate

1 = strongly disagree, 6 = strongly agree

Organization						
The organization has very well-defined contracting procedures	1	2	3	4	5	6
The primary focus is on profitability not performance	1	2	3	4	5	6
There are clearly defined roles and responsibilities	1	2	3	4	5	6
There are very traditional relationships with both customers and suppliers	1	2	3	4	5	6
The organization's goals and objectives are clearly defined and monitored	1	2	3	4	5	6
There is a firm focus on the financial outcomes of all actions	1	2	3	4	5	6
Personal performance is firmly structured into all incentives and KPIs	1	2	3	4	5	6
Every member of staff is empowered to make decisions within their area of competence	1	2	3	4	5	6
There is a high level of reporting within the organization	1	2	3	4	5	6
Management is very good at communications and shares what needs to be shared	1	2	3	4	5	6

When things go wrong the organization looks to learn rather than blame	1	2	3	4	5	6
There are clearly defined objectives and responsibilities	1	2	3	4	5	6
Management is always focused on why people don't meet their objectives	1	2	3	4	5	6
There are clearly defined standards of behaviour	1	2	3	4	5	6
There is a good culture in supporting people who don't meet their objectives	1	2	3	4	5	6

PART 1: Why?

Chapter 3 – Relationship risk and opportunity

> Relationships are a fundamental aspect of all business activities, yet they are seldom considered when assessing or managing risks. The inherent impact in failing to manage relationships effectively is likely to be significant. In this chapter the focus shifts to business risk and opportunity and the implications that relationships have on business outcomes.

Risk pervades every aspect of business, whether investment, product development, operational performance, reputation or supply chain. It is generally accepted that the more risk that can effectively be managed, the greater the competitive advantage. Simply seeking to transfer risk will frequently increase the potential likelihood of risk occurring, when the issues are outside the capability or influence of those holding the responsibility.

Risk is generally categorized by financial, performance, safety and external events, whether natural or social/political. The one aspect that is seldom mentioned in any risk brief is that associated with relationships. This should raise the concern of business leaders, since the most likely failure of any business activity will come from the breakdown of relationships such as with customers, partners or suppliers. The frequent assumption is that focusing on contractual conditions and liabilities places this risk in a manageable position, but perhaps ignores the reality that once the contract is invoked failure is largely assured.

Relationship risk

In most cases risk identification is driven by the perceptions of the parties involved. The issue of relationship risk is pragmatically ignored on the basis that we work with whoever we need to work with and they will manage their risks or those assigned to them. Effectively managing or mitigating the impacts of relationship risk will help to build stability and drive success by closing the gap between assumption and actuality – see Figure 3.1. Risk influences every aspect of the interaction between organizations and individuals, affecting both engagement and performance.

PART 1: Why?

Risk is frequently addressed from an internal perspective, based on current knowledge and often with a high degree of subjective perception. Understanding the other party's risk assumptions can help to smooth the way. It is their perception of risk that colours the way they see your organization, which traditionally leads us towards ever more complex contracting requirements. It is perhaps worth considering that one of the major UK construction projects, Terminal 5 at London's Heathrow airport, attributed its success to the way in which risk was centrally managed, which avoided individual contractors continually being focused on their own risks.

Integrate risk management

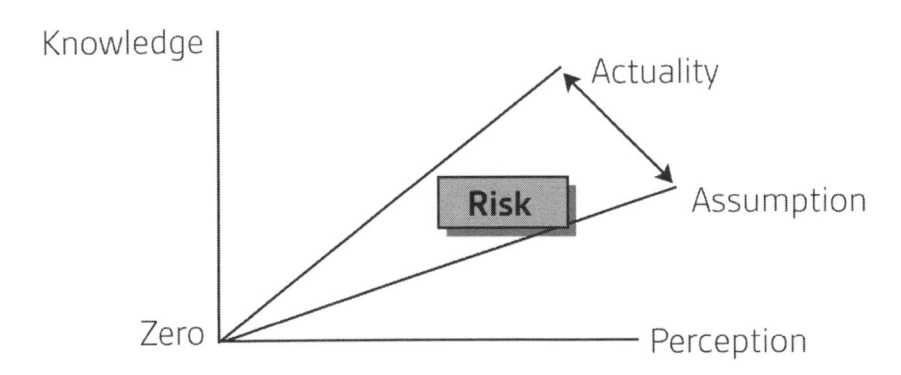

Risk management – closing the gap

Figure 3.1 – Risk management

At an individual level we each see risk in a variety of ways and how it may affect us; our enthusiasm for collaboration will be strongly influenced by the way we perceive it. Organizations need to consider the additional risks that integrated relationships may introduce, including aspects of business continuity through interdependency and the consequence of a failure in the relationship, together with the implications of reputational risk that come with increased integration.

Risk is both an opportunity and potential cause for failure, so effective risk management is a critical consideration. This is an accepted facet of business today, but the implications of relationships are a significant factor in the overall assessment of risk and thus should not be left to perception – or worse, left to pragmatism at an individual level to provide assurance of performance. Many organizations have

Chapter 3 – Relationship risk and opportunity

comprehensive risk management executives and teams with highly sophisticated financial modelling tools, safety programmes, insurance portfolios, actuaries and so on, trying to predict potential outcomes of risk, both man-made and natural, to develop appropriate mitigation strategies. What is less apparent is the consideration and understanding of the implications of business relationships and the inherent risk this can introduce, or the opportunity for joint mitigation strategies.

Business environment

As the business landscape becomes more complex and challenging, the relationships between organizations take on new and varied configurations. Often organizations miss opportunities by maintaining rigid risk boundaries between their internal functions; but as the market profile changes, so the complexity of these relationships increases, which generates a wider spectrum of risks that can be addressed through proactive integration of ideas and skills. The growing trends in globalization and convergence in many industrial sectors have expanded the range of trading relationships, both vertically and horizontally, within the value creation process. It is becoming more frequent to see competitors working closely together in specific ventures, as well as the complexities of mergers bringing together previous competitors into a single organization. The pressure to improve competitive edge has introduced a greater need to ensure that organizations can work in an integrated way to maximize potential benefits with various partners (see Figure 3.2). Integration has become a challenge for many business operations. Often multiple entities are linked within the value chain, which has evolved into a relationship matrix to create value and manage some aspects of risk while introducing new risks as a result of integrated relationships.

There can be few business ventures today that are not directly influenced by the spread of globalization. The multidimensional nature of the global landscape creates an environment that generates an ever-increasing profile of risk that must be addressed. The implications for organizations are far-reaching; they necessitate an increasing focus on risk mitigation and management to ensure successful outcomes from business ventures.

Risk and integration

It is difficult to consider any business interface where relationships do not play a significant part. As a business seeks to enhance its position or responds to the demands of the market, it creates an extended network of relationships, which interact to affect performance. In these integrated approaches they create an environment where the potential benefits are often constrained by the risk profile.

PART 1: Why?

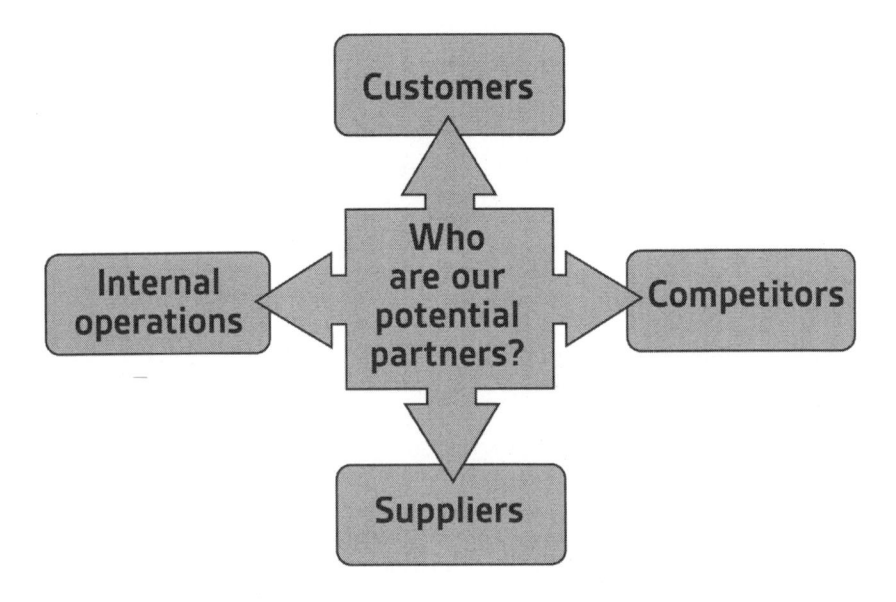

```
                    ┌──────────────┐
                    │  Customers   │
                    └──────────────┘
                           ▲
                           │
┌──────────────┐    ┌──────────────┐    ┌──────────────┐
│   Internal   │◄───│   Who are    │───►│  Competitors │
│  operations  │    │ our potential│    │              │
└──────────────┘    │   partners?  │    └──────────────┘
                    └──────────────┘
                           │
                           ▼
                    ┌──────────────┐
                    │  Suppliers   │
                    └──────────────┘
```

Figure 3.2 – identifying partners

Customers
As the demands of customers increase, so the pressure to perform both directly and through extended enterprises becomes more challenging and thus increases the risk of 'failure by association' when offering integrated solutions.

Consumers
Today's consumers are better informed than ever before and now look for competitive products and services, but they are also attuned to the broader profiles of corporate responsibility.

Supply chains
Global sourcing has provided increased competitiveness and choice; however, these extended supply routes introduce vulnerability to continuous supply.

Outsourcing
Outsourcing has offered many organizations considerable competitive edge but this opens up the impacts of third party performance on customers and consumers.

Alliance partners
Demand for integrated solutions increases the potential for integration of disparate organizations, creating 'go to market' alliances that are dependent on their cohesion.

Mergers/acquisitions
The increasing number of failed mergers and acquisitions prompts managers/investors/bankers to look beyond technical and financial modelling to assess effective integration.

Consortia/joint ventures
Developing multifaceted consortia or creating special purpose vehicles (SPVs) dependent on the strength of relationships in building uniform robust entities.

Academic research
Exploiting the power of academic research and drawing on a broader industry community. The trend is towards multi-institutional research programmes where historically independent and successful outputs carry significant relationship risk.

Research and development (R&D)
The high cost of R&D has over the past decade encouraged many organizations to seek more shared approaches where sound relationships and clarity of purpose are crucial ingredients for success.

Public sector delivery
As government bodies seek to reduce operating cost through integration with industry, relationships become critical to maintaining public service performance.

Voluntary sector
Harnessing the potential of the voluntary (third) sector highlights the need to consider how these relationships will operate outside traditional business or public sector environments.

Manufacture
As manufacture becomes more of a globally sourced activity, the interrelationships between various design, production and logistics networks introduce a significant relationship risk profile.

Services
Extended services such as facilities management and the integration of these often mission-critical services is a significant risk to overall operational performance.

Distribution/retail
In today's integrated marketplace it is frequently difficult to understand where one organization stops and another picks up the process; when performance fails, the underlying relationships present reputational and business risk.

Stakeholder management
The perceptions of customers and consumers, the confidence of investors, the integrity of partners and the commitment of personnel all create a

PART 1: Why?

business environment where relationships are no longer one-to-one but highly complex interactions where relationships are a key factor of stakeholder management.

Aspects of risk

Risk can be classified in many ways. All risk has an impact in terms of cost, time and profitability. To establish an effective approach it is important to analyse what the potential risks are and the potential effects. Risk may not simply be an issue of cost against today's business; it can also be an influence on tomorrow's potential business and the biggest risk to any business is the loss of customers through poor performance or global changes. Table 3.1 may provide a starting point for such consideration. For many of the traditional risk issues the introduction of partnering, collaborations or alliances may offer opportunities to aid the management of risk. At the same time many of the risks may well be removed or reduced by greater visibility and openness.

Table 3.1 – Risk impact types

Risk type	Impact
Operational	Greater interdependency increases vulnerability to the relationships it encompasses
Performance	In a collaborative operational approach overall performance comes from a commitment delivered by those facing the end-user
Knowledge fusion	The more integrated the business model, the harder it is to regulate what is transmitted between partners, creating a risk in terms of protecting proprietary information
Business continuity	As organizations focus on their core operations, they reduce internal capability where a breakdown in the relationship leaves one of the parties unable to meet its long-term obligations
Reputational	The blending of organizations' capability may have technical, financial and resource benefits; however, the relationship brings with it 'risk by association'
People	The attitude and behaviours of employees, both internally and externally, will reflect back on the

Chapter 3 – Relationship risk and opportunity

	organization and the impact of poor behaviour by staff is a potential risk
Culture	The different cultures of organizations are often ignored when considering how two or more organizations will work together, which can often become a single point of failure
Environmental	As regulatory controls grow, so the reliability of others depends on a shared perspective that is enhanced through a sound relationship of mutual respect and ownership
Technology	Technology developments may negate existing relationships and even those within a structured partnership or alliance may be hidden if the relationship is not sound
Business processes	If the relationship is loose, then the potential for operational breakdowns to occur is high and thus a risk to benefits realization if processes are inherently separated into 'silos'
Efficiency	Efficiency gaps can occur when integrating one or more organizations; this inefficiency can be multiplied by influences from their partners
Effectiveness	The effectiveness of an operation on paper may appear to be aligned and functional, but is highly dependent on the relationships that provide the cohesion
Innovation	Maintaining a competitive lead – whether scope, technology or delivery process – relies on organizations being innovative with their approaches, requiring relationships to be open and transparent
Future proofing	A failure to share future plans places constraints on the overall capability of the relationship, where each organization developing their plans individually impacts on joint performance and future investment
Change	Over time internal or external influences will affect the value proposition and market changes will affect

	the dynamics of the business; to maintain agility they need a robust relationship
Transition	All arrangements will come to the end of their potential to add value either for partners or customers; without a strong relationship, both may be damaged by a failure to construct a viable exit strategy

Risk analysis and management

The management of risk depends on the nature of the situation; in many cases the answer is simply a case of insuring the risk. In a collaborative relationship it may prove that jointly focusing this area of insurance cover can provide economic advantage, even before addressing consequential impacts or mitigation approaches in areas of interruption and liabilities. Managing the risks can often be mitigated through greater integration, ensuring that the aims of both partners are shared and protected through their business dealings.

Analysis of risk may be focused into three main areas of attention. The first area groups those issues that can be identified by source, in terms of where the risk comes from. In many cases this may provide the ability to reduce some risks by changing (say) supply options. Others may be natural (environmental) risks, which generally are subject to insurance cover – or, in certain cases, the need for design adjustments.

The second area is the risks that emanate from the actual operations, whether this is an internal or external function, by customers or suppliers. They may result from production processes and in many cases can be neutralized through re-engineering. In this case the ability of collaborating organizations to share working knowledge can often provide a wider range of options and solutions.

The third area is that of impact, in terms of being clear what the repercussions may be, which can generally be subdivided into impact on people, property or earnings. In each case the risk manager is seeking to find the most cost-effective mitigation, and then balancing the future actions to reduce the risk profile to acceptable levels, considering the liabilities in addition to impacts on customers and competition. A collaborative approach has the potential to provide an open platform that can focus on real (rather than perceived) risk, where in many cases competitive edge is lost through the accumulative impact of risk contingencies. Thus perception of risk may in itself be a significant risk factor. The earlier a risk is identified, the more opportunity there will be to manage the situation and certainly the less costly it will be to mitigate or eliminate the risk. What cannot be seen is unlikely to be managed effectively; the more integrated that organizations become, the greater importance to ensure that all those involved understand the risks being faced and – more importantly – allocate responsibility for action.

Conclusion

If we are to exploit the potential of alternative business models we cannot ignore the potential impacts on risk management. More importantly, in the broader sense of managing business risk the implications of relationships are not something that can be left to chance. Relationships link every aspect of business and yet for many they have a limited focus for those who are tasked with managing risk and delivering performance. If we do not recognize the implications of relationships then much of what is put in place to drive business outcomes and create more effective opportunities for stakeholders is inherently flawed.

Relationships are an integral part of business, which in turn should make them a key aspect of risk management. Effective joint risk management offers considerable advantage in a marketplace that is becoming more volatile in many aspects of its business culture. Risk in most organizations represents a significant cost consideration; by developing an appropriate approach, organizations can gain competitive edge.

PART 1: Why?

Checklist

Consider the following checklist by rating each element in terms of the business impact on your organization to develop an initial collaborative relationship risk profile (Table 3.2).

Table 3.2 – Initial collaborative relationship risk profile

Initial collaborative relationship risk profile			High/ Medium/Low
	Focus point	Rationale	
1	Operational	People operating in a collaborative environment can have a significant impact on effectiveness and efficiency. A key facet of BS 11000 is allocation of roles and responsibilities through transparent joint management to drive the appropriate behaviours	
2	Performance	A breakdown in relationships between collaborative partners will have a major impact on performance and thus create a risk in meeting objectives. Effective collaborative management through the principles of BS 11000 provides a basis to ensure that the relationships remain positive and sustainable	
3	Knowledge	Information and knowledge can be effectively exploited through collaboration; but they may also be dissipated through uncontrolled transfer of knowledge. A failure to share information may influence behaviours and thus affect performance. BS 11000 highlights the need to ensure required information is effectively used while protecting defined proprietary intellectual property rights (IPR)	

Chapter 3 – Relationship risk and opportunity

4	Reputational	In an integrated collaborative venture the parties are inextricably linked, both operationally and through their individual reputations. The action of one party reflects on the other, which may harm reputational profiles – particularly in areas like corporate social responsibility and environment impact, as well as exposing each other to third party or regulatory liabilities. Partner selection is therefore a crucial activity incorporated into the standard
5	People	Collaboration is not an easy concept to adopt for many from a conventional business background. People selection, coaching and development are critical aspects of any collaborative venture and therefore a potential risk to performance and successful outcomes
6	Culture	The nature of organizations is a combination of management ethos and their people. While partners may offer the appropriate resources, skills, knowledge, technology and financial profile there remains a key risk of whether the partners can effectively work in tandem
7	Business processes	Lack of compatibility of systems, procedures and processes presents a significant risk when overall delivery performance has to be integrated. Joint process assessment is a principle of BS 11000
8	Change	Change is a common area of failure in any business venture. Managing change effectively is a key risk alongside future-proofing outcomes; transparency and openness in collaboration are essential ingredients
9	Innovation	Sharing knowledge and capability allows organizations to harness value across the relationship and potentially extend their contribution to overall success.

29

PART 1: Why?

		However, this has to be balanced through joint management against the risks of undermining current processes
10	**Business continuity**	The customer is the ultimate beneficiary of the combined service or product from the collaboration or may themselves be part of the business venture. Either way, the failure of any partner affects all associated parties, and is thus a risk that has to be assessed, managed and (where appropriate) mitigated

Chapter 4 – Culture

> The subject of culture and cultural change has been perhaps one of the most debated and documented issues of all time. In the context of organizational development it has become a catchphrase for every business improvement initiative in modern times. This can be simply validated by typing the word 'culture' into an internet search engine, where two million plus hits is the norm. The focus for this chapter is the influence of organizational culture on effective collaboration.

What is culture? How does it develop? Perhaps more importantly, how can organizations harness cultural change to create the environment for collaborative working and project this to potential partners? We live in a global trading community, where almost every commercial activity encounters by its very nature some form of cultural exchange. National traits or cultures are something that every business traveller encounters; being aware of the nuances is a crucial aspect of success, based on how we act or interact by giving due deference to the local protocols and customs towards building the right relationship.

The more different we look to each other, the more aware we become of the potential differences of approach, language and signs that influence the way we do business. One only has to travel across Europe to appreciate the complexity of business styles and national traits. While English may today be accepted as the business language it remains the second language for most of the globe. If you travel to the USA, where Shaw famously remarked that the UK and USA were two countries separated by a common language, it becomes apparent that it is not simply an issue of language but a spectrum of influences that shape the way we assess those we are dealing with. Communication is crucial, but the art of communication is not simply about the words we use; it is also about the context that helps to form the message.

What is culture?

So what is culture and how does this translate or shape the nature of an organization? In the context of collaborative working, how does it drive the behaviours, both corporately and at a personal level, between organizations? Culture is a term that has many meanings but is derived

PART 1: Why?

from the Latin *cultura* (literally 'cultivation'), which infers that it can be developed. It is, however, more commonly used in three basic senses:

- the arts and other manifestations of human intellectual achievement regarded collectively;
- the customs, civilization and achievements of a particular time or people;
- shared attitudes, values, goals and practices exhibited by an organization or group.

Culture is frequently attributed to national aspirations or ideals; it is generally accepted that after 1945 the term started to attract more focus in relation to organizational psychology and business management. Since organizations are populated with people, it is often difficult to see how organizational culture is not an amalgam of all three definitions, since each individual's perspective and behaviour will be coloured to some degree by all three.

Given the interaction of individual and corporate values, it is reasonable to focus organizational culture as being a product of both; organizational change will only progress if we take a more holistic perspective. This leads us to consider the dynamics of relationships and the challenge of blending structure and people to determine behaviours (both internally and externally) to create an environment for collaborative working.

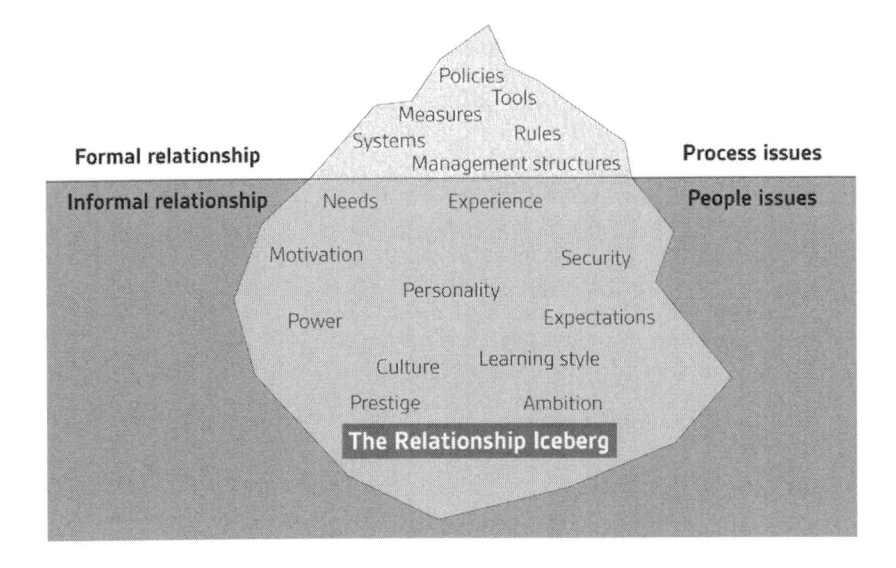

Figure 4.1 – The relationship iceberg

Chapter 4 – Culture

This can perhaps be appreciated more readily when considering the relationship iceberg (see Figure 4.1), where the underlying influence is not in the governance structure and process but in the people issues below the water line. This is amplified in terms of organizational culture: consider the implications of objectives and values reflected by an organization and evidenced by behaviours, where these issues take on differing degrees of importance when viewed from three separate perspectives: corporate, social and personal.

Constituents of culture

To address organizational culture, we need to break down the constituents, to evaluate these aspects and (where necessary) to modify them to drive the desired behaviours. For collaborative working, the organizations involved need to position their partner selection and governance to support a set of cultural principles that will underpin the relationship. Defining the key elements of culture prompts a wide spectrum of influences (see Table 4.1). The following cultural principles most readily provide a framework to focus organizational change. They specifically exclude the arts, literature, food and recreation, which are frequently associated with culture; while these are clearly important, they tend to be a by-product of local heritage.

Table 4.1 – Internal and external influences

External influences	Internal influences
Government/political	Leadership/objectives
National/regional	Market reach
Ethnic/religious/heritage	Diversity/quality
Social/customs	Visions/values
Language/education	Capability/competencies
Economy/environment	Business sector/CSR
Legal/regulatory	Governance/ethics
Technology maturity	Innovation/change

The external elements can be seen to have a significant degree of influence on any business activity and impact on perceived behaviours. In a collaborative working enterprise these external influences must be understood, whereas internal influences can be managed to develop the appropriate behaviours that will underpin performance and mutual objectives.

When considering the organizational culture there are many definitions; in a collaborative relationship, where two or more organizations are forming a subset of their organizations, they create a third level of culture. Strong cultures exist where individuals respond to stimulus because of aligned values; conversely a weak culture is one where there is limited alignment. A sound organizational culture should improve performance and suppress poor behaviours. A variety of characteristics might include:

- mission – strategic direction, vision, goals and objectives;
- adaptability – creating change, customer focus and learning;
- involvement – empowerment, teams and capability development;
- consistency – core values, agreement coordination and integration.

All of these would be inherent aspects of developing a sound collaborative relationship. The success of a strong collaborative approach is strongly dependent on the alignment of the partner organizations' cultures.

Cultural crunch

The cultural divide is not only between organizations, but also within them. Many established organizations have considerable difficulty in integrating collaborative concepts against a background of traditional internal practices. At the individual level there is a need for education and development of new thinking at all levels of operation. Most organizations tend to do what they know and have done for many years. Collaboration opens the way to radical thinking by 'breaking the mould'; the potential for developing and capitalizing on these concepts is limitless, providing that cultural 'tunnel vision' can be overcome.

Knowledge management

Knowledge management has become part of the business vocabulary and is regarded as the next generation of key issues to be addressed by the business community. Exploiting the intellectual capital of organizations is seen as a major opportunity; but the converse situation exists, as organizations seek to protect what rests not in their IT systems but inside the minds of their people. Despite the advent of the technological age the real value that is created within organizations is not generally contained within its IT-based intellectual property but held in the minds of key staff. As organizations move towards the integration of global networks and strive to harness low cost opportunities worldwide, the risk of lost intellectual capital becomes a potentially increasing threat to long-term stability. Focusing on what needs to be shared, in order to provide new value propositions and achieve lasting cultural change, means addressing the business environment, organizational structure, business processes and – most importantly – people. Knowledge is power; but hiding knowledge away is inherent in many corporate cultures. Instead, sharing it will be fundamental in creating a culture to support alternative business models.

Technology

The emergence of 'smart' systems gives rise to implications for many operations. There is a drive towards the integration of disparate organizations. These will form interlinked virtual entities, with variable lifespans, being created and dispersed in line with market drivers. This offers great potential for organizations of varying sizes to match their specialist talents and skills and forge new trading alliances. In developing these networks there is a common need to link systems and share knowledge to an extent that has not yet been fully exploited. The counter position is that with the technology that is now being harnessed there is also the ability, as never before, to soak up information; therefore the greater the integration, the higher the possibilities of knowledge spreading informally, without adequate controls. This fusion of knowledge and intellectual property may inadvertently pass between organizations who are working together; subsequently they may disperse, with the eventual outcome being the loss of intellectual capital.

Challenging traditional thinking

In the past, redefining a process was a challenge to traditional thinking within the organization. If the process is now taken outside the organization, with ownership vested in several disparate organizations, the challenge may be even greater. Now it is the joint perspective that has to be developed and sanctioned, which means that those outside may look upon what has previously been seen as protected territory and challenge its validity. Processes can become enshrined in tradition and maintained in line with people's established 'comfort zones'. Developing innovative value propositions requires freedom from past restrictions to open up the possibilities. Creating this environment requires a multifaceted approach, starting with a clear focus on education and training. For many employees coming from a traditional command-and-control culture, mentoring and coaching will be crucial to build up competencies.

PART 1: Why?

External influences

The relevance of Michael Porter's Five Forces model[4] and the implications of market entrants, competition and the power balance between buyers and sellers are clearly applicable to all aspects of organizational culture. Each industrial sector has its own 'biorhythms', which reflect the economic investment and development in that sector. The shift between customer power and supplier power will vary, depending on the traditional impacts of supply and demand. Clearly these variables will significantly influence the nature of any discussions or negotiations. Addressing internal drivers in this environment means deploying adaptable approaches. The competitor landscape is equally crucial, since clearly the greater the options available to the customer the higher their confidence level to negotiate a more robust deal for themselves.

Many organizations are affected not only by local pressures but also by the impact of wider changes in the market. There can be few organizations in the industrialized world today that are not affected by the financial markets and shareholders. In recent years there has been a significant change in the valuation process to reflect greater consideration for corporate structures, as opposed to assets. The move away from the traditional assessment of a company's balance sheet of assets, revenue, expenses and liabilities now includes a focus on brand, market channels, employees, suppliers and partners, with greater attention to the structure and nature of organizations.

At the same time the growing trend in recognizing CSR has created new dynamics in the interdependence of buyer and seller. In recent years one only has to look at the implications for companies like Nike, B&Q, Marks & Spencer and other high street names when they come under unfavourable scrutiny from the regulators and the media. The impacts of these commentaries on corporate culture are clearly identifiable. It may seem obvious to suggest that different national cultures require different approaches; but sadly very often organizations fail not because of the issues but a failure to recognize the cultural aspects of the business environment that are different from their own corporate culture. Effective relationship management is now a crucial factor in the global marketplace; when developing alternative business models to operate in this environment, partners may be drawn from a range of cultural backgrounds.

Corporate culture

It is perhaps best to consider separating corporate culture and organizational culture, particularly in the context of collaborative

---

[4] Porter's five forces analysis: a framework for industry analysis and business strategy development formed by Michael E. Porter of Harvard Business School in 1979.

working, which may only apply to certainly aspects of the business operations. Corporate culture is frequently typified by brand recognition – for example, we can all recognize the golden **M** of McDonald's or other high-profile brands. These we associate with consistency, quality, value etc. and they are generally supported by a strong outward-focusing culture that defines and reinforces these internal standards. We may not necessarily associate these organizations with concepts such as collaboration, since their brand profile is largely based on enforcement driven by robust training and conditioning of personnel. It should be recognized that in many cases there may be a corporate image that has to reflect local conditions; this is a challenge in many parts of the world. Local contradictions can prove difficult to moderate and perhaps in some cases reinforce the need for even greater command-and-control or power-driven cultures. The opposite can also be true: when visiting some parts of the world we make assumptions about the local culture, only to find that corporate training and education create a profile that is more globally recognized.

Nevertheless, if it is seeking to harness collaboration it is important for an organization to understand that its outward style and approach will be a crucial element of attracting and developing the right partners. This point is often lost on organizations that are traditionally focused on command-and-control models. Even when approaching the market with the expectation of developing a collaborative model such as innovation, past performance can be a deterrent for those considering responding. Many organizations today look for the 'intelligent customer' and undertake behaviour analysis before committing to the first stages of collaboration. It is important to understand one's own capability and image and to evaluate potential partners. If we consider organizational culture to be important, then we need to reflect on those influences we can manage as opposed to those which are externally imposed. The recurring theme through most literature related to organizational culture stems back to a focus on leadership. Roger Harrison[5] described organizational culture in four types:

- **power culture** which concentrates power on a few;
- **role culture** where authority is delegated within a highly structured organization;
- **task culture** focused through specialized teams and competencies;
- **person culture** where individual perceived superiority can be highly unstable.

---

[5] Harrison, Roger (1972) *Understanding your organization's character*, Harvard Business Review

Managing internal influences

A critical factor for collaboration is how behavioural traits are managed to optimize performance and satisfaction through effective self-management, within an organizational ethos based on building trust. Every organization is made up of people and how it is perceived outside is very much a reflection of the behaviour they display. The importance of understanding the key behaviours is crucial in every aspect of business operations. There are many aspects of behaviour but perhaps these can best be captured in the following respect model.

Respect model:

RESPONSIVE
ETHICS AND INTEGRITY
SERVICE TO CUSTOMERS
PROFESSIONALISM
ENTHUSIASM
CREATIVITY
TEAMWORK

Market reach

In most cases the failure of external relationships is directly rooted in a failure to understand the internal profile; a lack of clarity leads to confusion and misdirection, resulting in the failure of those outside the organization to appreciate the implications of their actions. Forming a successful collaborative strategy depends on the nature and culture of the organizations it will serve; it must encompass the main drivers of the corporate visions and values, and the visible support of the leadership at the highest level. Collaborative working will lead to change, which will affect all the organizations involved. Development of a collaborative approach must be integrated into the wider objectives and ethos, even though it may be viewed as only initially affecting one part of the operation.

There are many factors that the business community has to continually adjust and adapt to. In the global business environment these issues can create both opportunities and risks. When the relationship is sound, then this appreciation of significant change can be handled effectively. This includes the accommodation of changes in regulatory demands or political structures, which can create constraints that cross organizational boundaries. Economic variations alter the customer perspective and can provide advantages to competitors. The more global the operations, the greater the risk that changes in the business landscape can dramatically clash with internal cultures.

Diversity and equality

It is important to recognize that organizations are generally made up of differing groups of people. Many will want to stay in their 'comfort zone' and choose not to see why change is necessary, while others will be passive and seek more direction. The more progressive individuals will want guidance and a few will be more visionary. Each of these characteristics will create differing dynamics in terms of how they react to others, and this consideration must be high on the collaborative leader's choice of players. The organizational culture may be constrained by a number of factors that create obstacles to implementation. This situation can be observed in both the public and private sectors; it arises through a number of common parameters, such as traditional thinking and processes, levels of understanding and experience, legal frameworks, accounting and auditing concerns and regulation.

Conclusion

The future holds increasing challenges; organizations must consider in their long-term strategies how to address the changes and maintain their business profiles and profitability. In a changing and volatile marketplace, where competition is growing, there is continuous pressure on organizations to find alternative options to competitiveness, which is increasing. Corporate and organizational cultures can be the bedrock for sustainable business or a millstone in a dynamic market. The prospect of developing alternative business models, which are focused not on traditional contracting relationships but formulated around collaborative concepts, offers opportunity and further challenges to the business community. The proposition that a number of independent organizations form themselves into a virtual operation has many benefits but is likely to meet the barrier of traditional institutional thinking. These integrated relationships may be greatly constrained by their inherent cultures.

Culture is both a consequence of the environment within which an organization operates and a construct of the way it is organized and operated. The former aspect is partially beyond the control of business leaders; other than in understanding the organization's visions and values, its strategic objectives and direction can be selective. In understanding the desired direction and drivers, senior managers can take steps to refocus their traditional culture and improve their ability to function more effectively in areas where opportunities do or may exist. BS 11000 provides a foundation on which to consider those aspects of culture that can be addressed in order to facilitate clarity of focus and a platform for cultural understanding and integration. Understanding the cultural picture (whether national, regional, corporate or organizational) helps build confidence to expand the degree of interaction, with the aim of creating longer-term relationships that are mutually beneficial.

PART 1: Why?

Checklist

Culture is a key factor for success. Table 4.2 helps you to consider how you may interpret the culture of your organization and, more importantly, how it may be viewed from outside by customers, potential partners and key suppliers. Some examples are provided in italics.

Table 4.2 – Cultural perceptions – examples

Internal perception	Customer perception	Partner perception	Supplier perception
Success focused	*Challenging*	*Demanding*	*Aggressive*
Financially astute	*Rigid*	*Risk averse*	*Intrusive*
Customer focused	*Patronizing*	*Demanding*	*Aggressive*
Well organized	*Constrained*	*Controlling*	*Dictatorial*
Reliable	*Limited innovation*	*Inflexible*	*Bureaucratic*
Quality focused	*Expensive*	*Unimaginative*	*Compliance driven*

Chapter 4 – Culture

Now insert your perceptions of your organization, then a pragmatic view of how others may see it (Table 4.3).

Table 4.3 – Cultural perceptions – your own viewpoints

Internal perception	Customer perception	Partner perception	Supplier perception

Chapter 5 – Creating trust

> As organizations further investigate the application of a collaborative approach the issue of trust will soon be raised, so this chapter will examine the concept of trust. Trust has long been recognized as a key aspect of business success, yet it is a very personal attribute that is not given easily. If trust is important but is a personal perception, then how does it become an integral part of an organization's profile? And where trust is created between individuals, how sustainable is trust for the organization? If trust exists, can organizations validate, measure and manage the building of trust?

There are many aspects to trust; this chapter will look at the implications between individuals and organizations working together. To set the theme, the following are definitions of trust:

- the firm reliance on the integrity, ability and/or character of a person or organization;
- the condition and resulting obligation of having confidence placed in one;
- the reliance on something in the future: hope;
- the reliance on the intention and ability of a purchaser to pay in the future: credit.

The fourth definition is of particular interest in a commercial environment because it affects the very foundation of business. Trust is a key element of all business relationships, but it is seldom (if ever) visible as part of a contract, at least not directly. In one form, however, trust is defined as commercial credit. 'Credit' comes from the Latin *creditum* (loan), which comes from *credere* (belief) and is thus a link to contracts. In many ways trust is only recognized when it is given as the reason for a dispute because there is a breakdown between the parties.

Trust is the cornerstone of business; from the earliest of times the relationship between buyer and seller was driven by the ability of both parties to be able to develop confidence in the other. A shake of the hands was enough to put a contract in place and this freedom from complexity often provided a solid platform on which to create value and build trade. It is therefore a key factor when building collaborative relationships. As commerce has moved on, the scale of trade has significantly increased and so have the stories (good and bad) around the failures between organizations and individuals. Certainly once there has been a failure of performance it becomes less viable to trade, based purely on trust. This quickly takes us to a point where a lack of trust is probably the starting point for many relationships, rather than the other way around.

The complexity of the business community today and the very public demonstrations of what can happen when trust is assumed or exploited by unscrupulous businesses (such as Enron, WorldCom and others) has increased controls to the point where it has become in many cases virtually impossible to work on trust alone. Lack of confidence has added a huge burden to business operations – for example, in the case of Sarbanes-Oxley,[6] which created an environment where governance and regulation could be seen to be stifling growth.

As business seeks to find opportunities for trade, avenues to exploit competitive edge, or simply to constrain costs, the need for trust has grown. It has become more than simply confidence in the product or the assurance that payment will be made; it becomes fundamental to the business proposition and the most valuable of commodities. Without trust, organizations are forced to depend on lawyers and accountants, backed by the courts, to navigate a complex environment that adds little tangible benefit but contributes significant costs and a minefield of risks to business effectiveness.

Internally, organizations can no longer simply depend on employees to do what is right; nor, for that matter, can many employees rely on organizations to do what is proper and fair. The Trade Union movement in the early part of the 20th century took on the task of defending workers and improving working conditions. Much of this became law and perhaps has become so strong in parts of the world that companies can no longer do what is practical but struggle to satisfy regulation. This is not intended to be supportive of unscrupulous employers nor a criticism of the role for collective labour relations, but a demonstration that even at an individual level trust is often handled by law rather than common sense.

Social interaction

Forward-thinking organizations understand that good employee relations are a crucial part of an effective business. They stretch beyond geographic boundaries in this global marketplace, and frequently beyond corporate boundaries to those external providers in the delivery process. The more remote the interface, the harder it is to develop trust in those who contribute to individual or corporate success. The rapid spread of

---

[6] The Sarbanes-Oxley Act 2002: www.soxlaw.com

communications technology has provided a wide range of opportunities to operate outside localized structures. However, these virtual communities are often constrained by the inability of the participants to build trust in each other or the organizations they represent. The importance of social interaction is frequently ignored in favour of wired connections, which allow instant communication but frequently hamper the development of any personal connection. We all appreciate meeting around the coffee machine and the further we move way from each other the weaker the levels of trust.

The internet has created a significant change in the trading community, but when you ask people if they would buy mission-critical items for their business or items for their family through an unknown website they immediately recoil. So trust remains the catalyst for trade, even in this high-tech age. Even Microsoft has started to advertise around the theme of people and relationships rather than technology solutions, suggesting that the pendulum is swinging back in favour of traditional values and thinking. The investment challenge and diversity of the marketplace is creating an environment where business propositions are more likely to be based on the development of alliances and networks of companies linked together to form virtual organizations, to exploit a particular product/service proposition or meet a customer demand. This is perhaps causing a resurgence of thinking to revalue the importance of trusted relationships as a key ingredient of success and a crucial factor.

The importance of trust

There is no doubt that trust is essential in any relationship; in business it is a key factor in being able to exploit the opportunities and manage the risks at the interfaces between individuals, groups, functions and organizations. By building trust we can remove many of the time-consuming and costly controls that businesses place between themselves. Management of others is mainly driven by a concern that they will not do what is expected of them, so we form contracts that are based on a presumption of failure.

The problem is that in most cases contracts are not clear, nor can they fully define every situation. Thus when issues arise they fail to deliver their objective of clarity. It is perhaps worth considering the adage that companies make contracts and people make business. The more effort we invest in and rely on developing watertight contracts, the less time we spend focusing on how to be successful. This is not to suggest that we don't need contracts, but perhaps they should be considered as a safety net and not the exclusive driver.

There are certain people we inherently trust, likely doctors and teachers, but people are usually either trusting until proved wrong or fundamentally mistrusting of others until they recognize that through performance of obligations they can be trusted. The more often you get your fingers burned, the less inclined you are to trust what others say. In business we generally build trust through incremental stages, which is perhaps one of the simplest forms of risk management. We allow only a small degree of freedom, based on a limited belief in others; we progressively increase the boundaries, based on how we see their performance.

Organizations in principle are reflections of the people that execute their aims; trust is driven not by organizations, but by people each having different thresholds of trust. Performance is the only real measure of others and thus the benchmark for trust. The culture of an organization is reflected through its people; so if they are not trusted, then how do we expect them to trust others or create an environment where others would trust them or their organization? It is this dilemma that faces many organizations. As we see a growing trend towards collaborative approaches and a breakdown of the traditional business models it is perhaps time to consider relationship management not as a 'nice-to-have' or something that we do as a matter of course but as a fundamental necessity for the future. The writer's research into the challenges of collaboration highlights three key factors for success, each having its foundation in developing trust:

- when two organizations enter any kind of collaborative relationship there are always three sets of objectives: 'Yours, mine and ours'. Failing to recognize these potentially very different positions frequently leads to confusion and conflict;
- second is the issue of disputes. It is not the fact that we have them but how we handle them that defines the strength of trust and the relationship;
- third is the question of an exit strategy. This is perhaps the most damaging, since not understanding the rules of disengagement tends to colour the way we interact.

The question of trust is as much about good open communication as anything else; as organizations move more and more towards alternative business models, trust becomes a major consideration. Trust seems to be something that is inherently understood at a personal level but not something that organizations currently foster as an operational platform.

Contracts and people

Traditional commercial 'trial by combat' has been considered the only way to deal with customers and suppliers. The foundation is firmly entrenched in that the buyer wants to pay the least for the most and the seller wants to provide the least for the most; 'Let battle commence' from that position. Yet beneath the bravado of sabre-rattling there is a key concept that affects every decision we make, and that is **'TRUST'**. The less we trust each other the harder the fight and the longer it takes to get a resolution. This underlying concept is crucial to successful business; and in an environment today, where technology and communications have changed the face of trading relationships, it is perhaps even more true.

Collaborative working is a growing phenomenon, reflecting the reach across traditional industry sectors or competitive boundaries to create alternative models of integrated products and services. Yet so many of these programmes are considered failures, because frequently the relationships are not strong enough. Underlying this is the fundamental truth that trust is a crucial ingredient that we rely on but cannot measure. We may recognize that it exists, but generally only recognize it when it is not there.

Impact of behaviours

The development of collaborative programmes is frequently focused on the blending of company cultures. Delivering customer satisfaction is founded upon organizations going that 'extra mile' in terms of performance. Every business relationship is a journey; understanding where you are in the development process is crucial in being able to maximize the benefits. The ethos of an organization is a reflection of its leadership and its people, who influence the overall culture and reflect that style externally.

In any circumstance where people need to work together to deliver a product or service, success largely depends on the behaviours of the people involved. Exploiting collaborative relationships derives success from integrating business processes and sharing knowledge to create additional value and innovation. The way in which people interact with each other is a key factor in delivering performance and customer value. It should be clear that how each individual behaves and performs their roles in the operation strongly influences the way in which others react in return.

Relationships are a fundamental part of any operation. In an environment where customer satisfaction is the focus of the activity, then success is very dependent on improving the behaviours that support those relationships. The relational issues can be fundamental barriers to integration. This is particularly the case when considering collaborative relationships that span regional cultural boundaries. The emotional issues in general terms will be the areas that make or break a relationship. It is these areas that will define the success of any collaborative venture. Behaviours will strongly influence the way in which others react; thus to stimulate success an organization must start by understanding individual characteristics, group dynamics and organizational culture, and building trust. The organization will need to adjust behavioural patterns and continuously focus on excellence to improve performance and enhance customer satisfaction.

The key to managing behavioural traits to optimize performance and satisfaction is through effective self-management, together with an organizational ethos that is recognized as a critical factor for success. It is important that organizations have clearly defined objectives and values that are reflected throughout the operation and accepted by all involved. This is not to suggest that organizations can always satisfy the perceptions of every individual, but clear rules of engagement will help to maintain direction and not dilute its focus.

Communication

Effective communication is about understanding how behavioural traits affect the way a message is given and received. The attitudes and approaches that individuals present to others are key factors in creating empathy and thus trust between the individuals or their organizations. The most common failing in the customer relationship is the manner in which complaints are handled; the way in which disputes are managed can be a valuable benchmark for the strength of the relationship. Many organizations see complaint management as a negative factor while those that seek continuous improvement see it as a key performance indicator.

It is important to recognize the flow of any communication and influences that will define its effectiveness (see Figure 5.1). It is frequently not the words that are used but the peripheral influences that determine success. Recognizing the message is a factor of the actions and the context within which it is being delivered. It will be interpreted based on the personality and expectations of the receiver, where the perceived message will result from influences and manipulation within these factors. Balancing and managing these traits is an essential part of building an effective and trusting relationship.

The behaviours of organizations are frequently driven by their operating structures or corporate 'silos', which can often dictate the way in which individuals are allowed to perform. This is particularly apparent when considering operations that bridge national or cultural boundaries. The key influences are often part of operating processes such as financial reporting and incentive schemes, whether group or individual. Performance requirements that dictate the measures of success will also set benchmarks for knowledge sharing and collaboration. The more rigid and localized the performance measures, the more likely it will be that these will promote attitudes that create a blame culture, so it is

Chapter 5 – Creating trust

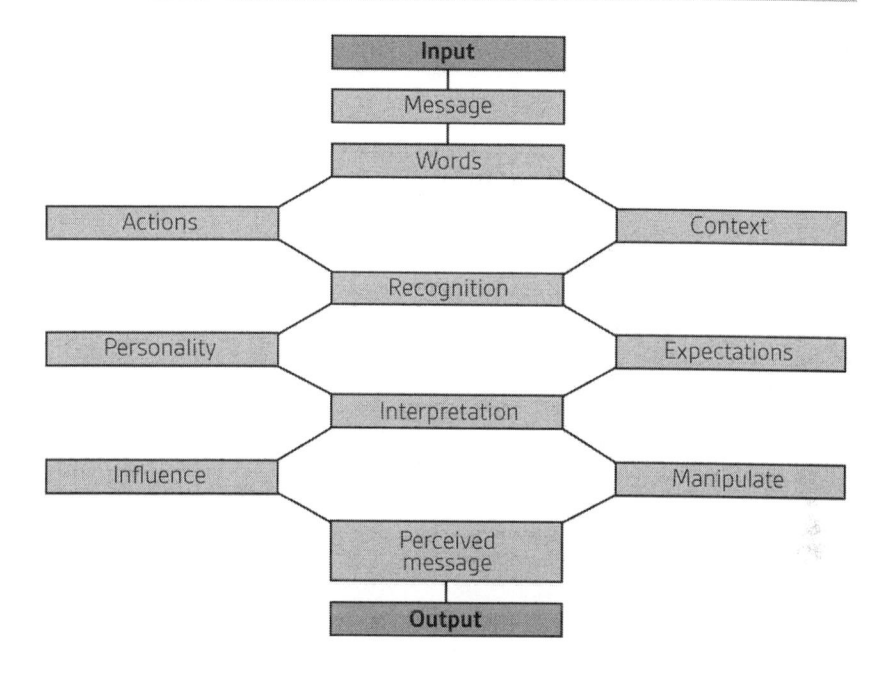

Figure 5.1 – Communications flow

Communications flow diagram: Input → Message → Words → Recognition (with Actions, Context) → Interpretation (with Personality, Expectations) → Perceived message (with Influence, Manipulate) → Output.

impractical to consider the behavioural traits of individuals without taking into consideration the business environment within which they are required to operate.

There can never be a single complete solution to the behaviour dilemma within organizations, whether considering external relationships or internal interfaces. There is a need to assess and balance the 'hard' issues of procedures, processes, systems and policy against the softer issues that reflect the personal traits and styles of those who are charged with delivering within these processes. The balance is **trust** through which individuals and organizations are able to rely more on common performance than on rigidly enforced processes.

In high performing organizations the key traits are facets of managing behaviours and thus lead to success. Leaders demonstrate commitment to goals and values, meeting the needs of stakeholders with ethical and transparent decisions, while encouraging innovation and harnessing diversity. Effective managers will in turn provide performance feedback against clear goal-setting, supported by risk and reward. They should also reflect consideration for developing skills and promote a work–life balance. Staff will take responsibility and contribute fully with commitment, initiative and support for corporate goals and values.

PART 1: Why?

Bridging the relationship divide

Most people who work in large organizations have suffered at some point with the internal conflicts that detract from the outward-facing relationships, whether they are with customers, suppliers or partners. Trying to improve performance by working with strategic relationships creates pressure because other internal functions fail to support the relationship effectively. The adoption of collaborative models can be constrained by a number of factors that create obstacles to implementation. This situation is observed both in the public and private sectors and arises through a number of common parameters, such as traditional thinking and processes, levels of understanding and experience, legal frameworks, accounting and auditing concerns and regulation. In a collaborative relationship the benefits arise from exploiting the interfaces between organizations and the ability of disparate groups to focus on common objectives and implement a joint programme. It is therefore imperative that organizations invest the time to embed the collaborative approach in their business processes and into the ethos of the organization to build trust.

Dispute resolution

In any business venture where people are involved there is always the possibility of differences; this includes a collaborative culture. Managing conflict towards a constructive and mutually beneficial outcome is a crucial element of effective collaboration. Although organizations and individuals may choose to operate in a more open manner, at times there will be circumstances that generate some degree of differences in everyday operations. It is inevitable that differing views will arise in the focus of groups, either within the teams or in the wider organizations that constitute the relationship. In the conventional trading relationship these issues are often suppressed until it is too late to defuse the conflict. In a collaborative arrangement it is important to ensure that there is a dispute resolution process that provides a mechanism and escalation route where appropriate. Certainly the strength of a relationship can often be judged on the way it is able to face and solve disputes; trust develops through effective management of disputes. Establishing this simple guiding process can help to focus on the issues and not on the personalities, starting by validating what is happening and what needs attention. Inside a viable collaboration there should be no power bases if it is to really operate with a focus on added value. In looking at any potential conflict there is always a chance that it will be seen as 'them and us'. In simple terms this is about the 'win–win' approach versus the 'win–lose'. These two conflicting positions can be explained as shown below.

Table 5.1 – Win–win versus win–lose

Win–Win	Win–Lose
Conflict as a mutual problem	Conflict where one party wins and the other loses
Team looking for joint solutions	Both sides looking for individual solutions
Satisfying both sides	Power owner forces solution
Mutual interdependence	Power through independence
Open and honest dialogue	Misleading information
Threats avoided	Threat is power
Flexible	Rigid

If not managed these situations can completely destroy trust, therefore once you have the issues out in the open (in the middle ground) then they need to be dissected by the team. You cannot solve a problem if you can't see the real cause, and so often we address the symptom – not the root cause.

Moving forward to trust

If we acknowledge that relationships are important, then the obvious connection is that trust (which is what fuels good relationships) must be high on the agenda, since to make relationships function effectively there must be trust between the parties or they will be constrained by rigid and inflexible systems and contracts. The latter is a situation which will be familiar to many in the business world, but which (as has already been said) is perhaps not the model for the future. The challenge, however, is how to build relationships that foster trust. In these times of business reporting, it is perhaps even more important to ask how we can measure trust. The issue of trust comes up time and again in cultural programmes, and even more frequently when organizations try to measure the resilience of their business relationships. Yet trust is perhaps the most intangible of concepts and is more often than not something that each individual defines and develops from a very singular perspective. It is difficult to measure, yet frequently it is included in cultural monitors, when in fact it is may be more of an outcome than a driver.

How can organizations define 'trust'?

To develop an approach for looking beyond the loose adoption of terms like 'trust', you have to try to get an appreciation of how others see the subject. If trust is an intangible perception, then how can you measure it? What you could perhaps measure is the *output* of trust and how this reflects the perceptions of those involved. Clearly some organizations – or at least their brands – carry a high degree of trust and every organization would wish to be recognized as a trusted brand.

Research carried out amongst ICW executives clearly identified trust as crucial; but the research also recognized that this was an output of behaviours, which had to be developed and not assumed at the outset. Trust was personal; so in general the organization's perspective on trust was based on its people, not its processes. Trust was developed incrementally, starting from a range of knowledge factors that might include personal experience, recommendations or public reputation. Trust was given in degrees based on a combination of knowledge and risk assessment. Thus, if trust was an output of performance and behaviours, then the next question was: 'What are the factors that govern your level of trust?' The many anecdotal responses were analysed to identify these outputs, which largely fell into three categories:

- **compliance** – which tended to come from very process-oriented and structured organizations, reflecting perhaps the nature of their management;
- **culture** – which in general came from organizations with a broader global operation;
- **commitment** – which had a wide focus for individuals who were more fully appreciative of partnering and alliance concepts.

Table 5.2 – Indicators of trust

Compliance	Culture	Commitment
On-time delivery	Open to negotiation	Early warnings of problems
High quality	Customer focus	Responsive
Contract compliance	**Going the extra mile**	Fairness
Meeting schedule	Adaptable to change	Flexible
Concise reporting	Good communication	Dependable
Factual	Openness	Empathy
Punctual	Honest reputation	**Clear commitment**
Risk averse	Share information	Accessible
Reliable	Friendly	Problem solving
Structured access		Continuous improvement
Sound planning		Sustainability focus
Meets performance targets		

Chapter 5 – Creating trust

Robust policies Health and safety Regulatory adherence Process driven Proven performance Strong administration Low level of complaints	Strong people focus Staff retention Innovative Creative Service driven Win–win Collaborative	Do what they say they will do Conscientious

Those aspects most often occurring during this study have been highlighted in Table 5.2. It is not surprising that there was a strong focus on performance for compliance in most cases, and many different ways of interpreting this. The other responses, relating to the aspects of culture and commitment, were more focused.

Measuring 'trust'

Critical behaviours are a key element of building a trust-based operation. The higher the degree of trust, the more efficiently the operation can move forward, releasing management time and effort to focus on value-adding activities. So, finding a simple model to measure trust across a relationship would seem a valuable idea. Distilling the variety of comments collected was relatively easy, since in general the key issues dropped out from the number of times a subject was raised. There is probably no absolute answer, but if these key aspects reflected what reassured people, then these would translate into some measurement or 'trust' index.

It is easy to place a high value on trust, but at the same time it is difficult to identify trust as the principal catalyst for performance. If people are open, honest and responsive, demonstrating fairness and commitment, then others will be likely to trust them. Building a robust approach, which harnesses the culture of collaboration, will facilitate trusting relationships within a framework that brings out the best performance. In the end it will be performance *and* trust that are the benchmarks of collaboration; as trust increases, accordingly it will add greater value to the participants.

Conclusion

Relationships and the behaviours that drive them are dynamic and will vary in depth and change over time. The ultimate objective is to strive for excellence in all cases, but this process has to be progressive. Excellence is unlikely ever to be achieved; the bar should be constantly raised to achieve greater levels of trust in order to drive efficiency and effectiveness.

PART 1: Why?

We may understand the value of trust-based relationships, but maintaining these in good times and bad is frequently a contest between short and long-term pressures. The next decade and beyond offers a complex and shifting vista of relationship challenges as we struggle with the conflicts of economics and service delivery. Relationships are the cornerstone of business; projecting these challenges into the future, our conclusion is that strategic thinking must build on a foundation of relationship management, which will be crucial to success.

The question we have to ask is whether organizations have the ability and skills to build and exploit trust to deliver these solutions effectively. A good starting point may be to look to the new BSI collaborative business relationship standard BS 11000. This may help to establish a foundation, put some consistency and rigour into trading approaches and help to underpin the value of 'trust'.

Chapter 5 – Creating trust

Checklist

Based on a current critical business relationship, try to assess how your customer or partner may currently view your organization (Table 5.3).

Table 5.3 – Assess customer/partner views

Subject	Rationale	High/ Medium/ Low
Performance	There will always be a strong influence in any business environment in relation to meeting the demands of the market. Trust will never be apparent if organizations or individuals continually fail to meet their obligations. This it is not simply about contract compliance; it is about doing what you say you will do at every level	
Openness	If there is any concern that partners are not being open then trust is put in doubt; it stimulates a protective reaction, which in turn will create a reciprocal reaction	
Honesty	A belief in honesty is fundamental to any trust-based relationship, but in a business context this is often disregarded in favour of game-playing – particularly in negotiations	
Responsive-ness	There is a general acceptance that questions may not be answered immediately. But if requests are ignored this frequently leads to frustration and concern that the answers are being manipulated or interpreted as shielding some aspect, and thus the level of trust becomes questioned	
Commitment	The question of commitment is often a reflection of the prevailing attitude rather than a failure to act. A lack of action may be reflective of other issues but the way this is conveyed will influence the perception of willingness to act	

PART 1: Why?

Fairness	The business world can be a tough environment but in general this is understood by those engaged in it. The outcome of any engagement will be judged by the parties in relation to how it affects their objectives and how fair it is perceived to be, given the circumstances
Information sharing	The benefits of integrated working are the value created by sharing information. The implication of information not being shared is that some other driver is influencing the decision to share and thus opens the way to concerns about the motives, which in turn will affect the level of trust
Communication	Most disputes between individuals or organizations stem from poor communication, which introduces concerns that the other party is not interested or is seeking deliberately not to communicate for some hidden reason. Either way the impact on trust is obvious
Early warnings	Trust breeds confidence and when that confidence is high each party will feel able to share bad news as well as good news. Problems shared after a failure will be interpreted as poor performance, whereas when conveyed early they offer the opportunity to find joint solutions, which increases the perception of trust
Extra mile	The perception that individuals or organizations are prepared to 'go the extra mile' is one of the strongest observations on trust. It conveys a genuine desire to excel and satisfy, which enhances the concept of a trusting relationship

Chapter 6 – Collaborative leadership

> To support change we need to address leadership, the theme of this chapter. As we increasingly adopt alternative business approaches (whether alliances, consortia or partnerships) to meet the challenges of the 21st century, hierarchical structures fail to provide the agility and flexibility to optimize the effectiveness of interdependent operations. The failure of many of these relationships stems from a lack of dynamic leadership to build the environments where the benefits of collaboration can be harnessed and exploited.

With a growing trend towards alternative business models versus traditional operating concepts, based on command and control, leadership is a principal catalyst for success. Leadership is a topic that is debated, discussed and analysed in every academic, political and business forum. From the time of Adam Smith the success of business has been focused on the implementation of strategy by innovative and charismatic leaders. To gauge the interest in the subject, simply log into an online bookstore and type in 'leadership'; there is an enormous number of excellent titles. Yet if you do the same using the term 'collaborative leadership' you will find a very limited number and fewer still with a focus on business.

Dynamic leadership is a key facet of every successful business venture. When managing any partnering alliance or collaborative programmes, where the delivery process crosses organizational boundaries, the role of the leader is even more crucial. Developing an effective focus is a challenge in most business environments but where the traditional command-and-control structure is replaced by cross-functional operations, the coordination and direction of the team is even more complex. Motivation and influence become vital to success.

Collaborative leadership

'Leadership' is often confused with power and control, yet in the environment of integrating relationships across organizational boundaries the most effective outcomes emerge from a pooling of resources, knowledge, skills and capabilities. Where the leaders seek to use their relative power they will inevitably create friction and a lack of

PART 1: Why?

trust that will undermine the potential benefits and development of opportunities. The implementation of alternative business models for operations requires cross-organizational management and effective relationship management to underpin processes and drive success. Leaders need to be able to draw on support, not only from their own organizations but also from those of their partners. The operational role is also likely to be stretched over distance and geographic boundaries, which requires that management rely more on trust and local initiative. The coordination and motivation of remote teams towards common goals is far more complex than co-located operations.

Leadership
- Creating strong values
- Vision
- Strategic thinking
- Motivation
- Energy

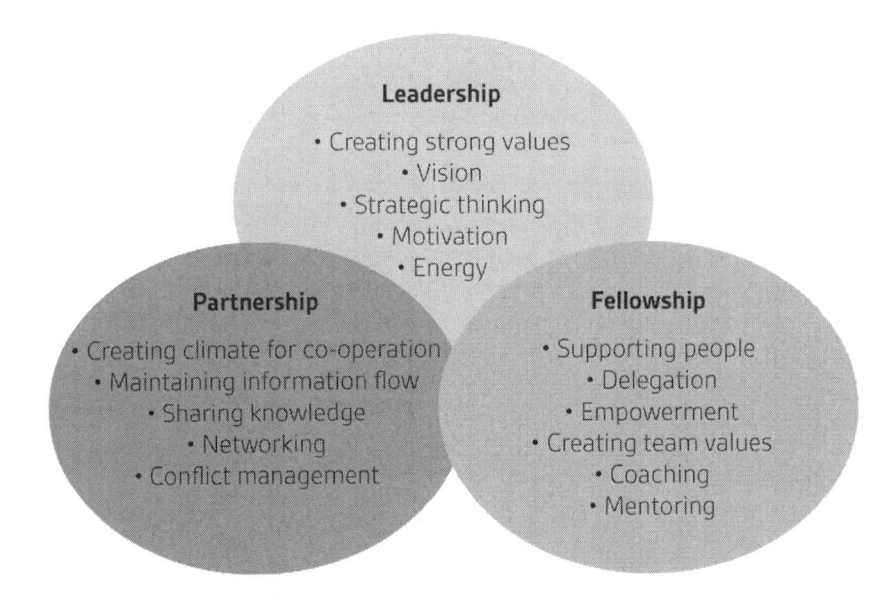

Partnership
- Creating climate for co-operation
- Maintaining information flow
- Sharing knowledge
- Networking
- Conflict management

Fellowship
- Supporting people
- Delegation
- Empowerment
- Creating team values
- Coaching
- Mentoring

Figure 6.1 – Elements of leadership

Executives and collaborative leaders need to recognize that their role is to be the advocate of the collaboration within their own organizations (see Figure 6.1), which may often be in conflict with internal structures. Making the shift from a traditional 'master-and-servant' relationship to co-creators often demands both organizational and personal realignment of thinking and approaches.

Identifying collaborative managers

The challenge when looking for effective collaborative managers is that the range of abilities and attributes necessary produce a profile that is

Chapter 6 – Collaborative leadership

hard to fill. However, this role is crucial in the process of building effective collaborative relationship programmes and driving them to deliver strategic and commercial advantage to the maximum benefit of the partners. Historically, management has drawn its power from position, resource control or professional standing but in a collaborative environment the emphasis must be on inspiration and motivation (see Figure 6.2).

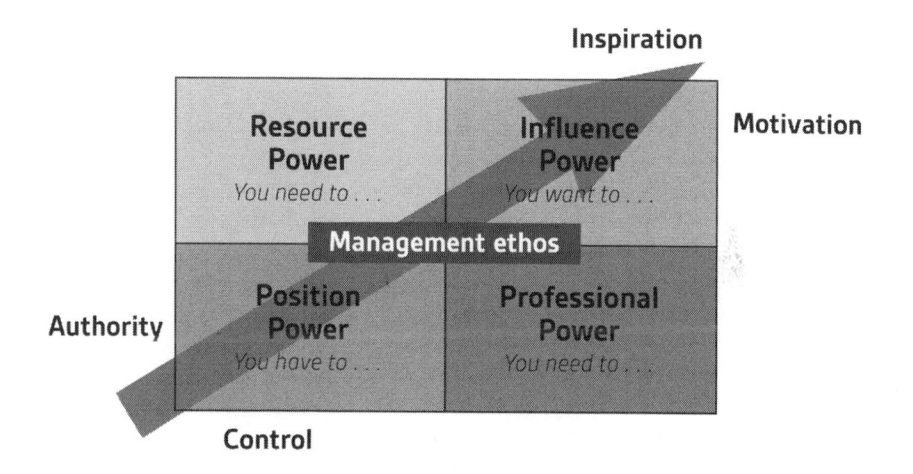

Figure 6.2 – Management ethos

The effective leader will operate not from a position of power but from the ability to influence and inspire, with a good understanding of his or her relative power. The most successful leadership takes its strength from being able to draw parties together and create solutions that use the full potential to optimize performance outcomes, which could not be achieved in isolation. Effective leadership must focus across the interfaces to exploit the potential of collaborative teams irrespective of their individual organizations, while acknowledging that each partner also has to satisfy management and development drivers within their respective organizations. The challenge in the arena of collaborative relationships is to bring together the individual members to contribute to the overall benefit of the team, focused on joint objectives. The recognition of individual contributions is a major factor in inspiring innovative approaches and fostering collective ownership.

PART 1: Why?

The changing nature of leadership

The nature of leadership has changed over time (see Figure 6.3), from a position that was principally based on strength. As the business landscape has changed, so has the influence and skill set required for bringing out the most effective performance. The development of business models from hierarchal wholly owned structures to the more flexible and fluid network of capabilities has led to the need to develop more adaptable management styles, focused on empowering innovation across a range of business relationships.

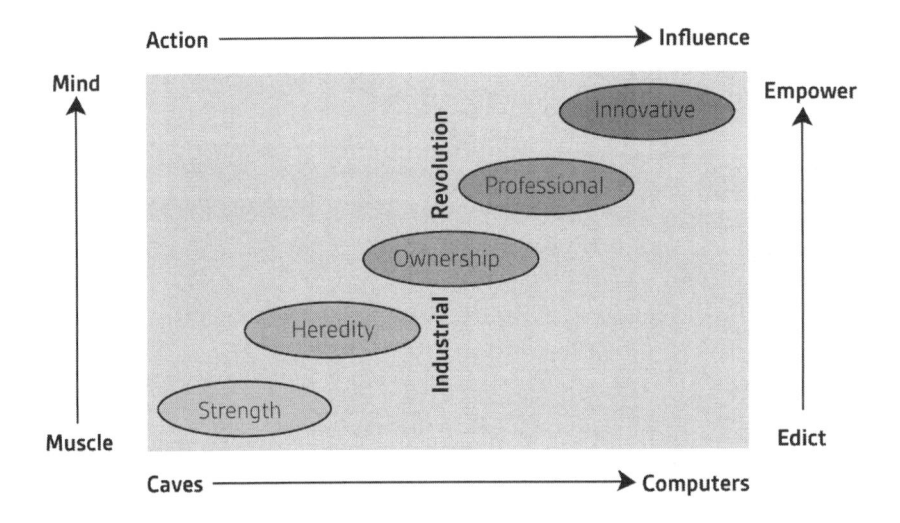

Figure 6.3 – Changing style of leadership

Collaborative working requires leadership that can take management beyond localized internal goals and direct the outcomes towards mutual return on investment within a culture of trust and cooperation. Organizations frequently focus their attention on the qualifications of their people to provide an indicator of potential performance and value. In terms of behavioural performance this may not be the best measure of suitability or reflect a communicative and collaborative style that motivates integration. As collaborative working becomes an established part of business operations, there is an increased emphasis on managing effective relationships – both internally and externally. It requires a foundation on which collaborative leadership can be developed, for those leaders to go on to create the right environment for collaboration and for the development of collaborative leadership skills to meet the strategic challenges of tomorrow.

Chapter 6 – Collaborative leadership

The challenges of leadership

Within many organizations the role of leaders is generally defined by what is expected of them, rather than the skills and capabilities they may need to achieve those results. There is often confusion between *management* and *leadership*. As a result the role of managers is frequently filled based on technical skills and experience. This situation in a traditional command-and-control organizational structure is less problematic than in a collaborative-based environment, where the various parties involved do not have direct ownership or responsibility for each other.

The probability is that in any organization there will be a need to assess and develop the skills and knowledge that are available, then mentor and coach teams to build on the capabilities that exist. The role should not be treated lightly, since the interfaces between organizations can produce significant opportunities and risks, but many of these will probably only surface under effective leadership. The leadership role in a collaborative environment is far more complex than for traditional organizations. Not only do they have to meet the normal demands of team building and motivation; in a virtual context this has to be achieved against the variable background of time, power, distance and cultural diversity. This demands creative leadership with the ability to establish the visions and values that will support a collaborative model, which broadens the essential elements of leadership.

The idea of collaborative integration may be one that offers many organizations the opportunities to develop alternative business models. It is not, however, a simple solution; it challenges many organizations and their leaders to change their operating methods, training, strategies and overall organizational approach. Underpinning collaborative programmes must be a focus on behaviours. From the executives 'walking the talk' to the front-line operators understanding their personal impact when working together to meeting joint objectives, this requires individuals, groups and organizations to understand and manage their behaviours.

To consider the exploitation of the potential benefits of collaborative operations and streamlining of processes, the significance of trust will be obvious. This issue is not simply one of greater openness in the external relationships; it is a major factor when considering the harnessing of internal networks by building a structure for collaborative alignment, monitoring and measuring performance and managing disputes. The concept of 'total cost of ownership' (TCO) has been around for several decades and has prompted many organizations to look beyond the traditional selection criterion of price. At the same time, as customers have sought to exploit 'solutions' rather than products, increasing their use of outsourcing and offshoring to reduce cost, so the integrated nature of managing TCO through a spectrum of external relationships highlights the need to focus on establishing greater cohesion throughout the value chain. The introduction of collaborative relationship management should be seen as a key element of the TCO equation. For leadership this means recognizing interdependency, developing concepts of joint ownership and harnessing collective capability. Understanding strengths and weaknesses will provide background on the areas of risk assumed by collaborative leaders, which they may need development plans to address.

Managing behaviours and disputes through influence

The ethos of an organization is a reflection of its leadership. In any circumstance where people need to work together to deliver a product or service, success largely depends on the behaviours of the people involved. The way in which people interact with each other is a key factor in delivering performance and customer value, and how each individual behaves and performs their roles in the operation strongly influences the way in which others react in return.

Internally there are many interfaces that affect the performance of an organization. It is important to recognize that while many of these may not be directly in the process of delivery they will significantly affect the way individuals react and perform. Customers and external organizations tend to view the whole operation, and effective performance comes from an integrated approach. This is particularly important when considering collaborative ventures that may affect numerous internal boundaries. These background pressures will significantly influence the way they respond to others. Understanding these issues and being aware of how critical behaviours are reflected in the operation is the crucial step towards fully optimizing performance.

Individual and collective performance need to be considered, together with a recognition that through their behaviour each individual can undermine the trust that is building between groups or organizations. It is unlikely that people can effectively reflect a style that is different from their natural traits, and be convincing. The importance, therefore, of understanding the key behaviours is crucial in every aspect of business operations. There are many aspects of behaviour, but in functional terms the key principle is *respect*. Authority can be bestowed but respect can only be earned. So while it may not be possible to change the basic nature of an individual, it is possible to manage how that nature is reflected to others.

The essentials of managing behavioural traits to optimize performance and satisfaction are effective self-management together with leadership, through an organizational ethos that ensures it is recognized as a critical factor for success. Personal and corporate expectations are crucial facets of the collaborative relationship. It is relatively easy to define how we

Chapter 6 – Collaborative leadership

expect others to behave, but it is frequently less common to find those same expectations being reflected in the way in which leadership and organizations present themselves.

The challenge for leadership is to ensure that collaborative programmes remain relevant, as over time new ways become a way of life and need to be regularly reassessed. At the same time, it is important to recognize that collaborative relationships should not only be delivering on the initial objectives; to remain energized they should also be focused on adding additional value.

Working in a collaborative environment may not come easily to everyone; developing the skills can make a significant contribution to overall integration. In most operating environments the route to effective learning is driven by exposure and sharing. It is, however, important to recognize that people learn at differing rates and through a multiplicity of styles. Learning is also a constant process and is essential to the development of effective relationships. It is a two-way process that only adds real value when it is a shared journey. The collaborative leader should be a catalyst for behaviour development programmes; intelligent learning is a fundamental part of the management process to support individual development and confidence.

In a changing world, the internal and external pressures on any collaborative relationship will inevitably lead to impacts on effectiveness. As relationships evolve they will undergo change. No two relationships are the same; the dynamics of organizational and people changes can influence performance. It is important to recognize that as relationships progress they need to be monitored to ensure that appropriate focus is maintained on areas where perhaps convergence is not happening to maximum benefit. Appropriate performance measures will need to be established, to ensure that behaviours and their impact are recognized and addressed. The longer the relationship is in place the greater the risk that complacency will build between the various parties.

In any business venture where people are involved there is always the possibility of differences; the same is true of collaborative programmes. Managing conflict towards constructive and mutually beneficial outcomes is a critically important element of effective collaborative leadership. In a collaborative arrangement it is essential to ensure that there is a conflict resolution process which provides a mechanism and escalation procedure where appropriate. In a commercial environment some issues may eventually lead to a contractual impasse between the parties. This will be likely to have a direct impact on operational performance and, if not addressed effectively, may lead to the breakdown of the relationship. While many issues may be resolved within the collaborative teams, some will inevitably need particular support. The value of the relationship and the investment made should stimulate a joint desire to find an effective outcome.

PART 1: Why?

Collaborative leadership self-assessment

Leaders must adopt an approach that is focused on helping the teams to master collaborative working and meeting their objectives. This starts by collaborative leaders supporting individual development and managing non-aligned behaviours. Success relies on a cluster of competencies and behaviours that build on those of traditional leadership, but are specifically aimed at collaborative working. The assessment of collaborative leadership can be focused on two key aspects: *ability* and *attitude* (see Figure 6.4). 'Ability' is about business-related experience in areas that would be supportive to functioning outside the traditional command-and-control structure. 'Attitude' is the individual's style of operating with others in a collaborative environment. These two distinct but interrelated aspects, when combined, together create a collaborative leadership profile.

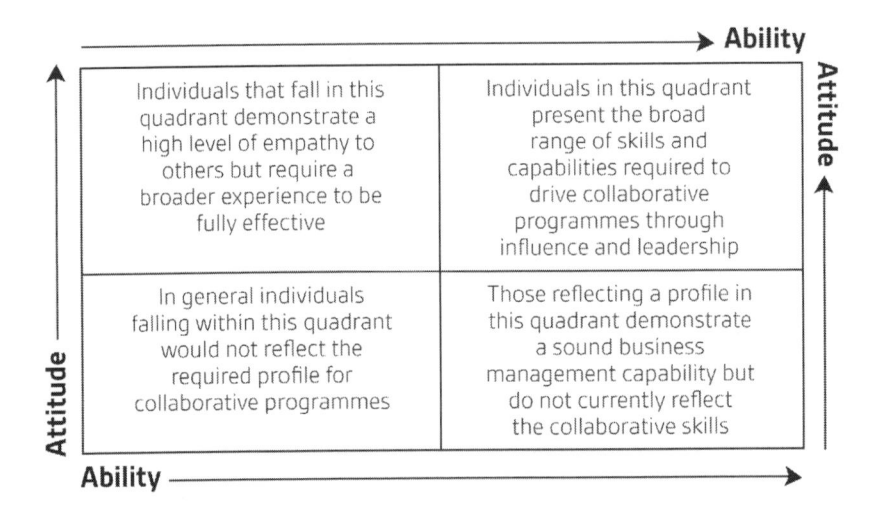

	→ Ability	
Attitude ↑	Individuals that fall in this quadrant demonstrate a high level of empathy to others but require a broader experience to be fully effective	Individuals in this quadrant present the broad range of skills and capabilities required to drive collaborative programmes through influence and leadership
	In general individuals falling within this quadrant would not reflect the required profile for collaborative programmes	Those reflecting a profile in this quadrant demonstrate a sound business management capability but do not currently reflect the collaborative skills
	Ability →	Attitude ↑

Figure 6.4 – Ability versus attitude

Table 6.1 contains some attributes that organizations and prospective collaborative leaders should consider as a basis for self-assessment, combining both business skills and their individual traits.

Table 6.1 – Abilities and attitudes

Ability (skills and experience)	Attitude (personal approach)
Business leadership	Communications
Contract management	Interpersonal skills
Risk management	Management style
Change management	Self-awareness
Planning	Business approach
Strategic thinking	Expectations of others
Relationship management	Importance of relationships
Performance	Team working
Team building	Leadership traits
Benchmarking	Sustainability
Partnering experience	Training and self-development
Product development	Decision making
Service delivery	Personal focus to others
International trade	Performance failure
Qualifications	Management of disputes
Customer management	Motivation
Market knowledge	Positioning
Project management	Working approach
Value chain	Learning style
Financial management	Key success factors

Conclusion

The challenges of working in a collaborative environment should not be underestimated and prompt us to look closely at personal attitudes. In a command-and-control structure the leadership position provides a degree of security and confidence, but self-awareness is crucial if collaborative leaders are to be successful. They need to be able to recognize their own strengths and weaknesses and understand how these aspects affect others. Directing through influence rather than power or position requires increased self-management to maintain control while at the same time creating trust, being adaptive and innovative. They will need to manage disruptive influences and maintain honesty. Collaborative leaders need to be self-motivated and drive innovation to focus on the improvements that will achieve organizational goals.

There is a need to maintain empathy by being actively interested in others, ready to share knowledge and mentor those individuals who are less confident in a collaborative structure. Many businesses are organized along traditional lines where command and control is the default situation. In a collaborative venture the leader must satisfy the mutual objectives of the parties and create additional value through innovation. The leader's skills are focused on influencing the relationship to achieve these outcomes, being unable to rely on hierarchical power and unilateral authority.

Leadership is a complex and crucial role; in a growing environment of alternative business models it is one that will largely define success or failure. Many can lead, but those who have the capacity to influence outcomes when they do not have control are less obvious. Too frequently the role is one that is assigned by default or based on technical skills and experience, an approach that has potential flaws when driving a collaborative programme. It is essential that organizations considering alternative business models expand their selection and development processes to encompass an alternative leadership profile which recognizes the challenges of leadership outside the traditional structures.

Checklist

To create an initial profile of a collaborative leader it can be useful to ask a few simple questions and analyse their inputs, such as shown in Table 6.2.

Table 6.2 – Initial collaborative leadership profile

	Score 5 high 1 low
I don't need to change the way I work	
I don't find some people hard to tolerate	
My thinking is intuitive	
I find it easy to see others' point of view	
I don't get anxious and know how to deal with change	
I have more control over my activities than others	
I adapt my behaviour to achieve my objectives	
I am not rigid once I have made a decision	
Friendship at work is a bonus, not a necessity	
I maintain my position even if it upsets others	
I am optimistic but keep my eye on things	
I only show my feelings when I need to	
Generally people live up to their promises	
I think constructive criticism is useful	
Building relationships is easy for me	
I know my strengths	
I understand where I am weak and need to be vigilant	

PART 1: Why?

I enjoy working as part of a team	
I expect others to follow without question	
I believe you need to listen to others	
Scores 0–25 The individual has difficulty managing personal behaviour; translating this to effective relationship management, the individual finds it hard to trust others. 25–50 The individual is comfortable with their own attitude but recognizes that there are areas which require development. The individual can deal with most problems but expects others to follow. 50–75 The individual is good at managing people and believes in developing trust and support from others. The individual tends to manage by consultation and openness, recognizing others' needs. 75–100 The individual has a good approach to leadership and management that is based on developing effective relationships. The individual will handle conflict well and react well to change.	

Chapter 7 – Positioning relationships

> Having considered some of the major influences in the development of collaborative relationships, the focus of this chapter turns to evaluating appropriate relationships to concentrate resources for maximum business benefit. Many organizations underestimate (or ignore) the investment required to achieve the full potential of collaborative working, because they do not take a focused approach to evaluating and targeting the right relationships.

Historically terms such as partnering, alliances and collaborative working have been used in a variety of circumstances, covering a broad range of relationships. Frequently the use of such labels has been inappropriately assigned to conventional trading arrangements, with the result that they set unrealistic expectations. This creates the perception that these models are simply cosy relationships – or the latest trend – and are deemed to have failed. Collaboration can make a valuable contribution to business operations, but it has to be recognized that these approaches can require a significant investment of time and resources, so it is important to establish the potential return on investment.

It is equally important to understand that every organization is different. While there are many common themes, any collaborative programme needs to be aligned with specific business objectives and challenges. By segregating the profile of external relationships, these can be grouped to ensure that resources are most effectively deployed. Consideration should be given not only to the current relationships, but also to the potential developments within the marketplace or anticipated changes in the overall business strategy. This will enable any implementation programme and investment in collaborative relationships to capture potential benefits in the future.

Applying collaborative concepts and approaches across the value chain can help to integrate horizontal and vertical relationships to create value. For most businesses their external spend may be a significant proportion of total operating cost; planning their supply needs early will direct efforts to the optimized outcome. Understanding the capability of providers and their drivers is crucial to developing an effective partnership. In today's market the adoption of alliances is equally important in terms of business development when considering the

PART 1: Why?

creation of complex multifaceted solutions. Assumptions during the early stages may prove both costly and time-consuming. Establishing the right partner is crucial to the success of the venture, so organizations should not take any relationship for granted; this is particularly relevant when moving into a new style of trading that could have long-term implications. The process needs to be carefully considered and developed in a managed way to support a good commercial and competitive position. In assessing a strategic partner there is a need to look much deeper than quality compliance to a contract. There is a need to evaluate more intensively, since once the relationship is in place organizations will operate in a more open manner. They must be able to support the intended markets and have appropriate experience, ethos and style as learning organizations (see Figure 7.1).

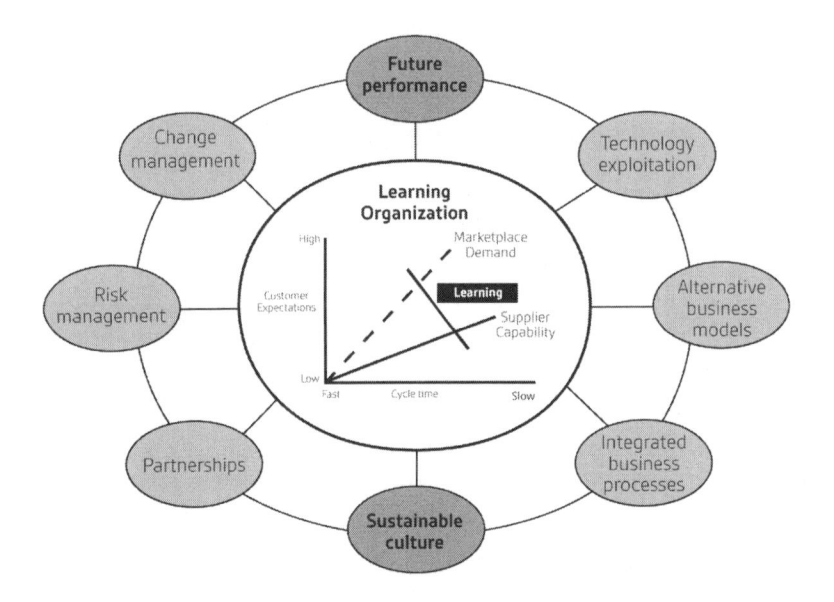

Figure 7.1 – Learning organization

Targeting collaborative benefits

Organizations should have a clear understanding of what collaboration means to them. The term has been misused in becoming the watchword for marketing people across the globe. It is not partnering if all you do is to speak politely to each other. Nor should it be used to disguise what in many cases are cost-down contracts. There are many contracting approaches that can be deployed that clearly work better under a collaborative umbrella. We may be looking at options such as target contracts, blanket contracts, preferred suppliers, cost-plus contracts, call-off agreements or joint ventures; if these will provide the required outcomes, they should not be confused by calling them a partnership. In developing BS 11000 the aim was to create a collaborative framework that could be used across the contracting spectrum, where partnership may be an eventual goal but that could also support more traditional relationships. The objective has to be focused on enhancing overall business performance. This enhancement is driven by all of the key drivers that make up this business cycle, starting with focusing the organization on the 'total cost' of doing business, as opposed to the price you would normally pay at (say) point of sale. It must encompass the sharing of risk, to get organizations looking beyond previous norms to understand why they should even consider partnering as an option.

The concept of collaboration has a very wide remit in terms of the joint potential that can be developed. Being clear on how far you want to go is extremely important to the development process. Setting the scene can often be just a simple process of assessing the advantages and disadvantages associated with any alliance. Consider the example below.

SELEX Systems Integration Ltd – case study

SELEX Systems Integration Ltd expected the standard would strengthen our business benefits by building and maintaining relationships throughout our supply chain, and we were not disappointed. The economic challenges of the current market, place even greater emphasis on the value of collaborative relationships. For us, therefore, attaining BS 11000 was never a 'quick fix' or 'simply another approach to supply chain management'. This standard offered an innovative, structured approach to relationship management, which, in addition to dedicated board commitment, had the potential to yield transformational long-term benefits. SELEX Systems Integration Ltd is rightfully proud that it was one of the first companies to be accredited to BS 11000, which is testament to our corporate ethos of building long-term relationships based on trust and transparency.

Anita Broadhead
Commercial Manager
Selex ES Ltd

To make a collaborative relationship work, there has to be clarity on all sides as to what each expects to gain and is prepared to support – joint objectives, not the individual scores. So organizations must be clear about their real goals in an environment of openness and this is often where

PART 1: Why?

the concepts start to break down. Developing collaborative programmes requires real commitment and a structured approach for finding the appropriate partner to work with.

Performance based collaboration

When should an organization consider the benefits of effective collaborative relationship management? In the first place it should be focused on being cost-effective and has to be evaluated as the most appropriate tool. There should be consideration as to whether the relationship lends itself to repeat business and whether it can benefit from lessons learned within the time frame that the relationship needs for it to develop.

Looking at collaborative arrangements requires a degree of filtering. It is unlikely that a direct copy of one company's programme would fit another organization exactly in any event. There are, however, some common traits that fall out from investigation. These are the traits that organizations should be looking to mirror, recognizing that the traditional adversarial approach diverts resources away from focusing on the mutual benefits of optimizing cost and time. Collaborative approaches do to some extent force organizations to look at how they share risk, monitor performance and share cost reductions, as opposed to traditionally subcontracted work based on a fixed price contract, which frequently results in conflict and claims. In a collaborative relationship the driver has to be targeted towards measurable performance and value for money, where the incentive is to perform well and share the benefits.

Skanska Civil Engineering – case study

At Skanska we a have a long history of collaborative working with our customers, our joint venture partners and our supply chain. Collaboration in business is not an easy option as it always involves additional effort to ensure that the terms and the direction remain clear to everyone, and to ensure that trust remains at all times – even when time and money are tight. However, we are convinced it is absolutely the right way to deliver best value to our customers and to our stakeholders – the benefits far outweigh the disadvantages.

Many of our flagship projects, such as the M25 widening, have been delivered through joint venture relationships that extend back decades. Our supply chain delivers most of our project output; it is essential that we work with them to continuously improve our combined efficiency and productivity. Since Egan and Latham[7] our public sector customers have recognized that collaboration is the best way to deliver the continual improvements demanded by those holding the public purse, and we have worked on many pioneering collaborative contracts including the Channel Tunnel Rail Link, Early Contractor Involvement schemes for the Highways Agency and Network Rail, and the @One Alliance for Anglian Water.

BS 11000 provides a framework and a language to improve the way we create and sustain our collaborative business relationships. It reflects our existing best practice, but some of this is not formally captured and in other areas we know we can yet collaborate more effectively. We view BS 11000 implementation as an opportunity to record, rationalize and improve our approach to collaboration so that everyone in Skanska understands how we should manage our collaborative relationships.

Jonathan Morris
Business Improvement Director
Skanska Civil Engineering

Defining your expectations

The reason to look at expectations before deciding on the focus of collaboration is twofold. Firstly, it is on the assumption that the organization already has some interest in collaboration and has ideas of where it could help; and secondly, without clearly establishing benefits the focus can be diluted. Throughout the commercial marketplace, you are unlikely to succeed unless you know where you are going – and it must make commercial sense. If you cannot define what success looks like, how can you strive for it or know when it has been achieved?

Examining the potential wider aspects of a business relationship will provide useful background thinking when it comes to deciding the suitability of the approach and the commercial benefits of collaboration. With the ever-increasing moves towards solutions (rather than products or services) the traditional view of an organization is changing. It may now depend as much on integrated capability as it does on traditional products or services. Cost reduction provides true opportunities that traditional relationships are unlikely to achieve. This is logical, for why should a provider pass back cost reductions when they have competitively

---

[7] Major reports in the 1990s leading to significant recommendations for better practice in public sector construction projects.

PART 1: Why?

won a contract? In a traditional relationship the buyer seldom (if ever) provides the flexibility to generate these savings, perhaps because they do not believe that they would get a fair share of the saving for the effort involved.

In a more open relationship the rules can change, and across industry they are being changed through partnering deals. To remain at the leading edge, organizations have to change the rules and collaboration offers one of the approaches. When both sides can see real return for their effort then the enthusiasm for trying increases, particularly if this can be done without eroding margins and profitability. This offers better benefits compared with the traditional negotiating of contract changes or variations, where both sides lose interest as each tries for the major slice. If you have the right partner you can look to see where there is duplication of effort and what really does add value. Once organizations 'cross the Rubicon' in making a collaboration decision it is surprising what opportunities come to light.

In many fields of engineering contracting much of the time is spent in reviewing and questioning the output of providers and suppliers. So one might ask: is it not better to apply the effort upfront to validating the partner than sitting looking over their shoulder? The effort should go into looking for opportunities, not failings. This gives a much greater return on investment but involves a much greater degree of responsibility on both sides to make it a success. The development of joint responsibility opens up the possibility for joint management and as a result lower costs. However, avoiding duplication of effort does of course raise the issue of risk management – but the potential to improve competitiveness through collaboration risk sharing is a major consideration.

Having looked principally at the operational benefits, the next benefit comes from taking a longer-term perspective. These opportunities may not be immediately appropriate but could in time be the basis of a true winning combination through optimization in its many forms. The long-term stability of a true collaborative partnership provides a platform on which each party can grow, working within a team environment that encourages the focus to be on total cost (not individual order volume) while maintaining profitability for all and increasing orders. These are some of the concepts that are being used to improve the competitiveness of previously established adversaries in the value chain.

Segregating relationships

The spectrum of relationships, specific needs and strategic requirements will be many and varied. Within this context the following generic model

Chapter 7 – Positioning relationships

(see Figure 7.2) based on the Kraljic model[8] provides a basis for initial positioning of relationships. In some cases there will be a progression from one sector to the next, based on changes in demand or the development of an opportunity. At the end of this chapter there is a brief checklist, which may help to focus development.

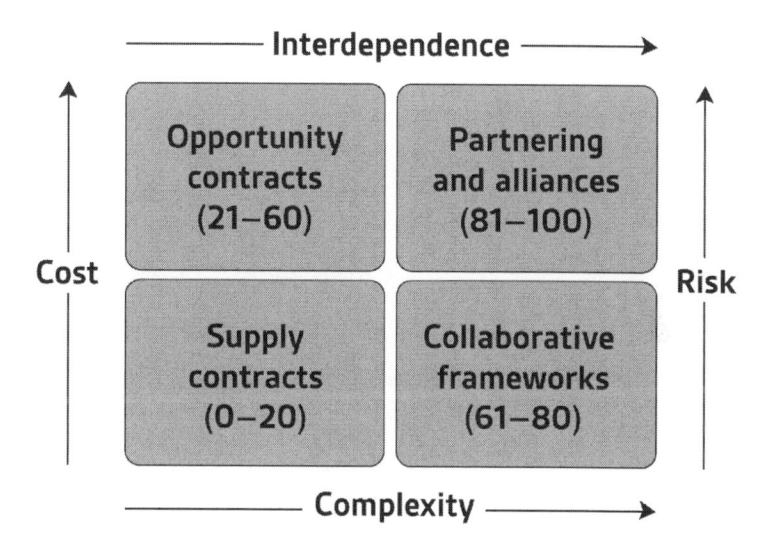

```
                    ——— Interdependence ———▶
        ▲
        │   ┌──────────────┐  ┌──────────────┐   ▲
        │   │ Opportunity  │  │  Partnering  │   │
        │   │  contracts   │  │ and alliances│   │
            │   (21–60)    │  │   (81–100)   │
  Cost      └──────────────┘  └──────────────┘   Risk
        │   ┌──────────────┐  ┌──────────────┐   │
        │   │   Supply     │  │ Collaborative│   │
        │   │  contracts   │  │  frameworks  │   │
        │   │    (0–20)    │  │   (61–80)    │   │
            └──────────────┘  └──────────────┘
                    ——— Complexity ———▶
```

Figure 7.2 – Relationship focus

Supply contracts would be those that will generally cover products, commodities or simple services that are relatively low value, limited complexity and low risk but, more importantly, not of strategic impact to the business. Opportunity contracts would be those that while of significant impact are generally one-off type requirements, where the most likely best outcome would come from a traditionally developed arm's-length contract arrangement. Collaborative frameworks would be those that while not initially strategic in nature are of significant cumulative value, where overall cost and performance can be enhanced through the development of a framework agreement that fosters a more integrated approach. Partnering and alliances would be strategic requirements where the long-term potential for an integrated approach could provide significant advantage and benefit through the exchange of knowledge and resources.

The challenge for most organizations is to establish and communicate a clearly defined set of criteria to help those involved in the selection

---

[8] *Purchasing must become supply management*, Kraljic P, Harvard Business Review, 1983.

PART 1: Why?

process to understand the different models and applications. However, these alone should never be the only criteria when considering any contracting arrangement. There needs to be a balance against aspects of performance and overall risk to the business. Every organization is different and thus the spread of activities may vary significantly; however, in most cases the cost and risk profile tends to follow a pattern.

	Criteria	Supply	Contract	Collaboration	Partnership
1	Cost, delivery and quality only	x	?		
2	Single site service contract		x		
3	Multi-site service or maintenance contract		x	x	
4	Outsourcing BPO programmes			x	?
5	Customer facing outsourcing programmes				x
6	Fully defined supply requirements	x	?	?	
7	Solution development programmes				x
8	Repeatable construction programmes			x	x
9	Product development programmes			x	x
10	Integrated distribution and logistics programmes			?	x
11	Performance critical activities			?	x
12	High levels of knowledge transfer required			?	x
13	Clear opportunities for joint value creation		?	x	x
14	Limited market supply capability			?	x
15	Open ended development requirement				x
16	Opportunity for cost aggregation			x	x

Figure 7.3 – Contracting types

The matrix shown in Figure 7.3 provides an initial basis for establishing a relationship route to ensure that collaborative programmes are focused appropriately, defining how they will function and deliver additional value. Structured correctly, it will provide a platform for measuring success and provide clarity on resources, risk and contribution. Before looking at setting up a collaborative approach, there should be a hard debate around the life expectancy of the agreement. Contract duration will have a major impact on the thinking process and the structure of arrangements. Over a period of time the market position changes; if agreements are not flexible there will be problems downstream.

Chapter 7 – Positioning relationships

What should your partner look like?

Creating an effective strategy must be based not on desires but on a firm foundation of capabilities and sound assessment of the arena that will be encountered. There needs to be a framework within which organizations can undertake a systematic approach to consolidating their internal expectations and views of potential partners, then deploy these findings to create the appropriate strategy (see Figure 7.4). Through a process of categorizing the key issues, organizations can focus on the fundamental issues that will drive the relationship towards a successful implementation. Certainly there will be some opinions about the issues that have greater weight, simply due to the personnel involved, or at an administrative level this may be a factor of the organizational style of the potential partner. In the later stages of assessment there has to be a focus on setting action plans for improvements and any corrective actions; no one specific issue is likely to be a 'show-stopper'. This is because in most cases the potential partner is already part of the existing trading network, where common performance issues will have already been assessed.

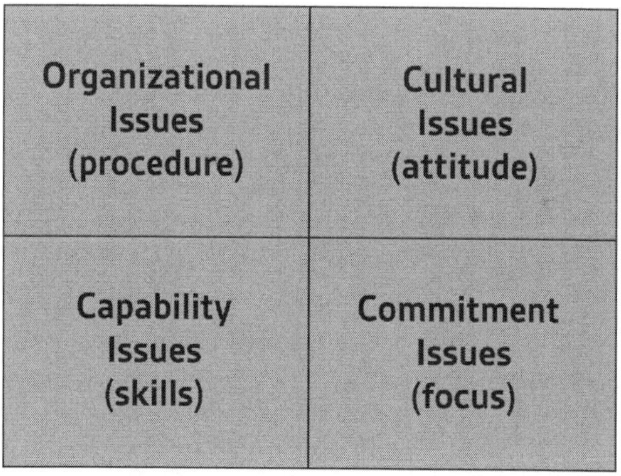

Organizational Issues (procedure)	Cultural Issues (attitude)
Capability Issues (skills)	Commitment Issues (focus)

Figure 7.4 – Development areas

The process is to develop the criteria that will be used to make the assessment, aimed at compiling a sound overall picture of the potential partner and then focusing on the areas for exploitation and improvement. It is common that certain functions within an organization will have greater emphasis than others, but if the relationship is to be effective then each primary functional group must be represented in the evaluation. Sample criteria for assessing potential partners is shown below.

PART 1: Why?

Typical partner profile questions:

Level of commitment
Level of capability
Dynamic culture
Appropriate organization
Level of communication
Total cost approach
Quality programme
Commitment to our vision and values
Customer focus
Attitude to partnering

This will result in identifying those potential partners where there is an obvious fit. The remainder are those organizations that may need time to develop in order to become partners and those where it would clearly be in the best interests of the parties to remain in a conventional contracting relationship.

In general, the custom and practice of organizations and their traditional relationships will support the views identified in partner assessments. The intended outcome of this process is to initiate a more integrated relationship; the views used to this point have been those from within the organization, so it is often useful to consider testing the validity of the filtering process on the prospective partner. Clearly, many of the views expressed from inside the organization are likely to be critical, since that is the objective of the process. Even though the aim is to highlight strengths, it is common to focus on the negatives.

Conclusion

If segregation is approached in a structured manner, then the outcomes will be focused on creating a platform for exploiting the relationship and defining areas where joint attention could produce benefits to both parties. In most cases the tensions between organizations are seldom one-sided; the structure of the assessment can be very useful in opening up possibilities for improvement. The feedback from such discussions can often strengthen the analysis and improve the overall process, as recognition of internal constraints is not something that most organizations can easily identify.

Collaboration is about exploiting the joint potential of partnering organizations in an open and positive manner, so feedback will also test the validity of the potential partners' resolve to participate proactively. This should be developed into suitable action plans to address the short-, medium- and long-term issues that result from the overall analysis. This process is crucial to get in place the key issues that need to be addressed with potential partners. These consolidated perspectives generate a realistic and recognizable profile that should only encourage improvement.

The application of collaborative approaches takes time and valuable resources, so it is important to focus on deploying organizations' assets to maximum effect. A structured approach helps to ensure that these capabilities can be focused on where they will deliver maximum value. It is also important to ensure that approaches such as partnering or collaboration are not applied to situations where more traditional approaches are adequate to meet the operational need, since if they are not managed properly the likely outcome would be counterproductive.

PART 1: Why?

Checklist

The general profiling approach shown in Table 7.1 helps to develop a specific strategic approach that addresses internal concerns and external influences. The matrix is based on a simple scoring model to gauge the importance of specific identified issues. By assessing these 20 parameters the organization should be able to start the process of segregating its existing or projected future relationship requirements.

Table 7.1 – Identifying key parameters for potential partners

		Low = 1 – High = 5	
1	Scope	Standard product – New development	
2	Overall risk assessment	Low risk – high risk	
3	Engineering design	Fully developed – solution required	
4	Market profit	Highly competitive – specialist field	
5	Number of suppliers	High – low	
6	Supplier capability	High – limited exposure	
7	Quality requirements	Market standard – mission critical	
8	Cost baseline	Fully validated – estimate only available	
9	Complexity	Plug and play – high integration	
10	Frequency of requirement	One off requirement – multiple need	
11	Delivery performance	Low impact – strategic needs	
12	Knowledge transfer need	Low – high level of exchange needed	
13	Performance improvement	Low potential – high opportunity	
14	Scope for risk and reward	Low – high potential for improvement	
15	CSR implications	Limited – high risk	
16	Internal reference data	High – limited data available	
17	Management requirement	Light touch – high supervision need	
18	Past experience in this area	Good – poor record of performance	
19	Procurement driver	General requirement – strategic focus	
20	Business criticality	Low impact – business critical	
		Total	

PART 2: How?

Chapter 8 – Background and introduction to BS 11000

> In Part 2 of this book the aim is to assess how to use BS 11000: where the BS 11000 framework can add some structure and benchmarking for an organization's capability to exploit collaborative approaches. Part 1 considered the background and positioning of collaborative relationships; potential benefits were also identified. This chapter introduces the reader to BS 11000; subsequent chapters in this part focus on the various 'how' aspects.

The aim of BS 11000 (the world's first relationship framework, developed in association with a pan-industry group) was to establish a national and sector-neutral framework that captures best practice in collaborative and partnering programmes to support the implementation and management of collaborative relationships. The drive to develop a route map for collaboration came from the experience of working on alliance and partnering programmes, some of which delivered significant benefit and others that failed. Experience highlighted that when relationships did not deliver or hit upon rough times it was clear that the foundations were weak. There are many sound methodologies available to support collaborative or partnering programmes, but most of these focus on the point of engagement and beyond, whereas the standard is based on a life cycle model from concept to closure.

The major challenge highlighted was that the principal constraint would be the lack of skills within the business sector to develop and manage these networks. The traditional command-and-control management training was inadequate to address the complexity of exploiting this relationship-based community. Developing the more fluid structures and training of future managers has also brought out a significant number of associations and organizations focused on trying to raise the professional standard and benchmarking for these new skills. It was this trend that instigated the development of BS 11000 through the adoption of the

PART 2: How?

CRAFT methodology,[9] which was the foundation of the standard. The driver was to identify the key requirements that would provide a sound platform to collaborate, then develop the principles that could be embedded in operating processes to give organizations a more effective foundation. The result of this research was the eight-step model that now forms the backbone of the standard (see Figure 8.1).

Figure 8.1 – Eight-step life cycle model

Awareness: changing the way we relate to external organizations can be challenging to overcome. There may be internal constraints where collaboration is viewed as 'soft and fluffy'. It is equally crucial to ensure that efforts are focused on those relationships where collaboration will

---

[9] CRAFT: Collaborative Relationship, Assessment, Fulfilment, and Transformation – methodology developed by the author with PSL (now known as the Institute for Collaborative Working).

deliver real value and avoid using titles such as *'partnering'* that can complicate traditional contracting relationships.

Knowledge: creating effective collaboration needs strategies focused on the business objectives. The strategy must recognize the risks associated with greater integration, together with aspects of knowledge management and business continuity. It is particularly useful to consider your exit strategy at this stage, as this will help to identify key concerns.

Internal assessment: understanding the strengths and weaknesses of our own organizations is critical if collaboration is to be successful. We frequently focus on what we want from others, rather than ensuring we can meet our side of the arrangement.

Partner selection: finding the right partner is critical and frequently we assume that long-standing traditional supplier relationships can simply migrate. Often this is not the case, so it is important to understand the partner profile you are looking for and how you will evaluate their capability to collaborate.

Working together: establishing joint governance for collaborative programmes and integrating these into effective contracting arrangements requires careful attention. There must be consideration for both the joint objectives and those of the individual partners, together with ensuring that the performance incentives and measurement will support collaborative behaviours.

Value creation: the key to maintaining a sound relationship is to ensure that it remains current and drives innovation to bring additional value to the relationship through joint continual improvement programmes.

Staying together: relationships need nurturing. Changes in people and the business environment must be monitored, along with performance and behaviours. Issues and disputes will be inevitable but can strengthen relationships if handled effectively.

Exit strategy: nothing lasts for ever and business relationships will eventually reach an end. Maintaining a joint exit strategy is important, to keep the partners focused. At the same time, clear rules for disengagement will frequently improve active engagement throughout the life of the relationship.

A foundation for collaboration and partnering

The concept of a virtual organization is not new; early references go back to the 1950s, when the computer was a new business tool. Taking a broad definition, perhaps the grouping of different specialist trades to create a customer-focused product has been common, rather than exceptional, throughout history. In today's wired world we focus on computers and internet technology, linking companies across the globe and offering opportunities for value propositions that independently would not be practical. Another significant movement towards integration of business relationships began in the 1980s. This was partnering or the use of alliances, which showed how independent organizations could operate within the 'umbrella' of a single objective. Crossing traditional contractual boundaries, the model develops a more integrated approach than that of old-style consortia.

As business moves from an industrial economy towards a network economy, exchanging a portfolio of products for capabilities and new relationships, we see an evolution embracing virtual integration. This is given further impetus by globalization; organizational structures and skill sets must be re-evaluated to relate better to the relationship-based value chains of the future.

So why did this 'new' enthusiasm start to drive in different directions? The truth is that, despite the 'soft and fluffy' perceptions, the foundation of collaborative thinking was based on hard commercial needs and challenges – reducing costs to maintain position in an ever increasingly competitive marketplace. Unfortunately it also meant that pressure to reduce costs at the top of the supply chain placed pressure on those further down to take on higher levels of risk. In many cases the result was less reward, despite the sales pitch that shared risk would be balanced against increased potential profit. The idea of 'no pain, no gain' takes on a whole new meaning.

In fact the real exponents of collaboration in recent years were those at the supply end of the production manufacturing markets. Concepts such as just in time (JIT) supply programmes required the forging of new relationships between suppliers and manufacturers. In many cases the major retail sales outlets developed approaches which ring-fenced such a large part of their supplier's production that in practice they had almost total management control without taking any equity. These may have been called partnering arrangements but in reality they were traditional master-and-servant relationships. The move towards outsourcing brought with it new problems, for while it did reduce in-house costs it also meant a greater dependence on third parties, who themselves needed to provide returns to their shareholders.

The evolution of the supply chain became a strategic imperative and the idea of JIT relationships moved towards finding new ways of remaining competitive; the prospect of cost reduction across the supply chain became the major driver. These arrangements triggered the start of looking at much tighter relationships, where interdependency opened doors to eliminating duplication of effort and investment. The essential component of these relationships was a need to introduce incentives for

Chapter 8 – Background and introduction to BS 11000

improved performance on both sides of the trading boundary. Risk and reward had to be acknowledged and trading terms had to be long enough to allow investment return.

Unfortunately for many, at least in the short term, they launched into the concept with a somewhat uninformed approach. Their new way was outwardly based on teaming, bonding and a search for those who claimed the same desires. The view that your attitude and that of partners was in fact more important than having a sound working relationship opened up a whole vista of problems. The collaborative alliances became stretched as conflicts of interest and individual company profitability came under pressure. As with any relationship, there will always be times when differing views and drivers create the pressure for self-preservation. But some cases, which are now often held up as the benchmarks for promoting the concepts of partnering, not only established working alliances to enable a sound business case to be made for previously uneconomic developments. They have shown that by working openly together with their supply chain, development costs can be reduced by 30 per cent as was the case for BP Andrew. The reality is there and so is the potential risk: if any company heads into the world of collaboration thinking it is easy, they will very quickly fail. Those who have been successful shout a lot, those who have failed keep very quiet.

Changing the rules of the game requires alternative thinking that may be suppressed within the confines of current contracting practice. This transition can seldom be achieved purely based on internal actions. The development of an integrated relationship must be based on exploiting the complementary skills and resources that potential partners can bring to the arrangement.

The objective of increasing value to the partners and to the ultimate customer must be based on the key ingredients that that are considered to represent and support the end goals. The objective when undertaking an organizational analysis is not simply to rank organizations, but to remove the outer layer; and establish if the potential partner shares the long-term objectives and targets that will deliver benefits to the arrangement over time.

The traditional benchmarks that accompany supplier selection such as financial strength and historical performance should not be ignored, but should be balanced against the underlying ethos that will ensure that as the relationship progresses the parties can become focused on joint aims to their mutual benefit.

Successful collaboration rests on a common drive to exploit the joint potential of two or more individual organizations. BS 11000 standard provides a structured platform for organizations to realize their capabilities and those of its partners to provide an integrated solution that creates value and optimizes existing relationships. Organizations are

PART 2: How?

beginning to appreciate that integration can deliver valuable contributions; however, this means that traditional contracting boundaries and perceived safeguards need to be complemented with a more focused view on the type of organization being collaborated with.

Costain – case study

For Costain the main drivers for collaborative working were already there – it is fundamentally the way we work, and is key to our 'Choosing Costain strategy'. So adopting BS 11000 was a 'no-brainer'. Doing so will demonstrate to our customers that we do what we say, and our collaborative capability has been independently verified by BSI.

Another key driver is that BS 11000 provides a standard approach with a common language that (as more organizations adopt the standard) can be adopted and readily understood by all parties. It has helped bring structure and process to a subject that had in the past been a little intangible and is particularly important as we form many joint ventures, alliances and relationships.

One of the first challenges was to map our existing collaborative processes to the standard, and not to reinvent the wheel or cause duplication, and then looking to see where any gaps were. For example, planning for 'disengagement' before selecting a partner was something that was not formally done at this early stage of a relationship.

Tony Blanch, Business Improvement Director
Costain Group

Effective performance is created through integration of the organization's internal environment and its external customers and suppliers. Holistic management has to extend beyond the traditional functional boundaries within organizations to ensure that opportunities are fully exploited. Building on the strengths of the organization, it is critical to establish the current level of knowledge and skills to ensure that suitable training is developed that will provide an effective platform to move into collaboration with confidence.

Creating the future of collaboration

In collaborative business relationships, the advantage of developing more effective relationships is in exploiting the joint knowledge and capabilities of organizations to create added value for the partners, and for the end-customer or consumer, which could not be created individually. This sharing of knowledge is at the core of effective collaboration and is the catalyst for creating value.

Value creation is about stimulating innovation and capitalizing on the realization of what may have been known by all but not recognized because of organizational barriers. It is probable that much of an

PART 2: How?

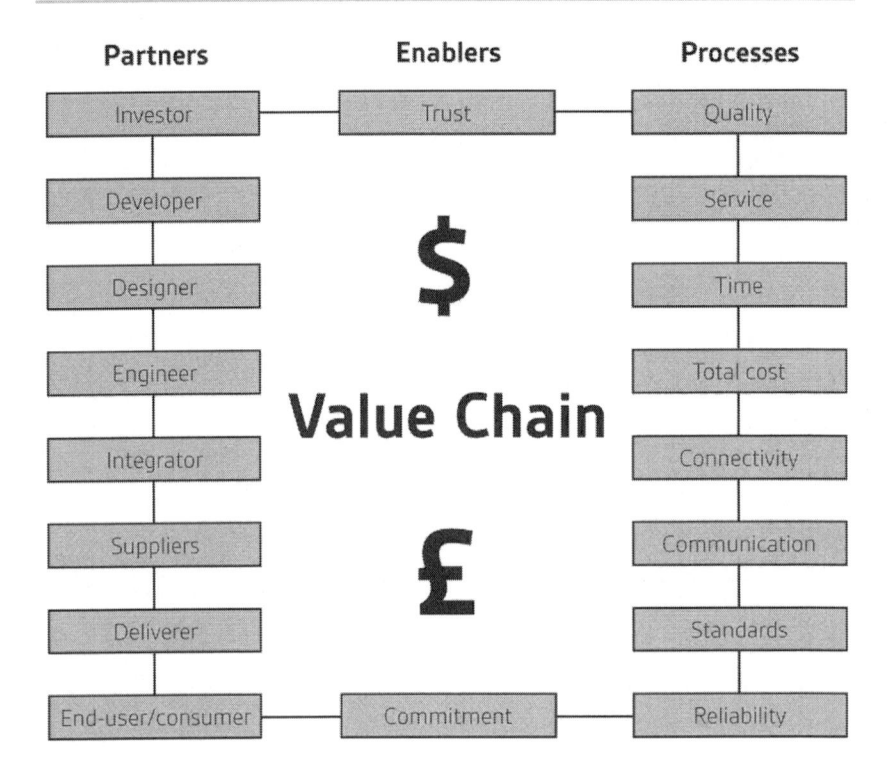

Partners	Enablers	Processes
Investor	Trust	Quality
Developer		Service
Designer	$	Time
Engineer	Value Chain	Total cost
Integrator		Connectivity
Suppliers	£	Communication
Deliverer		Standards
End-user/consumer	Commitment	Reliability

Figure 8.2 – Value chain

organization's business processes and interaction has been established because of organizational boundaries and lack of trust. The process of seeking out competitive advantage through collaborative interaction is a major opportunity throughout the value chain (see Figure 8.2). The exploitation of collaborative approaches must have a foundation that is based on delivering added value to the parties, through capitalizing on the synergies. This will enable organizations to share resources or remove non-value added activities. Longer-term benefit is in moving the arrangements forward to provide more competitive options for the end-customers and creating even greater value. In different organizations value may be derived from satisfying a variety of differing challenges and needs. These are often common across organizations, but they may vary and ensuring synergy is crucial to maintaining joint focus on outcomes.

Every relationship is different, whether vertical or horizontal; however, the key issues will be common to most. BS 11000 creates a platform for developing and managing collaboration from concept to completion. The challenge for many organizations is firstly to ensure the effective initial engagement of the stakeholders and then to maintain this engagement over the life of the programme, particularly where it is likely that there will be changes of personnel during the operational phase. The introduction of the relationship management plan (RMP) provides a framework to document the development process and create a dynamic record as the programme evolves. In this way it is intended to provide a focus and background for operational personnel; where appropriate, it also provides a centralized record for any process audit or assessment for organizations seeking accreditation to BS 11000.

Raytheon Systems – case study

Raytheon Systems recognizes the importance and significance of achieving success both for customers, suppliers and the company. This understanding is reflected in the company's core values, embedded in Raytheon's Vision, Strategy, Goals and Values. They serve as the road map for our achievements and the benchmark by which we measure our performance each year.

BS 11000 complements these core values; it underpins and sustains Raytheon's approach to relationship management, both internally and externally. BS 11000 provides an independent and reliable benchmark against which each participating entity can rely on a common set of measurable relationship principles, outlined against a balanced and equitable process of relationship management. While Raytheon has always had a strong collaborative working culture, adoption of this standard has provided 'structure to our culture'.

Certification and full adoption of BS 11000 supports Raytheon's strategic aims. More customers seek to reduce cost and risk through various efficiency measures. This includes positioning more complex and lengthier contracts, necessitating collaborative industry solutions. Through certification to BS 11000, Raytheon believes it is strongly placed to meet customer demands in this environment. Adoption of the standard has supported the necessity for significant self-realization in the form of mandating internal due diligence as well as the obvious external due diligence before entering a collaborative arrangement. From experience, we know that application of the standard has added significant value to existing and new relationships.

Mike Woodstock, Commercial Executive
Raytheon Systems Limited

PART 2: How?

Conclusion

Clearly each organization has different drivers and strategic needs; for many organizations collaboration and partnering is not the answer. But it should be part of the strategic thinking to identify where there could be investment opportunities, which expand the enterprise without creating complex and rigid legal relationships or joint ventures.

There is no single solution to the complexities of collaborative ventures but the characteristics are common. It is these common features that the development of BS 11000 has captured to provide the route map to creating individual solutions, which are based on mutual understanding and benefit. The neutrality of the standard provides a bridge to help forge robust and sustainable relationships.

Chapter 8 – Background and introduction to BS 11000

Checklist

Table 8.1 provides some initial ideas to help identify where collaboration and BS 11000 may add value initially and beyond. It is important to define the expectations, not assume them.

Table 8.1 – Identifying relationship drivers

Wider aspects of relationships	Competitive tender	Preferred supplier	Alliance	Partnership/ consortium	Joint venture
Long-term stability				X	X
Joint research and development (R&D)				X	X
Reduced total cost		O	X	X	X
Focused team			X	X	X
Risk sharing			O	X	X
Innovation				X	X
Optimization			O	X	X
Reduced quality cost		O	O	X	X

91

PART 2: How?

Reduced support cost			o	x
Reduced engineering cost		o	o	x
Back-to-back terms			o	x
Realistic liquidated damages (LDs)			o	x
Real guarantees			o	x
Cost reduction		o	x	x
Inflation hedging			o	x
Lower tendering costs		o	x	x
Reduced cycle time		o		x
Winning prices			o	x
Improved cash flow			o	x
Finance/funding support				x
Global supply	o	o	o	o

Chapter 8 – Background and introduction to BS 11000

Customer support		O	X	X
Currency risk management			X	X
Reliable delivery	O	O	X	X	X
Market pricing	O	O	X	X
Enhanced service support		O		X	X
Extended skills base			X	X
Enhanced supply options		O	X	X
Integrated propositions		O		X	X
Customer focused solutions		O		X	X

X = likely
O = possible

Chapter 9 – Awareness

> Collaborative approaches will cut across every function in an organization; in order to achieve success there must be awareness of the new approach – the subject of this chapter. The initial key is to ensure that an organization has a clear mandate and strategy to undertake a collaborative engagement. This has to be demonstrably aligned with the visions, values and objectives of the business.

It is essential that the adoption of a collaborative approach is clearly aligned with the business goals and objectives. In this way the concepts, aims, and the potential for a value chain or value network approach can be appreciated across the organization. Promoting collaboration may be at odds with current thinking, so its benefits often need to be explained. These benefits must be articulated and understood, including the long-term advantages; this may be particularly difficult where integration with external organizations could affect internal resources. Adopting a value chain approach must clearly offer greater tangible benefits than a more traditional ownership model. It should be focused on a robust analysis of a cost-effective solution.

Executive sponsorship and policy

For many organizations the view of traditional trading relationships is seen as one of exploiting power. Implementing collaborative approaches needs strong support from the top to overcome internal concerns and constraints and to support appropriate provision of resources. Successful collaboration must be based on establishing realistic and achievable aims that are clearly defined and meet the objectives of the whole organization. As the implementation progresses there may be opposition to the change; the challenge and potential objectives will need to be understood. The appointment of a senior executive sponsor responsible for supporting these collaborative initiatives is seen as a crucial starting point to reinforce implementation, support the allocation of necessary resources and ensure that clear policies and processes are in place to underpin the visions and values of the organization.

PART 2: How?

Business objectives

Aligning collaborative approaches with the business goals and objectives ensures that there are clear linkages between adoption of a collaborative approach and the organizational change that may be required. When should an organization consider collaboration and the benefits of effective relationship management? In the first place it should be focused on being driven by measurable outcomes. Collaboration may be a good way to work but it should be deployed where it adds value. There should be consideration as to whether the targeted relationships lend themselves to sustainable business, then whether the arrangements will facilitate the sharing of resources, can be based on shared risk and reward, and can benefit from lessons learned. To set the overall business strategy, you will need to address not just the local objectives, but also understand the wider perspective. Whether collaboration is at company, group or international level, each has an influence on how the players may react or what options and safeguards may have to be integrated. Understanding what drives your organization and that of the customer or supplier are important features of the development process. The whole spectrum of the marketplace will influence events; if these are not understood, then opportunities may be missed and the risk profile increased.

Benefits and business case

Adopting a value chain approach must clearly offer greater tangible benefits than a more traditional ownership model. It should be focused on a robust analysis of a cost-effective solution. There needs to be a sound business case established; despite what many people suggest is just a change of attitude, effective collaborative working requires investment of resources to develop the processes and skills to deliver success. Its success will very much depend on the attitude and commitment of those involved to drive the right behaviours. Collaborative working is not a 'soft option' but one that can deliver real tangible benefits. Implementing any organizational change programme must be balanced against the costs and impacts on the current business model; the same is true when implementing collaboration – in fact, potentially it can have a greater fundamental impact across the organization. Understanding, explaining and raising awareness about the costs and benefits are crucial to creating the right environment.

Segregate relationships

Historically terms such as partnering or collaboration have often been used too liberally and frequently when not necessary or appropriate. This can lead to confusion, misalignment of goals, failure based on expectations and lack of robust management. It is important to focus only on where collaboration can add real value. So if existing approaches will provide a competitive outcome, then avoid the complications and efforts of a collaborative model. Collaboration should be clearly focused on those relationships where it will clearly deliver real value; using the term where it really has no true value can complicate a traditional engagement. Perhaps the most crucial decision is how organizations differentiate their relationships and focus their resources effectively. The spectrum of relationships and specific needs and strategic requirements will be many and varied. Consideration should be given not only to the current relationship profiles but also to potential developments within the marketplace or expected changes in the overall business strategy. This will enable any development programme and investment in partnering or collaborative relationships to capture potential benefits in the future. Understanding the parameters of existing relationships provides the platform for building effective engagement.

Evaluate key individuals

Working in a collaborative environment may not suit everyone; while they may be excellent in one domain, the capability and skills for operating in a mutually beneficial relationship may challenge some individuals – however, it can represent a development opportunity for many professionals. When potential areas for the application of collaborative approaches have been established, the next key stage is to consider the internal capabilities to deliver such a programme. Collaborative working and management are not easy tasks and frequently they are outside the experience of many people. If collaboration is to deliver value it has to have the right leadership and skills. This may be a significant constraining factor even at this initial stage; the assumption that everyone can handle the nuances of collaboration can lead to inherent failures. As part of the overall business strategy that is encompassing a potential collaborative approach, it is essential to understand what skills are available and what development may be necessary.

Initial risk assessment

Every business venture carries some risk and managing risk is a key aspect of sound business. Collaborative approaches can introduce alternative ways of managing risk, including a joint approach with partner(s), but can also introduce new risk elements that need to be identified and carried forward.

Building new business models or refining the current value chain must be driven by clearly identified opportunities and realistic identification of

PART 2: How?

the potential risks involved. A collaborative relationship offers broad opportunities to expand the business profile, but at the same time brings a level of integration risk. A collaborative approach encourages organizations to look at how they share risk, monitor performance and share rewards. Traditionally, if you subcontracted work, you issued a fixed-price contract, then fought with the provider to get them to meet their obligations. In a collaborative model the driver has to be targeted towards measurable performance, value for money and shared objectives. Research into collaborative programmes highlights the problem with performance standards: in many organizations the performance of internal services groups is always criticized, but there are few major critics, as most issues get solved locally or at a personal level. Once you bring in a 'partner' to provide the service the level of performance is expected to be substantially higher.

Relationship management plan

The introduction of the RMP provides a structured approach for documenting the development process and creating a dynamic record as the implementation evolves. In this way it is intended to provide a focus and background for operational personnel; where appropriate, it also provides a centralized record for any process audit or assessment for organizations seeking accreditation to the standard. This may be a separate process or the requirements can be integrated into existing standard approaches such as customer management programmes, key account management, programme management, procurement plans or contract management plans. Implementing BS 11000 should not be about writing many new procedures, since this tends to leave it outside the mainstream operational processes.

The RMP can be used as a corporate model to establish processes to be adopted, in the case of partnering or collaborative programmes, and as a model for individual relationships or specific collaborative relationships. This establishes a consistent model from which delivery teams, with their partners, can establish a tailored RMP to suit the specific needs and requirements of individual programmes. Each RMP is expected to evolve over the lifetime of a programme, providing a core record of the pre-contract development as background information to programme team members. Subsequently it establishes a working platform for relationship management through the life of the programme, ensuring that relationship management is effectively communicated at all levels and integrated into contract execution and delivery for all stakeholders.

For a collaborative arrangement to be successful there has to be a clear focus and understanding for those involved of the broader aspects of the programme, over and above their individual roles and responsibilities. Thus, while it may not be practical for every member of the team to fully understand all the detail of the contracting arrangements, an executive summary will help to position their activities and how they interact with other stakeholders or partners. This overview should contain a brief description of the initiative, its rationale, aims and objectives to ensure that individuals are focused on the overall desired outcome.

Effective relationship management is all about embedding the right behaviours within an integrated team. It is doubtful that the right behaviours can be driven solely by contract conditions, though one possibility could be to incorporate the RMP into any contract to establish an agreed platform to encourage the appropriate behaviours. This would ensure that the strategic mission, vision and values, governance, collaborative charter, behavioural expectations of the partners and their teams, together with an agreed process of monitoring and performance measurement, are in place to support a sustainable relationship.

When the organizational structure and strategy are set in place, the next phase is to address individual relationships or initiative through the knowledge phase of BS 11000.

Conclusion

Collaborative working in any form is not an easy option. It requires investment and resource and it frequently changes within an organization, so it needs sustained backing and focused direction. For many organizations the view of traditional trading relationships is seen as one of exploiting power. Implementing collaborative approaches needs strong support from the top to overcome internal constraints and to support appropriate resourcing. Without this high-level support, efforts to harness collaborative working will most likely fail to deliver.

PART 2: How?

Checklist

To start the process of considering where BS 11000 may fit your business operations and, perhaps more importantly, at what stage the organization is currently set up to exploit collaborative working, consider the checklist given in Table 9.1.

Table 9.1 – Awareness initial parameters

Awareness		Yes/No
1	Are the objectives of the organization clearly defined and visible?	
2	Is there a defined responsibility at the executive level to support a collaborative approach?	
3	Does the current business strategy support the overall objectives and include the opportunity to exploit collaborative working?	
4	Is there a unified focus across the organization for adopting collaborative approaches?	
5	Is a collaborative approach essential to the achievement of the business objectives?	
6	Have the benefits of collaborative working been evaluated and clearly defined within the organization?	
7	Has there been an assessment to consider if there would be internal constraints to adopting a collaborative approach?	

8	Has there been an assessment of the market to identify the market reaction to a collaborative approach?	
9	Is the focus of the organization based on developing long-term relationships, either vertically or horizontally?	
10	Has the organization defined its focus of value and what would be the measure of success?	

If the answer to each of the above questions is 'Yes', the organization is well positioned to deliver success through collaborative approaches.

Chapter 10 – Knowledge

> When you have identified the potential for collaboration the next stage is to develop specific strategies and risk management that will deliver the required outcomes; this is the focus of this chapter. What do you want to achieve and do you have the skills to support the complexities of these integrated approaches? How will you manage knowledge and information flows? What will your customers and markets make of a collaborative approach? Who could you partner with? What would be the impact of withdrawing from collaboration? The exit strategy is often seen as negative but in fact understanding the rules for disengagement focuses the attention on the key issues to make a relationship work. Most importantly, what do the specific risks look like?

Every relationship is different, whether vertical or horizontal; however, many of the issues will be common to most organizations. These are the key factors that BS 11000 captures and thus provides a common and consistent foundation for collaboration. While there may be many common factors, each relationship will be likely to have varying drivers, which will shape the relationship. It is important to understand these and ensure they are transparent to the organization and stakeholders. As the relationship progresses these must remain at the fore, as they will influence every aspect of the development.

Identify objectives and drivers

Understanding the objectives and drivers for collaboration is essential, since if these are not well defined it becomes difficult to communicate the rationale for seeking external partners – particularly where these relationships may affect internal functions. Building new propositions or refining the current value chain must be driven by clearly identified opportunities and realistic identification of the potential objectives and risks involved. As the development process proceeds there may be internal opposition, which needs to be managed. The effectiveness of a collaborative approach depends on integrating with the business environment within which it will operate, and validating the capabilities and skills of an organization to build and operate an appropriate solution.

Skills and competencies

It is important to consider the available resources to support a collaborative approach and, where appropriate, ensure development programmes and support are in place. As previously mentioned, collaborative working may not suit everyone and the right people may not be the traditionally obvious ones. It is important to consider the development needs at both an organizational and individual level, putting the emphasis on selecting and developing those individuals who can support the environment and respond with appropriate behaviours. This may be simply awareness of the approach, more detailed use of tools and techniques or collaborative leadership.

Knowledge management

One of the significant benefits of collaboration is the ability to share knowledge with partners. This frequently creates a challenge for many organizations to identify what can and cannot be shared in order to avoid clashes later. The effective exploitation of knowledge is the key to success; creating the environment necessary to ensure the sharing of knowledge should have a clear focus. Collaboration provides the catalyst and platform for organizations, both internally and externally, to create an ethos that encourages the sharing of knowledge and the creation of new thinking for mutual benefit. Collaborative principles are focused on shared resources and skills being optimized and directed towards common objectives. Through effective collaborative relationships, organizations can capitalize on the knowledge pool which may have been constrained by traditional contracting boundaries.

How will knowledge and information be managed in a relationship that is more integrated? Sharing ideas and information sounds good but this is also an area where 'knowledge creep' can lead to unplanned disclosure. Most companies have intellectual property rights (IPR) that they want to retain, but this is only a small part of the knowledge base. If we want people to work closely together then they need to understand what can and cannot be shared. In particular, we need to engage the rest of the organization to support the flow of information outwards to collaborative partners and inwards to ensure that internal groups have the information they need from external partners. Knowledge mapping is one way to assess how far collaboration can make use of the knowledge and information that organizations have. By

Chapter 10 – Knowledge

identifying what we are prepared to share, we can structure our approach accordingly when engaging with partners.

Perhaps the most important factor in the behavioural patterns of organizations and individuals is the desire to control through knowledge. The importance and value of knowledge are understood by most people, but to harness the energy and force of that knowledge requires organizations to first understand the diversity of knowledge that exists. Understanding the difference between know-how (experience) and explicit (recorded) knowledge is only the first step. Building an environment where individuals, groups or external organizations are encouraged and empowered to share knowledge must start from a perspective of identifying clear objectives and driving the development of knowledge sharing from the executive level. We need to develop organization-wide cultures and processes that ensure appropriate access to explicit knowledge; however, recording and facilitating the distribution of personal knowledge know-how rests with individual members of the organization.

Strategy development

The success of any business venture depends on the strategy that is behind the approach and the depth of risk evaluation that precedes action. Developing collaborative strategies should start by establishing the influences that will stimulate success. To exploit the potential it is essential to fully appreciate the drivers, risks and pressures of the marketplace being addressed; adopting collaborative approaches requires investment from all parties and thus should be focused where it offers most benefit. The challenge is to develop an effective strategy that integrates the ideas into a practical approach to meet the business objectives and expectations of the potential partners. The four key areas for strategy development are environment, organization, people and processes; these define the parameters for developing an effective strategy and focus the process of collecting and validating the approach, together with the major challenges to be considered. These issues are interconnected and each is a major factor in strategic thinking.

Market analysis

Understanding the dynamics of the market is important – how competitors and suppliers will see collaboration and also how this may be viewed from a customer perspective. Strategy development in many organizations can be a sophisticated approach, but for others it is often an ad hoc activity. For an organization to be successful it must first understand its own requirements before trying to develop those of an external organization. In most cases the failure of external relationships can be directly rooted in a failure to understand or define the internal route map. This lack of clarity leads to confusion and misdirection, which in turn will result in the failure of those outside the organization to understand the implications of their actions. The scope of where a relationship is expected to operate today and where it will operate in future is important in defining the parameters for potential partner selection; setting the scene for collaboration has to be scalable and transportable.

Collaborative partners

Adopting the collaboration concept is the first step, but then you have to consider who might be collaborative partners. The starting point is often existing traditional relationships, taking account of their traditional stance and their potential to change the rules of engagement. When they have developed the outline of a proposed collaborative proposition, organizations need to consider who is out there in the marketplace to fill the gaps as potential partners. In some cases these partners may come from existing relationships, or partnership potential may evolve from a mutual agreement to work together. Whatever the catalyst for collaboration it is important to understand the principal elements that drive the association. How will collaboration enhance our position? What sort of partner do we need and where do we need them? Who has the resources we need and can we work with them?

Initial exit strategy

Part of the overall strategy should include the implications of exiting the relationship at some point. This is not simply about having a process for contract termination but should incorporate transition (to a new partner or even a new service) and acquiring key assets or knowledge. This may highlight key aspects that must be part of the overall plan for implementation (e.g. ownership of intellectual property). A key aspect of developing a strategic approach is to consider the exit strategy as an essential component upfront. Understanding the issues that will arise from disengagement will highlight aspects to be addressed in development. However, experience suggests that a defined approach will enhance engagement in the future, by identifying the issues that are likely to undermine the process of opening up the organization to a third party.

Risk management

In developing an effective strategy it is essential to integrate risk management into the overall programme. It is the skill in managing this risk that generally distinguishes between those organizations that are successful and those that are not. To be successful, the management of risk should be high on the agenda of all parties – both in terms of mitigation and sharing of risk. Failure to identify the risk element of a relationship may ultimately undermine the programme and thus build up greater risk. Development of a strategy must be linked to the creation of a risk management strategy that addresses the concerns of all parties, together with identifying a profile of the levels of acceptable risk.

Business continuity and CSR

Two aspects that are often overlooked are concerned with greater integration. First, how can business continuity be assured if the relationship breaks down? Second, as partners may now be synonymous with your organization, how could that affect internal CSR policies and values? These are two key risks associated with a collaborative approach that need to be considered. The nature of a collaborative approach is that the partners will establish an integrated operation. This will naturally create a linkage where corporate policy needs to be understood and shared to avoid conflict or a breakdown. Clearly business continuity will inevitably be part of any exit strategy.

Relationship management plan

When a strategy has been established, the creation of a specific RMP will help to capture the key principles. This will provide the communications and information platform that will help to raise awareness across the organization.

Conclusion

Organizations may have management support for collaborative approaches, but there is often a tendency for people to say: 'Collaboration is the answer; what was the question?' so as to be seen to be following the party line. These alternative business models take time and resources to develop, so should always be adopted against a robust business case that can be tangibly measured. If organizations cannot validate the rationale then as the engagement progresses it becomes difficult to harness appropriate support to drive success.

PART 2: How?

Checklist

Focusing on moving to the next stage of developing specific collaborative relationships or programmes, consider the knowledge-related issues given in Table 10.1.

Table 10.1 – Knowledge initial parameters

Knowledge		Yes/No
1	Does the organization have specific strategies in place to exploit collaborative working?	
2	Is there an established policy and appropriate processes for collaboration?	
3	Is there cross-functional support for collaborative working?	
4	Will specific collaborative approaches fit with the current market?	
5	Has there been an internal assessment of the impacts on staff and their development needs?	
6	Are there triggers in the business systems to identify potential risk associated with collaborative working?	
7	Is there a focus within current risk management programmes that addresses relationship risk?	
8	Is there a clearly defined linkage between collaborative programmes and business objectives?	
9	Is there a process in place to ensure a cost–benefit analysis is undertaken whenever considering collaborative business models?	
10	Does the current business process identify the need for an exit strategy to be developed that recognizes the impacts of interdependence?	
If the answer to each question is 'Yes', then there is a sound foundation to consider adoption of collaborative business models.		

Chapter 11 – Internal assessment

> Organizations that want to build robust collaborative programmes need to ensure that appropriate rules of engagement are clearly embedded in their operational approaches, as explained in this chapter. This ensures that over time behaviours remain aligned to the agreed objectives and goals. It is useful to take a step back and consider whether current operating practice may constrain effective collaboration and get these issues addressed. These can vary widely but may relate to programme ownership, cross-functional barriers, incentive and performance measurement policies, together with systems and procedures.

Most organizations are very good at defining what they want from others but perhaps less willing to recognize their own capability to meet the demands of collaboration. A collaborative relationship is a two-way process and to achieve the desired goals it requires commitment on all sides. This is not just about processes, procedures, systems and contracts (the 'hard' process issues). It is also a question of the 'people drivers' (the 'soft issues') such as leadership, skills and motivation, which will govern the behaviours and approaches at the working level. It is important to understand the internal enablers that build trust between the parties based on mutual benefit and equitable reward.

In developing a collaborative programme there must be a clear linkage between how to develop the business strategy for the market and how this may affect the vision and values of the organization. Any such programme should integrate with the policies and processes in order to ensure clarity for those involved. This becomes even more crucial when you start to consider the long-term nature of collaborative approaches, where development will be based on exploiting the complementary skills and resources that potential partners can bring to the arrangement.

Collaborative working operates outside traditional boundaries and is far more sensitive to the level of commitment that is brought to the table. As a result it is important that the whole organization is behind the programme. This may sound easy but experience suggests the reality is often very far from being simple. Working in collaboration with third parties opens up many possibilities and opportunities, but is totally dependent on ensuring that internal teams are fully supporting the

PART 2: How?

initiative. Many see the approach as just another new trend, while others close their minds to the possibilities of working in collaboration or view it as a threat.

The collaboration model opens the way to radical thinking at every level by breaking down pre-set conventions and removing previous limitations. At the same time there is a need for the institutional side of commercial operations to understand these new virtual models and cross the barriers in thinking. A successful collaboration will be driven by the attitude and expectations of the players; if real value is to be created, then the first step must be to assess how well equipped an organization is in relation to the challenges. This assessment has to take a hard look at many different aspects of the organization to identify whether there is really a fit and – more importantly – an opportunity to be developed through partnering.

Self-assessment starts with the executive board since they will set the tone and support. If they are traditional in their thinking this will influence the management to be strongly focused on functional boundaries and vertical management structures. The problem with organizations that are structured around traditional functional operations, rather than with business processes that are well defined and developed holistically across all operations, is that it will be difficult to introduce collaboration effectively. However, organizations that have a continuous improvement programme in place, focused on performance improvement, will be more open to alternative thinking at every level of operations.

Policies and processes

Organizations that want to build robust collaborative programmes need to ensure that appropriate rules of engagement are clearly embedded in their operational approaches. This ensures that over time behaviours remain aligned to the agreed objectives and goals. Establishing the appropriate policies and procedures is essential to laying down the right foundation. Policies and procedures are not simply about defining rules around compliance to systems and processes, but also about recognition of the balance between the 'softer' aspects of adopting appropriate approaches to support engagement. In undertaking this assessment it is essential to look at the enablers and ensure that these are in line with the overall aspirations. Consider, for example, how individual incentives may influence behaviours. The holistic nature of collaboration means considering the attributes of the organization, its ability and experience to work collaboratively and the attitudes that prevail from the executive management to the front line.

Internal constraints

It is useful to take a step back and consider the extent to which current operating practice may constrain effective collaboration, then address these issues. These can vary widely but may relate to programme ownership, cross-functional barriers, incentive and performance measurement policies, together with systems and procedures. Most people who work in large organizations have suffered at some point with the internal conflicts that detract from the outward-facing relationships, whether they are with customers, suppliers or partners. As part of developing a collaborative approach there is a need to identify traits and indicators that reflect an organization's ability to collaborate. One aspect of the assessment is the requirement not only to look at the operation but also to evaluate the customer and supplier relationships, to establish if the desire and ethos of collaboration actually spans the internal functions of an organization. Even a simple SWOT analysis to assess the strengths, weaknesses, threats and opportunities of the organization will be useful – in particular, identifying the weaknesses and threats, as these will need to be assessed during the process of developing a partner.

Collaborative profile

Undertaking a review of the organization's collaborative profile – and there is a variety of models that you can use – will provide a platform on which to consider if your organization would make a suitable collaborative partner when viewed externally. For collaboration to work effectively, potential partners must see you as an intelligent partner they can work openly with. BS 11000 is a benchmark for collaborative capability and a useful model on which to test the current position. The maturity matrix has been developed for this purpose, since it can provide evaluation criteria for partner selection and also works to assess internal capability. From these assessments, organizations need to be able to identify what are likely to be the internal constraints to collaborative performance and, where appropriate, implement the necessary change management programmes incorporating policy reviews, process development, systems changes and (most importantly) the development of resources and skills to meet the challenges.

Collaborative leadership

The key to successful collaboration comes from having the right leadership, which is a difficult role since on occasions the programme managers may be required to fight the partner's corner internally. In addition they need to be able to engender and maintain the ethos of collaboration by supporting and mentoring those involved. In any collaborative programme, effective leadership sets the tone, leading by example. Developing effective team focus is a challenge in most environments, but where the traditional command-and-control structure is replaced by cross-functional operations the coordination and direction of the team is even more complex. Traditional management tends to focus on control through position, resource power or technical standing; in a collaborative structure it is the ability to influence that counts, where individuals are able to draw on support not only from their own organizations but also from those of their partners.

Partner profile

As part of the internal assessment it is useful to establish in each case what your partner should look like. This enables the organization to set its agenda and also provides a basis for evaluation later in the process. There are many aspects that organizations may consider for their assessment of suitable partners, drawing these out to consolidate into a representative benchmarking profile. Internally it is likely that there will be many different viewpoints, but it is important to have a clear and agreed profile before launching into the market. Even if you are faced with a choice of only one partner it is better to establish a baseline to understand what may have to be discussed or changed in future.

Knowledge and skills

It is unlikely that every organization will have an abundance of skilled professionals ready to take on a collaborative role. Even those highly skilled people in a traditional environment may struggle when operating outside the command-and-control structure. This does not make them poor performers but may challenge them to work in a collaborative model. So, in selecting or developing a team it is important to focus on those individuals who will best respond to the challenges of collaboration.

In most operating environments the route to effective learning is driven by exposure and sharing. Understanding these styles of learning and assimilation is a key part of the communication process. It is valuable to consider these learning styles in terms of establishing the expectations and behavioural approach that may be most appropriate. Consider the implications of an individual who strives for precision, who is not prone to impulsiveness but focused on listening, compared with a person who is a risk-taker and innovative. The reflective type will seek accuracy while the creative individual will strive for ingenuity. Recognition is only the first step in the process of managing behaviours and it is important to implement a development route, particularly where there are clearly challenges ahead. The eight steps given in Figure 11.1 provide a framework against which to structure the development process.

Organizational needs and goals
Individual needs
Personal assessment
Tailored learning
People inclusion
Links to goals
Adjust expectations
Monitor progress

Figure 11.1 – Supporting individuals

There is always a danger that certain individuals may be found to be in the wrong outward-facing roles and this needs to be addressed. Behaviour is inherent in most individuals and while it may be amended it is seldom possible to change overnight. Behaviour is clearly linked to goals and targets; these must be validated to ensure that localization of incentives is not allowed to create a negative impact. At the same time the overall process must be focused on adjusting expectations at each interface, recognizing that relationships and the behaviours that drive them are dynamic – they will vary in depth and change over time.

Implement and review

The benefit of an internal assessment is to identify the capability of the organization to meet its obligations; it also sets the platform that encourages partner participation and commitment. Once the assessment has been done it is important to put the necessary steps in place to address any areas for development. At the same time these issues should be borne in mind when moving to partner selection; ideally they can be matched to external strengths to provide a strong joint resource and capability. With these building blocks in place, organizations can now move forward with a degree of confidence to address the market.

Conclusion

Collaborative propositions can place stresses on organizational processes and, more specifically, on individual capabilities. If the business case is strong then the resources need to be appropriately allocated and the best skills deployed to meet the demands. Adopting these alternative business models without recognizing internal weaknesses will leave the organization open to failure.

Of course, there is often no choice in terms of obtaining adequate capability, but recognizing the potential weaknesses provides a basis to seek further development or training to mitigate potential risks.

Chapter 11 – Internal assessment

Checklist

Organizations are made up of people. It is essential that each organization understands itself before collectively seeking to influence others, either internally or externally; the issues shown in Table 11.1 should be considered

Table 11.1 – Internal assessment initial parameters

Internal assessment		Yes/No
1	Has there been an assessment of the internal impact of collaborative working on overall performance?	
2	Has the organization reviewed its strengths and weaknesses?	
3	Has there been any benchmarking to validate the collaborative profile of the organization?	
4	Has there been an evaluation of the staff's experience and skills in relation to working in a collaborative environment?	
5	Has there been any structured approach to profiling the organization's culture and behaviours?	
6	Are there training programmes in place to support the developing of internal capability for collaborative working?	
7	Is there a process to identify those leaders within the organization that have the capability to manage collaborative ventures?	

115

PART 2: How?

8	Does the current market review process include considerations for collaboration?
9	Does the organization have a range of business and contracting models that support collaborative working?
10	Is there an established basis to develop partner evaluation and selection criteria?
	If the answer to all of these questions is 'Yes' then the organization is likely to be in good shape to take collaborative proposals to the market.

Chapter 12 – Partner selection

> Collaborative relationships can be used in many different circumstances and finding the right partner should not be left to chance. The selection process is discussed in this chapter; too often the selection process is by default or based on long-term experience in a traditional relationship. This may not always be the best criterion. Most collaborative programmes result from an evolution from more traditional trading interfaces. A good arm's-length supplier, for example, may not be the best choice when considering a more integrated approach.

It is important to understand the differing dynamics of a collaborative approach and assess the strengths and weaknesses, whatever the route to selection. Where an existing provider is perhaps a single-source option their collaborative capability is frequently ignored, as there is no other choice. It is clearly important to ensure that selection maintains the competitive edge that many see only coming from competition. To build confidence in the selection process, a competitive starting approach is always desirable – or a way of conducting a form of robust benchmarking. It should, however, clearly define the endgame upfront to avoid confusion later.

The process of considering collaborative approaches often starts from an internal perspective on the basis of what is wanted from such an arrangement. It is, however, equally important to recognize that if collaboration is to work successfully it has to give benefits to both sides. Before starting to consider moving forward with a collaborative programme, organizations should take time out to understand what might be expected by potential partners and (more importantly) what you are prepared to give. Matching strategic intent is an important part of understanding the potential for successful collaboration.

On one side, there is a potential partner who may be looking to develop markets or find a customer who is a strategic business opportunity. On the other side, there is a potential customer who may be looking to regularize supply, reduce a bottleneck, exploit long-term supply or integrate critical strategic needs. Each has a relative value; the combinations can be high risk if not aligned, so the partner perspective is a key consideration. If it does not work for them it will not work for you.

PART 2: How?

As the business landscape becomes more complex and challenging, the relationships between organizations take on new and varied configurations. Most organizations are both customer and supplier in relation to different aspects of the value chain, but often miss opportunities by maintaining rigid boundaries between their internal functions. However, as the market profile changes, so the complexity of these relationships increases.

Identify collaborative partners

Whatever the drivers for collaboration, it is important to have a clear perspective on who the potential partner(s) might be. Experience suggests that in many organizations there will be preferred contenders for a variety of reasons. Understanding who could be in the game allows a transparent process to be developed. It is unlikely that every potential partner would meet the aspirations and it is sensible to eliminate these early. Prioritizing the business objectives is critical, focusing on the necessary, nice-to-haves and finally the bonus issues. This provides a basis to drive the selection of the potential partners, while taking into account cases where sourcing restraints and choice are limited; this may make the process easier, but makes the selection more critical. In the previous stage the organization should have established what the ideal partner would look like and how the organization's visions and values can be identified. This now forms a cornerstone for the selection process.

The point, which many people may recognize and others need to address, is that the thread of effective relationships should be consistently woven internally throughout the organization and not localized simply to external interfaces. Bridging the relationship divide should be a key focus throughout every organization that wants to improve performance and be an effective collaborative partner. One approach that was incorporated within BS 11000 was the maturity matrix as a consistent benchmark to meet the needs of the business community. Getting below the surface of a company is not easy, but it is essential if you are going to join forces. Organizations need to have a degree of compatibility, otherwise there is little hope of meeting the expectations. While a company may be an entity in legal terms, it is the people within it that make it what it is and without their commitment the success of the venture is doomed. This is often the case where collaboration may result in some downsizing on either side and people are understandably protective of their own position.

How organizations expect they will be working together will help to define the nature of the contracting relationship and the style of integration and level of interfaces. This will have a significant impact on the development of risk management approaches.

Partner selection process

Most organizations will have established processes for provider selection and these should be followed as the starting point to seek out the ideal collaborative partner. Where this involves public tenders and so on the aims of the collaboration need to be defined, together with the relative value that will be placed on their collaborative capability. The reference point of BS 11000 can provide a valuable benchmark for assessing a potential collaborative approach.

In assessing a strategic partner, you must look deeper than compliance to a contract. Organizations may have the attributes to deliver a sound proposition and an established performance record that supports their ability to meet the required performance. However, they may have not progressed in developing an appropriate performance culture that would enable them to fit into the business process of other organizations. A more subjective evaluation tries to identify the attitude of a potential partner; this does not mean the corporate image that is portrayed, but understanding their internal business culture and the approach of those charged with delivering the programme. A MAP[10] triple A rating (as outlined in the BS 11000-2 guidance) would ideally mean that as an organization they would be able to operate as part of the organization they are proposing to serve. Clearly the optimum benchmark for collaboration would be certification to BS 11000.

Establish common objectives

Throughout the selection process it is advisable to work with the potential partners to understand their objectives, as well as building a dialogue around common objectives and outcomes. These may not always be the same as yours but should be evaluated for alignment and compatibility.

Negotiation strategy

Moving a relationship forward generally requires a process of negotiation before developing a contract base. This is frequently a significant weakness in the development of collaborative arrangements. The traditional negotiating models have been based on a combination of arm-wrestling and poker to extract maximum advantage, often referred to as win/lose. Negotiations will set a baseline for the relationship and need to be managed in a more structured way around the concepts of

---

[10] MAP = Maturity Assessment Programme which is based on a triple A rating, e.g. Attributes, Ability and Attitude.

win/win. It is important to recognize that trying to force a commercial advantage at this early stage will almost certainly damage the future relationship.

Conclusion

For a collaborative relationship the traditional contracting safeguards may be less applicable, so overall management and organization have much more relevance. The management style and capability are extremely important features of the selection. The partner's organization will probably become an integral part of your own processes. Even if this is not the case, you are likely to relinquish part (if not all) of your involvement in their day-to-day activities. It is essential to have real confidence in their structure and capability to manage the needs and harness the benefits of collaboration through avoiding duplication. This process should also highlight specific areas where some consolidation may be needed, to develop an acceptable level to meet requirements. Identification of these issues upfront is essential since they will need to be incorporated in any future agreement.

An effective strategy must be based not on desires, but on a firm foundation of capabilities and sound assessment of the business arena that will be encountered. This assessment will have identified the need to team or partner with others, to overcome the obstacles ahead or to complete a proposition that the marketplace requires. BS 11000 provides a framework within which organizations can undertake a systematic approach to consolidating their internal expectations and views of potential partners, then deploy these findings to create the appropriate negotiation strategy.

Checklist

Partner selection is clearly an essential step in developing any collaborative programme. Too often this evaluation ignores the relationship, behavioural and cultural aspects of a potential partner in favour of simple commercial assessments. The questions given in Table 12.1 should help to focus on this area of development.

Table 12.1 – Partner selection initial parameters

Partner selection		Yes/No
1	Does the organization have an established commercial selection process?	
2	Are there established evaluation criteria for potential partners?	
3	Is there a defined process to create a capability profile of potential partners?	
4	Is there a defined process and methodology to undertake a cultural and behavioural profiling of partners?	
5	Is there an established portfolio of prospective collaborative partners?	
6	Are there existing internal models of 'risk and rewards' contracting models?	
7	Does the organization have a structured approach that monitors and measures performance?	
8	Has the organization undertaken reviews of existing relationships to assess where these might be improved through collaborative working?	

PART 2: How?

9	Does the organization have a history of recognizing external partners' objectives and drivers that they can then support?
10	Is there a process in place to ensure that development and negotiation strategies take account of collaborative business relationships?

If the answer to all of these questions is 'Yes', then the organization is well placed to develop and select proactive partners and establish collaborative relationships.

Chapter 13 – Working together

> Establishing the right platform on which to create a collaborative relationship is crucial, as described in this chapter. Clearly there will need to be an agreed contract; however, it is important to work jointly on setting out the appropriate governance model that will support collaborative working. When finalizing the contracting arrangement it should (where possible) incorporate the key requirements and principles for collaboration. These include the need to address the operating practice and systems to be employed to manage the operations. Once the partner(s) are selected the focus shifts to ensuring that the relationship is placed on a sound foundation.

The key aspects of collaboration are trust, clear objectives and value creation. These aspects form a foundation for innovative approaches and the way to support integration, either internally or externally, across traditional trading boundaries. Collaboration is not an easy option; the more integrated the relationship, the higher the interdependence and thus the increased need for sustainable relationships. It is against these challenges that BS 11000 was developed to provide a sector-neutral and consistent framework to create this sustainable foundation.

Effective and sustainable collaboration requires a robust approach to both organizational development and personal behaviours; these factors are inextricably linked. This starts with a focus on individual and joint partner objectives, together with agreement on roles and responsibilities. To establish a working platform on which collaboration can deliver the benefits of combining skills, resources and driving innovation, there must be clear governance that is supported by integrated business processes, measurement and people development.

As organizations seek to optimize their own performance and provide customers with more comprehensive solutions, the challenge to manage through-life integrated operations becomes increasingly complex and has to look beyond the traditional criteria of price, quality and delivery. The introduction of collaborative relationship management should not be seen as a separate initiative, but as an integrated element of the extended enterprise. This should ensure that over time life cycle management is supported by effective joint management and sustainable relationships.

Joint sponsorship

As operations are likely to reach beyond those initially involved in establishing the relationship, it is important that there is joint executive sponsorship to provide overall support. There needs to be clear and transparent agreement on the desired outcomes and objectives of the relationship, which must also reflect joint ownership of the principles that will govern the behaviours of those involved. Appropriate governance models are crucial in supporting both corporate and organizational culture, backed by executive sponsorship to provide support. Creating organizational culture or change requires a robust approach to both organizational development and personal behaviours; these factors are inextricably linked through a sound governance structure, which must be supported by integrated business processes, measurement and people development.

Objectives and principles

It is in the blending of both common and individual objectives that organizations are able to remove many of the hidden agendas that may affect successful collaboration. It is equally important to establish the core principles upon which the relationship is to be developed and operated. The development of a collaborative charter can provide a basis to ensure there is clarity for all involved about the way in which the organizations will interact. The common failing of these charters is that they are frequently very abstract and vague. To be effective, these principles should define the aims of the collaboration; they should also define what is expected of those involved and how these attributes will be measured. The joint executive sponsors and management team must also determine the actions required if these principles are not maintained.

Capability/competency review

You should undertake a joint assessment of the competencies and skills of the partner organizations to be engaged in delivery and, where appropriate, agree a joint development plan; some aspects may have been identified during the partner selection process. Individual competencies can strongly influence behaviours and thus the success of relationships. This concept is not new but reflects an understanding of the importance of behavioural traits and capabilities, which is not a significant factor in traditional command-and-control organizations. Figure 13.1 highlights some of these competencies; they are further highlighted within BS 11000-1:2011, Annex C.

Chapter 13 – Working together

Competencies (upper triangle):
Stakeholder management, Communications, Strategic alignment, Leading by influence, Cultural awareness, Risk management, Problem solving, Governance development, Organizational development, Collaborative negotiation, Change management, Dispute management, Joint planning, Coaching, Responsive, Supportive

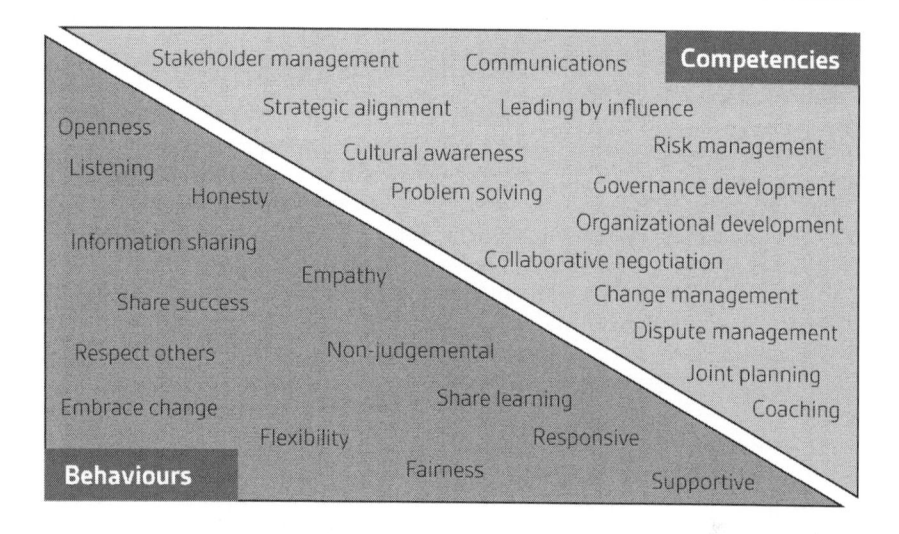

Behaviours (lower triangle):
Openness, Listening, Honesty, Information sharing, Empathy, Share success, Respect others, Non-judgemental, Embrace change, Share learning, Flexibility, Fairness

Figure 13.1 – Competencies and behaviours

Joint management team

Establishing a management team, together with a clearly defined profile of roles and responsibilities, ensures that all participants fully understand their contribution. The challenge for the leadership will be building a team without perhaps bringing all the players together. Many technologists will not see this as a problem, as they expect to operate in a wired world; experience, however, would suggest that in most business trading relationships it is important to have some face-to-face interaction. As we start to see the interdependence of organizations being networked and integrated, this social challenge will need to be addressed at personal and organizational levels to support the exploitation of collaboration. The collaborative team has to meet the everyday demands of the business landscape and contend with the internal stresses and strains of being separated from (or out of step with) its home organization. The team leaders must coach and motivate, while maintaining focus on the overall objectives. The organization and reporting structure should be defined and agreed. As the process moves forward the information and authority chain must be clear to all. Understanding who can do what (or not, as the case may be) is important in any organization; but inside a collaborative structure, with two separate business entities involved, it is crucial.

PART 2: How?

Information management

Effective management of knowledge and information is essential to ensure that the partners are clear on what information they need and how to share it. Identifying the key processes is an integral part of knowledge mapping, since it is the interfaces between functions or activities where the knowledge transfer becomes crucial to success. Information flow is a major benefit from collaboration, but frequently it is an area of conflict when working together. The gaps in knowledge and understanding are where most of the operational failures and frictions will occur, whether this is between customers, internal groups and individuals or external providers and partners. The true benefit of a knowledge-based approach is that real value can be identified and exploited by ensuring the appropriate interfaces are addressed.

Communications plan

A key aspect of maintaining a sound relationship between organizations and their stakeholders is to ensure that there is a solid process of communications. As the relationship becomes established it is advisable to establish a plan for effective communications across the stakeholder community. Keeping people informed helps to strengthen awareness and thus maintain the support for collaboration.

Joint risk management

Developing a robust joint risk management programme as part of the operating process is a crucial factor in being able to build sustainable and flexible operations. The exploitation of collaborative relationships within a business environment is often viewed as being the answer to some elements of risk. However, the relationships may address many of the challenges that are created by today's business environment, but in doing so they may also introduce new risks – so collaboration should not be seen as a reason to ignore the principles of sound risk management processes. Joint risk registers are often established, but these are frequently limited to those risks that are associated with the shared objectives. It is less common to find the recognition that individual partner's risks (whether corporate or individual) strongly influence behaviours. The evidence of a strong relationship is the fact that the partners support each other's risks where practical. In some cases this may not be possible, but even acknowledging these risks can have a positive impact.

Process review

When first establishing the relationship it is valuable to undertake a joint review of the delivery processes. This will establish the platform for effective performance and provide a basis to ensure that all key issues have been jointly addressed before formally contracting. Optimization of business processes is a key benefit of working in collaboration arrangements, but this can often create the next level of potential conflict. So it is important to define how the integrated team will deliver their objectives; this is an essential aspect of establishing a sound basis for working together.

The adoption of process mapping has become a standard tool for most organizations in understanding and developing their operational approaches. It provides a basis on which to challenge and enhance both delivery and service. Understanding how each party operates is a key stage in the process of evaluating where knowledge is lacking and how creating new knowledge may stimulate and enhance value. Working together to develop a TCO approach can be a complex process, which challenges organizations to understand the true cost and value of the operational processes. Moving towards integrated ownership takes much more complex analysis. It frequently requires greater integration with the parties involved to encompass a true through-life optimization, recognizing that long-term commitments may not simply be a question of extended contracts but also of maintaining joint commitments to resources, maintenance, product support and future product or service development.

Monitor and measure

In any relationship it is important to understand how the relationship and delivery performance will be measured, to ensure that performance incentives also support required behaviours. Creating a collaborative programme is only the start of a process; while targeted in the early stages, it can often lose momentum over time. The longer the relationship is in place the greater the possibility for complacency to build between the various parties, so agreeing a joint monitoring and measurement programme provides a valuable indicator of the relationship's current condition and future development needs. This ensures that overall performance is focused on continuous improvement.

Dispute resolution in the process is a must. In any collaboration issues will arise and it is essential that the relationship protects itself from these stresses. Generally this is handled by some form of escalation process, which ultimately ends with the respective Chief executive officers (CEOs). If it goes beyond that point, then the relationship has probably broken

PART 2: How?

down irretrievably, but nevertheless further action may ensue. By driving a dispute process down to the working level many (if not most) conflicts can be avoided.

Contracting arrangement

Every business relationship needs to anchor its contracting arrangements from the point of establishing what it hopes to achieve through the relationship. In developing a contracting approach it is essential to define the individual responsibilities and to place these obligations with the correct party. In the initial stages of developing a collaborative strategy the temptation is to set objectives that are too far-reaching and have varying chance of actually being achieved. Setting expectations too high will also influence the structure of the contract and probably place unreasonable demands on partners, which will ultimately result in contract conflict when they are not achieved.

Relationship management plan

When the decision is made for one or more organizations to work together the RMP becomes a joint plan, which will outline the way they intend to manage the relationship in future. There are a variety of ways this can be addressed as outlined in BS 11000. It may be integrated into contracts or alliance agreements; however, for many organizations a separate document often proves most manageable – either as a standalone document or as an annex to a contract. The principle, however, should always be that this is a mutually agreed approach between the parties.

Conclusion

Whatever contracting model is used it needs to be jointly agreed and evaluated against the relationship approach. It must be compatible with the joint principles, aims and objectives of the parties in order to establish the governance that will support a collaborative approach.

Chapter 13 – Working together

Too often collaborative arrangements are established in isolation to the necessary contracting arrangements and thus creating potential friction at later stages of the relationship. In a strong relationship that contract may not be predominant, but frequently as individuals change roles through the programme the collaborative concepts can become diluted and the contract takes precedence. Thus the relationship objectives and the contract should always be compatible. It is also worth considering evaluation of the contract against the 'contracting for failure' ethos – for example, reviewing the terms of contract as to whether they support success or simply drive towards accountability and blame.

PART 2: How?

Checklist

Table 13.1 will help you to assess your organization's readiness for working together.

Table 13.1 – Working together initial parameters

Working together		Yes/No
1	Does the organization have established commercial models to support effective management of collaborative programmes?	
2	Does the organization have established approaches to ensure that processes are reviewed to identify interfaces and implement actions to close gaps?	
3	Are there established models in place to drive joint objectives and measure the effectiveness of implementing a collaborative operating approach?	
4	Is the current organizational structure flexible enough to accommodate a proactive risk-sharing approach?	
5	Is there a structured platform of defined roles, responsibilities and reporting that can be adapted when working with external parties?	
6	Is there an established joint planning and risk management approach that recognizes both individual and joint risks?	
7	Does the organization have appropriate skills development and training programmes in place which can be jointly accessed by potential partners?	
8	Is there a process in place to manage issue resolution that promotes solutions being developed at the lowest level of the operations?	

Chapter 13 – Working together

9	Is the current commercial approach focused on developing joint early wins for the partners?	
10	Are there established contracting models available within the organizations that support collaborative engagements?	
If the answer to all of these questions is 'Yes', there is positive focus to establish collaborative relationships.		

Chapter 14 – Value creation

> Experience has shown that the benefits of collaborative relationships will tend to lose momentum over time if not driven to maintain continual improvement. Relationships that are particularly focused on long-term benefit must maintain a relevance to markets and customer needs. A major value from collaborative approaches comes from the ability to share ideas and harness alternative perspectives; those that look for additional benefit often exceed their original objectives and perform much better overall. Value creation is clearly important to success, as discussed in this chapter.

A parallel benefit that comes from introducing a structured approach to value creation is that it supports organizations and teams working together. How organizations choose to encourage innovation depends on a wide variety of factors, but is often managed well by establishing joint cross-functional teams that can be brought together to address specific challenges or ideas.

To harness this added value means challenging the traditional thinking and getting 'outside the box', creating new value or alternative value propositions. Value creation programmes should maintain a focus on the end-customer, while capturing potential benefits for all participants that may or may not directly affect the customer. Too often organizations seek to drive cost out of their operations and ignore the impact on the customer. Innovation is a critical factor in the value creation process, since simply reallocating costs or obligations does not bring new value to the table. Some relationships may be instigated for a specific objective but this should not prevent exploiting other aspects of the value chain.

Much of the resources that organizations spend on managing business processes are used to control or compensate for actions and risks in dealing with external organizations. It is to a large extent the rigidity of these processes that sets the culture of an organization. Given the opportunity to expose duplication or eliminate activities, the value creation process brings out improvements, benefits and savings that had never been recognized before. In the process of eliminating process and management controls, it can help to improve relationships and trust, which are catalysts for even more improvement.

PART 2: How?

Value creation process

While there is great value in a spontaneous approach to innovation, establishing a joint process that ensures both targeted support and encourages new ideas is very powerful. A structured approach will underpin sustainable engagement; it will provide a measure of integration and continual focus on driving greater value from the relationship. The advantage of developing a collaborative relationship is in exploiting the joint knowledge and capabilities of organizations to create added value for the partners, and for the end-customer or consumer. However, the exploitation of collaborative approaches must have a foundation that is based on delivering added value to the parties. Initially it will capitalize on the synergies in the relationship; subsequently it should be a focus for continual improvement and enabling organizations to share resources or remove activities that do not add value. The longer-term benefit is in moving the relationship forward to provide more competitive options for the end-customers they serve, and thus creating even greater value.

Innovation groups

Every organization will have its own specific targets to ensure a value creation programme that captures all opportunities. It helps to adopt a framework that provides a robust platform involving all aspects and functions within the organization. The value creation model (see Figure 14.1) captures the basic functional activities of a business operation or organizational process, which can be contained within one of six key areas (total cost, cycle time, business process, resources, specifications and performance). Within these there will be many individual issues and targets identified by the partners. It should also be recognized that many of the potential benefits and opportunities may cross between these areas. For example, cycle time reduction may have a cost–benefit associated with it, while process improvement may bring improvements in cycle time.

The value creation process may not necessarily deliver immediate returns, but for the new partnering team finding some early wins is quite important to boost confidence and encourage the team to become more innovative. It is important not to focus simply on cost, as this will tend to create friction, but focus on the causes of cost.

Areas for improvement

The key to optimizing this co-creation is to ensure that identified issues are regularly reviewed and, where necessary, removed if not delivering. This ensures resources are not wasted or diverted from the primary objectives. Value is only created if it brings benefit to those involved;

Chapter 14 – Value creation

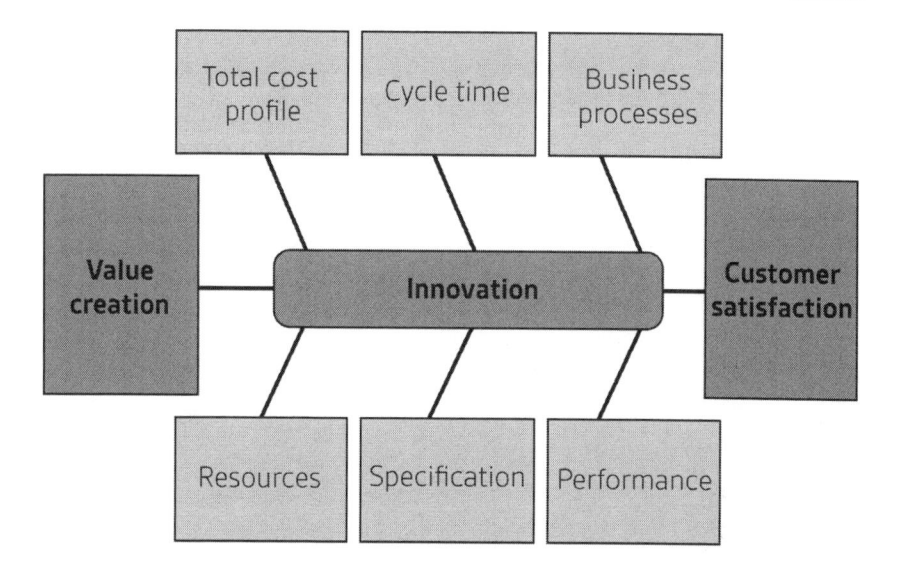

Figure 14.1 – Value creation model

when developing a value creation programme it is important to remain focused on the key priorities and evaluate every initiative in terms of strategic drivers. The opportunities for organizations to look constructively at their own processes, as well as the wider integrated processes that deliver products and services, opens the vista of creating new value for customers by improving current performance and exploiting new openings through the extended enterprise. In a collaborative environment, value creation is about delivering innovative solutions or releasing value that could not be generated by one organization alone. This evolves into introducing new value propositions that fulfil the future aspirations and expectations of customers, or perhaps those that have yet to be recognized.

Define value

One of the major challenges in any relationship is to define what value means for those involved. For every organization the focus for value creation will be different, since every business strategy creates different demands. Developing a collaborative innovation programme to deliver best value starts with the partners setting clearly defined definitions of value for their own organizations. When establishing value-based objectives, the parties have to recognize that within a relationship there will be joint objectives in addition to those which are partner-specific. Commonly when two organizations get together there are three sets of objectives: yours, mine and ours. It is crucial to understand these multiple aims and blend them into a joint strategy to deliver mutual benefit. Defining value is a focus that not only varies in different organizations; it also may change over time. As initial programmes develop, the wider aspects of improved service delivery and market growth strategies take the value definition to a broader level, along with the identification of operational improvements driven by increased confidence and trust. To implement effective value creation programmes, it is important to define value in the relationship, both to establish targets to strive towards and to identify benchmarks against which to measure success.

Value creation should be viewed as a continuous iterative process that provides a focus for development and a catalyst for change.

Learning from experience

As organizations begin to work together more closely it is equally important to capture the lessons learned. This is a key aspect of creating value and setting the agenda for innovation. The traditional competitive approach has been to focus on reducing price, but as many will appreciate, lowest price is not always lowest cost; certainly this approach is seldom a catalyst for collaboration and sustainable value. Developing new value propositions has to start from an understanding that the overall objective is to reduce total cost to those involved; this may require some transfer across what were traditionally trading 'battle lines'. To open up the full potential of integrated operations, there has to be a change in the whole organization on both sides of the relationship to ensure that existing rules do not constrain innovation. It may be that a small team is driving a programme but the bigger organization will influence many of the processes and decisions. Ultimately, the collaborative approach should be delivering alternative value propositions that have much wider implications and benefits.

Generating innovation

Few business activities will stay unchanged for very long; particularly in a technology-focused environment, innovation is crucial to maintain competitive edge for the relationship. While there may be many common opportunities, it is also important to recognize that some opportunities may only benefit one party – but joint support for these is equally important.

The development of innovative ideas has to be an iterative process that promotes a continuous cycle of improvement. Most organizations, particularly those partnering teams that are newly brought together, will only be able to focus on a small number of opportunities at one time. It should also be apparent that most opportunities will come by

Chapter 14 – Value creation

combinations of actions within the six key areas of total cost, cycle time, business process, resources, specifications and performance. Priorities must be set to ensure focus on the strategic objectives of the partnership. A major target for organizations is how to improve cycle time, without reducing control and quality. To provide some focus some key areas are listed below for consideration:

- product development time;
- integrated planning;
- information flow;
- delivery time to customer;
- reduced risk.

Each offers the opportunity for a value creation team to consider the cost–benefit analysis of what improvement would mean in terms of internal benefits, cost and resources, as well as customer and market positioning. Effective planning can provide substantial returns for what is often only the integration of critical factors within each organization. The longer-term benefit of integrated planning is the impact of reliable information flows that ensure actions are undertaken only when needed, thus avoiding wasted effort, late change and reducing the risk of delays. Cycle time is not only a market driver, but also a potential cost reduction activity, which in the early stages of a relationship does not involve significant exposure.

The main benefit of collaborative business relationships is to bring together teams from external organizations, as it provides a more holistic view of operational processes. Business re-engineering is a common aspect of internal improvement programmes, but is rarely explored across the borders of organizations – yet many of the processes have been established to manage external organizations. Looking beyond the improvement of existing activities, the future development of integrated approaches may provide new and innovative propositions that are only achievable through collaborative partnering ventures. Business processes involve resources and costs, so their improvement provides a real opportunity for organizations who are prepared to share their knowledge and skills.

The major area for investigation and development is to look at process flows in terms of duplication and recycling. These are potential benefits that often require only simple adjustments to the overall process, but may offer substantial benefits to both parties. The next phase of integration is rationalizing data flow. Duplication of activities and effort, and double handling, are common between organizations; when these processes are rationalized they create additional value, competitiveness and performance.

Resources are the major cost factor for most organizations after external spend, whether these are materials or skills. Exploiting the full potential of resource optimization has to start with the organizations involved partly releasing control in order to evaluate where each activity should be undertaken and by whom. This initial assessment requires the participants to see their role and function in terms of contribution to the process rather than personal responsibility and status. As with most relationship issues, progress is often smoothed by focusing on what all agree on and then moving to the more contentious issues, drilling down through the many resource-related activities that cross boundaries. Which party ultimately undertakes the activity should be defined through capability and risk assessment.

The potential for organizations to share information and develop new ideas is generally only constrained by their desire to retain knowledge within their own boundaries. Creating value from integration offers the opportunity to look constructively at what has been common practice, then disseminate the factors that may be adding to the cost and resources without true added value (see Table 14.1). Effective integration starts with the uncontentious issues that exist at the interface points between most organizations, whether manufacturing or service-related. There are always constraints that each would like to remove. Often, these are simple requirements that have either grown out of past problems or have never been appreciated by considering both sides of the supply relationship. Once the process starts the openness and trust will grow, as will the opportunities.

Table 14.1 – Value creation focus

Eliminate waste	Standardize materials	Enhance service
Rationalize documentation	Simplify specifications	Joint research
Reduce contingencies	Optimize production	Long-term investment
Remove constraints	Improve maintenance	Shared equipment
Integrate assembly	Enhance service	Shared product R&D
Phase development	Common outsourcing	

Conclusion

Improving performance clearly supports the initial objectives in different ways, including individual satisfaction that comes from achieving goals that stretch the organizations. In addition, getting improvement from a product or service for the same investment improves the relationships across the whole value chain and at the same time reinforces the value of collaboration.

PART 2: How?

Checklist

Table 14.2 will help you to assess your organization's approach to innovation and continuous improvement.

Table 14.2 – Value creation initial parameters

Value creation		Yes/No
1	Does the organization have a clear perspective on what value means and does this also recognize that external parties may have other value drivers?	
2	Is there a clear focus on customer satisfaction within the organization?	
3	Does the organization recognize the potential need for joint investment where additional value can be created?	
4	Does the organization have an internal focus on resource profiling to ensure that innovation can be developed alongside programme delivery?	
5	Does the organization have an established process to promote and develop innovation?	
6	Does the organization have an established business focus to review the effectiveness of its process?	
7	Does the organization have established processes to undertake cost–benefit analysis when considering process improvements?	

Chapter 14 – Value creation

8	When establishing collaborative programmes does the organization seek to develop benchmarks over time?		
9	Does the organization focus on implementing key initiatives to deliver additional value from its relationships?		
10	Is there an ethos of continuous improvement within the organization?		
If the answer to all of these questions is 'Yes', then the organization has a positive focus on innovation and continuous improvement. This is a strong platform to enhance relationships for mutual benefit.			

Chapter 15 – Staying together

> Market demands, organizations and thus business relationships will be likely to change over time. This may be as a result of internal and external factors or pressures. Even where partners have invested in creating a firm foundation and governance, the people involved will develop or move on, which will change the dynamics of the relationship. This is a strong reason for embedding collaborative practices in the operating model. To achieve performance goals continuously it is essential to establish a programme that works to maintain a sustainable relationship through ongoing joint management; this is the focus of this chapter.

In a changing world the internal and external pressures on any collaborative relationship will inevitably lead to impacts on effectiveness. It is also important to recognize that as relationships evolve they will undergo change, so to ensure the maximum benefit it is important to undertake regular validation to maintain focus and efficiency. No two relationships are the same and the dynamics of organizational and people changes can influence performance, so it is equally important to recognize that as relationships progress they need to be monitored to ensure that appropriate focus is maintained on areas where convergence might not be happening to maximum benefit.

Experience suggests that collaborative relationships have a minimum effective development cycle, which takes between 12 months to 24 months depending on the complexity of the relationship. Over this period of time many factors can alter, so it is essential that organizations recognize the need to revalidate approaches. This will include the need to readdress the original objectives and assess whether these have been (or are being) met and whether they should be modified, which in turn may create an impact throughout the collaboration. There are also likely to be changes in personnel, which may alter the dynamics of the partnering team and perhaps the wider organizations. BS 11000 can be regularly used to provide a benchmark of how the operation and the team are converging or diverging over time.

PART 2: How?

Monitor performance

It is common practice to use both service level agreements (SLAs) and key performance Indicators (KPIs); however, these are often confused, which creates tension between the parties. According to the IACCM,[11]

> an SLA typically identifies the fixed measurements for the delivery of the services and spells out measurements for performance and consequences for failure. It must include: levels of required performance; consequences for failure to reach or maintain these levels; and descriptions of the parties' roles and responsibilities in achieving the performance levels.

In brief, an SLA is a contractual commitment; it is a detailed and comprehensive description of the performance aspects of the service. In contrast, KPIs are high-level measures (quantitative or qualitative) that enable the overall delivery of a service to be assessed by both customer and service provider. KPIs should be few in number and focus on the service's contribution to the customer's business success; they are often linked to a balanced scorecard and typically monitor performance in terms of financial criteria, customer satisfaction, internal process quality and performance, and staff skills/competence.

It is important to understand and agree how the performance of the contract and the relationship will be jointly measured and ensure appropriate reviews are undertaken. In most organizations there will be established processes for monitoring performance; frequently, however, these are focused on outcomes, deliverables or even profitability. These are clearly very important, but where collaboration is an integral part of the business performance this should also include monitoring the strength of the relationship. All relationships are subject to change either from internal or external influences that affect the basis of the original programme, so if the relationship is delivering and remains a strategic approach then it should be periodically tested and adapted to reflect changes in the business environment. These may be as a result of internal changes by one or both of the partners or (more likely) market changes that may alter the value proposition.

Measurement

In raising the profile of collaborative approaches the challenge is always to show that sound relationship management aids effectiveness and efficiency while delivering extra value. We all know intuitively that it does, but proving the point can be more difficult and we often find ourselves struggling to make the links. There is a well-known saying that 'if you can't measure it you can't manage it', which makes absolute sense

---

[11] International Association for Contract and Commercial Management.

and is a position that most people would endorse. But there are times when the quest for measurement goes beyond common sense. Clearly we should measure performance, if only to see where we can improve or to judge that we are getting value for money. The challenge is to start from a point of understanding what is important in relation to the objectives, and translating this into realistic measurements that provide value to those managing the process. Frequently, when organizations look to collaboration, they drift towards aspiration-based objectives, which is why lawyers have consistently challenged the concepts of partnering. Alternatively, we revert to the lowest possible denominators where we are sure to be able to deliver exact measurement. Either way, we are deceiving ourselves and failing, while creating the conditions for conflict.

Joint team management

The principal key to sustaining any relationship is to ensure there is effective joint management of the approach. This should not be a task for executive management; it should be focused on the operational level, managing the day-to-day activities of the relationship and ensuring continued focus and support. Maintaining both delivery and development focus is crucial to ensure the relationship remains proactive. This must involve joint objectives for measuring and monitoring to maintain a dynamic approach across teams. Revalidating effective agreements and contracts is crucial to ensuring the appropriate platform for collaborative operations.

Support innovation

There should be continuous support and monitoring of innovation and continual improvement, to ensure that the partnering teams are exploiting their joint knowledge and, where appropriate, enhancing their skills.

Behaviours and trust

Developing trust in the relationships and ensuring the appropriate behaviours is a key aspect of joint management. As trust increases the performance of the relationship should increase the value it delivers. The wrong behaviours will quickly undermine the situation, with obvious impacts on output.

PART 2: How?

Maintain performance

Business relationships are created to meet the challenges and demands of the market and customers, whether internal or external – and clearly collaborative initiatives are no different. It should be recognized that while it is important to develop the relationship the prime business objectives must be met. A critical aspect of any relationship is that it delivers the performance that was initially envisaged and agreed; any failure by a partner in a collaborative environment will inevitably lead to a breakdown in the relationship. While this may seem obvious to many people, it is essential that the partners continue to meet or exceed their obligations; it is also important to recognize that a failure to provide early warnings of problems will significantly undermine trust. This ensures that overall performance is focused on continuous improvement. Creating a collaborative programme is only the start of a process; frequently while targeted in the early stages it can lose momentum over time, so it is essential to establish early on a programme of benchmarking that can identify areas of potential stress or conflict that may require intervention to optimize performance. The longer the relationship is in place, the greater the possibility for complacency to build between the various parties.

Dispute resolution

Managing conflict towards a constructive and mutually beneficial outcome is an essential element of effective collaboration. In any venture where people are involved there is always the possibility of differences; collaborative working is no different. It is important to ensure that there is a dispute resolution process that provides a mechanism and escalation procedure where appropriate. Frequently disputes, whether internal or external, become disproportionate to their real impact if not addressed early. Disputes may be created more from the positioning of individuals than from the relative positions of the organizations, so analysis of the various perspectives will help to generate focus. It is important not only to establish the perceived basis of the dispute but also to gain examples of how this dispute has shown itself; frequently the outward demonstration of a dispute hides an underlying problem. The most likely cause is a lack of trust, which translates into a hardening of interfaces and is then interpreted as a lack of cooperation. The next most likely area for dispute is a change in the market (by customers or external influences) that affects the partner(s). Conflict with business processes often becomes a challenge to the team, who find themselves operating outside their own organization. The most common cause of disputes is a simple breakdown in communications which, once re-established, dissolves the conflict.

Joint exit strategy

Developing a structured joint approach to formulating an exit strategy is an important facet of collaboration. There is a clear rationale for understanding on both sides of the relationship how each will act if or when the environment changes or when the agreement reaches the end of its natural time span. Even more important in the short term is that much of the exit strategy will bring to the surface issues and concerns on both sides; these will need to be addressed to help the process of building trust and openness, so that focus can be maintained on value creation and not defensive protectionism. Considering an exit strategy may be viewed as negative, but in fact it is one of the key structures that adds strength to the relationship and aids the building of greater integration.

The relationship health check

A relationship health check approach draws upon the key elements of BS 11000 and how these are viewed by both partners in the relationship. This is a crucial facet of the approach, since a relationship cannot be considered satisfactory unless it is meeting the objectives and aspirations of both partners. Trust is essential to business, so it is perhaps fitting to start from a perspective of looking at the issue of trust as a key factor in building more effective business relationships. There are numerous behaviour profiling tools, such as Myers Briggs, which look at the personal attitudes as well as those that are reflective of the organizations involved, as an indicator of the strength of the relationship; the perspective of the organization provides an overview of behavioural traits. Assessing how each individual sees the framework within which behaviours are developing provides a helpful benchmark of potential constraints.

Conclusion

Risk – and the perception of risk – is a major constraint to any relationship, and in particular one that is focused on innovation. Business in general and collaborative relationships must manage risk effectively, so the establishment of risk registers is a key tool in any management process. As a measure of the strength and effectiveness of a relationship, analysis of the current risk profile can provide a valuable indication of how well the relationship is performing. The test of whether a programme is engaging the operation is the additional initiatives that are developing complementary new ideas; the relationship will enhance its strength. Any relationship will inevitably face some disputes between the parties; the strength of the relationship is founded on how well these are addressed and resolved. Increases in disputes may not necessarily be

PART 2: How?

negative, since as organizations seek to exploit the benefits of collaborative working there is an increased tendency for conflicts in thinking to arise. What is crucial is that these are resolved to mutual advantage and not left to create a potential breakdown of the relationship.

Relationship maturity against organizational collaborative competence of an organization in its collaborative approaches can be used as part of the selection process, but more importantly it gives a measured approach to monitoring improvements. As part of the overall health check the annual validation of progress provides a benchmark in both measuring the strength of the relationship and assessing the development of capability against BS 11000.

Chapter 15 – Staying together

Checklist

Relationships need constant monitoring and support to achieve the full value of the collaboration, to ensure delivery of primary objectives through performance and to encourage the development of added value. Table 15.1 helps you to assess the extent to which your organization's internal processes are capable of monitoring performance jointly with partners.

Table 15.1 – Staying together initial parameters

Staying together		Yes/No
1	Is there an established basis for joint executive sponsorship and regular reviews?	
2	Is there a structured approached to establishing a joint management approach that recognizes the mutual responsibilities of collaborative programmes?	
3	Does the organization have a flexible approach to performance reporting that would accommodate the needs of external parties?	
4	Are the organization's incentive programmes conducive to working across organizational boundaries and supporting joint management of programmes?	
5	Is there an established management process that supports the joint management of collaborative programmes?	
6	Does the organization have established processes in place to monitor and measure relationships and behaviours?	
7	Is there a model issue resolution process in place?	
8	Do existing management models incorporate the need to jointly monitor market changes that might influence a collaborative arrangement?	

PART 2: How?

9	Do the current skills development programmes extend to external parties and do current processes recognize the needs for joint programmes?	
10	Does the organization have established guidelines for the development and monitoring of joint exit strategies?	

If the answers to all the questions are 'Yes', the organization has internal processes that recognize the needs to jointly monitor performance and manage issues. It is positively placed to achieve benefits from collaborative approaches.

Chapter 16 – Exit strategy

> The exit strategy is the last stage in the relationship life cycle, but is in fact a key aspect that should be addressed as part of the initial thinking and carried through the whole life cycle, as described in this chapter. The exit strategy should not be confused with contract termination; although this is important it addresses another aspect of relationships with suppliers. The strategy should focus on how the parties plan to disengage when necessary and ensure effective business continuity and customer support.

A strong relationship will recognize the value of looking to monitor the changes and ensure that the concerns and needs of each partner are duly addressed. It is important to ensure that while one particular initiative may come to its useful end due to a variety of factors, others may – and should – emerge from successful collaboration. The implication of terminating an agreement and how this is viewed internally (and from the market) is crucial to the reputation of the parties. While it may be appropriate to cease activity, how this is presented and interpreted will influence the way each party proactively approaches disengagement. This is particularly important in supply chain programmes where services and outsourcing programmes are involved, which may require periodic re-tendering for regulatory or competitive reasons.

The lifespan of any business relationship will vary between organizations and market influences; adapting to these changes is a crucial part of developing effective collaborative partnering arrangements. The development of effective integrated activities requires the building of trust between the parties, which over time will enhance the opportunities – those who expect to maximize their investment over a limited time will generally find that collaboration does not provide solutions. Many people may consider that to address an exit strategy at the outset of a relationship infers an acceptance that the relationship will fail, but this is not the case. Experience suggests that being open about all possibilities allows the partners to focus on every aspect of integration.

PART 2: How?

Maintain a joint exit strategy

Jointly developing and maintaining a focus on disengagement ensures that the partners have a clear focus on the value of the collaboration. Taking into account the potential problems of disengaging the relationship means that all parties can establish an exit strategy that allows them to define the limits of engagement. The development of collaborative relationships will often have a defined lifespan to meet specific project requirements, and alongside this the business environment is subject to change. It is therefore important in any development to take into consideration the impacts of time and the implications that an integrated operation may introduce. During its formation the relationship must take into account the process that will lead to the eventual disengagement of the partners. This may not need to be planned in detail, but should identify the key implications of sharing knowledge across organizational boundaries. What many people do not consider when entering into a more integrated relationship is that previous contracting interfaces can never be the same.

Establish boundaries

It is important to define the boundaries of the relationship clearly, though it is accepted that these may change over time by mutual agreement. This should include the business risks; in any business environment there are many factors and pressures that can have an impact on the operational drivers. When considering the need for an exit strategy and developing the appropriate approach, these can generally be focused into eight key phases of BS 11000, though every business and organization will eventually refine these to reflect their local issues and impacts. As part of the process of working together in the development of an integrated relationship, these primary concerns will influence the way that team members participate. Integration is a progressive process that grows as the team investigates value creation opportunities; having clear boundaries allows them to avoid potential areas of conflict that reach beyond their brief.

Monitor changes

There should be regular joint reviews of both the market and the relationship, to ensure it is still relevant and delivering value to the parties. After the implementation of an initial collaborative programme it is inevitable that changes will occur, both inside the partnership and in the wider trading environment. Many of these will be addressed by the team and adopted within their operations, while others may affect the long-term validity of the relationship. It is essential that partners recognize these changes and take action to manage the implications.

Chapter 16 – Exit strategy

There are many factors that the business community has to continually adjust and adapt to. In the context of the global business environment these issues can create both opportunities and risks; the potential advantages that collaborative relationships can deliver are often focused around the need to meet some of these challenges, but they can also be factors that relationships need to consider in terms of changing the premise for working closer together.

Change is what every business has to accommodate under normal conditions, but the implication for collaborative relationships is that these changes may affect only one partner – but as a result affect the other. Alterations in regulatory demands or political structures can introduce constraints that cross organizational boundaries; and economic variations alter the customer perspective, which can provide advantages to the competition. Any collaboration must be established against the background of the market environment. In the same way it can establish the parameters and benchmarks against which the partners consider being released from their obligations. Establishing clear rules of disengagement means that both parties can monitor the market and recognize the developing changes so as to take alternative options.

Establish triggers

It is essential to understand the triggers that would indicate the relationship has fulfilled its useful life. This does not mean that collaboration has failed; on the contrary, joint forward planning is the key to an effective relationship. Each organization is a constituent of the collaboration, so if one of them undergoes a significant change in structure or ownership this affects the overall proposition. This does not mean that relationships must fail under these conditions, but it needs to recognize the possibility that (for example) ownership could have a fundamental change in direction. This allows the partners to consider options.

In the trading marketplace many factors drive the shareholders and direction of business ventures. So restructuring and rationalization may often drive the need for partnering; it may also create a new working environment that is counter to the other partner(s). The value-added capability of the arrangement is crucial to its success; the more robust the relationship, the greater the probability that it will survive major corporate change. The area that presents the biggest challenge will come from mergers and acquisitions, where additional internal resources and capabilities conflict with external partners or where the strategy of the new organization takes a different direction from that when the partnership was established.

The effectiveness of an extended enterprise depends largely on the personnel who operate the activity on a day-to-day basis. There is always

PART 2: How?

a challenge when key individuals move on or are replaced over time. The robustness of the business processes that are put in place and the strength of the value propositions will be tested when there are changes to the influencing players. Every relationship faces these challenges at some point, but if the relationship is robust it can overcome some variations in the team. However, it has to be recognized that when there are major corporate changes the sponsorship of special relationships may also come under pressure.

Some personnel changes will certainly test the strength of the team and may result in the relationship having to look towards disconnecting the organizations. The greater difficulty comes in cases where staff have been transferred between partners or have been assigned to special programmes outside their organization's normal structure. When creating collaborative ventures that extend the organizations, it is important to ensure that staff do not see the arrangement as a cul-de-sac in terms of their individual careers. This factor must also consider the regulatory impacts of staff assignments and the long-term local impacts.

Business continuity

The foundation of a sound relationship is that while it continues to add value it must also recognize the implications of maintaining continuity for both the partners and their customers. Clearly, business operations do not simply involve the partners; they extend into the customer base and the wider marketplace. The responsibilities that operating organizations accumulate may remain after the partners have agreed not to continue the relationship. In any case where the parties agree that future joint activity may not be appropriate, there will be obligations that still require servicing and these may have been developed through joint participation and resources. When developing a collaborative concept it is important to understand the implications of the proposed market offerings, while it is generally one or other partner who actually contracts with customers. The manner in which the service or product is provided will be dependent on resources and input from several partners and their suppliers. In developing an exit strategy the partners must consider the way in which current liabilities will be fulfilled; the reputations of all parties are important and support to the customer is crucial for future activities.

Transition

The termination of any collaborative initiative needs to be effectively orchestrated by the partners. This is particularly important where service provision is being transferred to another party. The transferring of resources and production activities between partners often arises out of exploring the optimization of business delivery processes, but in doing so vulnerabilities can be created; thus these alternative value propositions must take into account the implications of future abilities to meet contractual needs. Clearly, under the banner of a robust relationship these issues can be accommodated, but in cases where the prime partner makes decisions outside the model then gaps can be left on all sides – to the detriment of both parties and their relationships with their customers.

Future opportunities

Collaborative integration offers the opportunity for organizations to extend their individual capabilities and market reach through combined operations. These may be time-limited or open-ended, but in every case there is a need for the parties to openly address what they need to do in the event that the relationship is no longer viable. Each party must consider what they will contribute for short-term gain and what may be at risk in the longer term. Finally, if the relationship has been well managed and has delivered its objectives, then the way should be open to consider future possibilities for collaboration. The future offers the perspective that more and more organizations will look towards this approach as a viable alternative. In time, competitiveness will be between business clusters rather than between individual organizations. This opens up the prospect of partners leaving one relationship and linking with competitive clusters, which again raises the prospect of knowledge flowing across competitive boundaries.

Conclusion

The exit strategy is frequently considered as being negative. However, from experience a well-defined strategy will help to support engagement and ensure clarity for the parties as their current business activity ceases or reaches the end of its usefulness. Experience suggests that effort during the development of collaborative programmes and throughout their life cycle (to maintain a focus on the endgame and perhaps the future) will underpin the relationship.

How we exit from a relationship says a great deal about the integrity of the parties, the strength of their relationship and their potential to collaborate in the future.

PART 2: How?

Checklist

Establishing an exit strategy can be one of the most positive aspects in developing a collaborative approach, since it allows the parties to consider the implications for those involved and ensure a continued focus on sustainable relationships (see Table 16.1).

Table 16.1 – Exit strategy initial parameters

	Exit strategy	Yes/No
1	Is there a recognized process for creating and maintaining an exit strategy?	
2	Is there a requirement for joint management teams to maintain a focus on the life cycle of relationships and its value to the organization?	
3	Does the organization clearly define those triggers that might necessitate the activation of an exit strategy?	
4	Is there a clearly defined process for the organization to secure intellectual property?	
5	Do current processes recognize the need to define ownership of IPR that is created through a collaborative working arrangement?	
6	In developing a collaborative approach do the current processes recognize the potential risks for knowledge transfer or loss of skills?	
7	As part of the development of collaborative initiatives, do the current business processes recognize the implications for both customers and suppliers in the event of having to exit the relationship?	
8	Do current development processes take full account of all stakeholders when considering the establishment of a collaborative model?	
9	Do current contract models incorporate clearly defined liabilities for all parties?	

Chapter 16 – Exit strategy

10	Is it part of the current business processes to incorporate a focus on future joint relationships with collaborative partners?	
If the answer to all of the questions is 'Yes', the organization has created a collaborative operating model that initially considers the implications of exiting the relationship, which provides a basis to assess risks and benefits. The organization is soundly placed to create more robust and successful programmes.		

Chapter 17 – Implementing collaborative certification programmes

> The aim of adopting a standard for collaboration is to provide a platform for sustainable relationships by integrating best practice into the operating processes of organizations. This will establish consistency of approach and create the foundation for driving appropriate behaviours and skills development. Certification to a standard should be seen as validation of those approaches; this chapter describes the process of implementing collaborative certification programmes.

For many organizations collaboration is an integral part of their make-up, but for others it may require a cultural shift and changes to their current operational approaches. This clearly may not be applicable to every business activity or relationship, so in developing an implementation plan for collaboration it pays to focus from the top as to where collaborative working will add value. It then requires an assessment or gap analysis to understand what it may be necessary to change or be complemented to make use of the BS 11000 framework. If your organization has given positive responses to the checklists in the previous chapters covering the BS 11000 framework, then it is likely that existing collaborative programmes already meet most (if not all) of the standard's requirements.

The focus for adopting any standard is to integrate best practice to enhance the operations of the business, so as to exploit the benefits. In most cases this will lead to some degree of organizational change. Certification should be seen not as the goal but as a consistent benchmark for sustainable performance and recognition that a capability has been established. There can be many reasons for seeking certification – customer drivers, differentiation, process improvement and so on, but primarily it should be seen as a means to ensure a sustainable approach, creating an environment where best practice becomes common practice for the organization. This is particularly applicable to collaborative business relationships, where implementation may be constrained by traditional thinking.

This chapter on implementation has been developed from BS 11000 to support organizations from concept through to implementation.

PART 2: How?

BS 11000 has been developed to recognize the individuality of organizations; it does not try to impose a structure on existing processes but rather to complement the best practice that may already be in place. The key requirements for certification are like many other business management systems standards, which are:

- there must be established and recognizable business processes in place;
- there must be evidence that these processes are being robustly applied;
- there must be a level of understanding for the requirements by those involved.

Figure 17.1 provides a model that outlines the five stages for development using the experience, knowledge and tools developed as part of the creation of BS 11000 and the experience gained during the piloting of the certification programme.

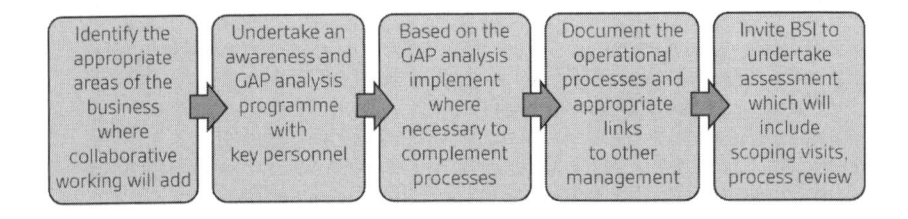

Identify the appropriate areas of the business where collaborative working will add	Undertake an awareness and GAP analysis programme with key personnel	Based on the GAP analysis implement where necessary to complement processes	Document the operational processes and appropriate links to other management	Invite BSI to undertake assessment which will include scoping visits, process review

Figure 17.1 – Implementation steps

The value of any standard or process should always be focused on establishing the identifiable value for the organization and the degree of integration, process and effort that is consistent with the value it can deliver. To benefit from BS 11000, organizations do not need to be certified; however, the rigour that the certification requires and the annual reassessments ensure that organizations maintain their approach.

Establish the background

Before starting any business initiative it is important to draw on a range of information against which to make a value judgement. You will need to obtain a copy of the standard and gather other publicly available material. The most important step in the case of BS 11000 is to establish the importance of relationships within the organizations – whether these are customers, suppliers or delivery partners. Then you will need to assess the level of impact these relationships have on business operations. This

Chapter 17 – Implementing collaborative certification programmes

will enable the organization to assess whether the standard's implementation is likely to bring benefit to current or future operations.

Undertake initial gap analysis

Using the standard's checklist, it is recommended that organizations undertake an initial gap analysis against current operating practice. At this stage it is likely to be high level, but it is also important to be honest about whether existing processes really are in place or are just perceived to be. Many of the standard's requirements may cover things that are done currently, but in an ad hoc manner and unscripted. Worse still, policies, processes and procedures may be in place but they are ineffective or not generally followed with any degree of rigour.

Obtain executive approval

As with any standard that crosses functional boundaries within organizations, it is important to ensure there is effective support from the top; if changes are necessary, support will be required. At the same time this provides the opportunity to validate the high-level benefits analysis.

Brief the executive team

It is important that the executive team has a fundamental understanding of the standard's scope and possible impact. It may be appropriate at this stage to bring in specialist independent advice to assist in 'walking through' the key requirements.

Identify potential internal pilot(s)

Introducing any standard can consume resources and disrupt day-to-day operations, with the potential to create a degree of negativity within the organization. With a discrete pilot application these impacts can be contained, while at the same time the pilot can be used to test existing operational processes and produce a blueprint for further deployment. The collaborative model may not be suitable for every aspect of the business, so piloting enables deeper assessment of value and impact.

Nominate a pilot leader

All change programmes need leadership and focus, so it is important to ensure there is a clearly defined role in place to drive forward the initiative. There is likely to be a high level of internal discussion and perhaps some selling to be done, so it is valuable to have a key point of reference within the organization who can act as internal champion.

Identify the key personnel involved in the pilot

Collaborative interaction will traverse the organization, so it is important to identify those groups who will initially be involved, whether functional or operational. Collaboration can be complex, so these key players should represent the roles that will be affected and they should be clearly established to provide cross-functional support and knowledge.

Undertake awareness and gap analysis

The key players should undertake a gap analysis to establish a sound baseline for development; if they are working with a specialist adviser this can also provide a more detailed level of awareness for the team. It is important to ensure that any external advice comes from a validated source. BS 11000 may appear on the surface to be straightforward, but experience has shown that understanding the depths behind the requirements is crucial to successful implementation. This gap analysis should provide a foundation for the evaluation of impacts and level of compliance, and the scope of change required. It may also challenge the initial pilot selection criteria.

Evaluate impacts

From the gap analysis, the internal champion and pilot team(s) should be able to provide a detailed assessment of the operational impacts, degree of change required and potential cost and duration for implementation. For organizations with well-established business processes and an ethos of collaboration, experience has indicated that perhaps as high as 80 per cent compliance may already be in place. This can vary greatly, of course.

Develop benefits analysis

Based on evaluation of the impacts, the implementation team should now be able to develop a benefits analysis to assess the value of moving forward and the potential wider benefits of deployment beyond the pilot.

Chapter 17 – Implementing collaborative certification programmes

Define the scope of assessment

If the business case stacks up, then the next step is to engage BSI and seek to agree both the scope and cost for assessment of the pilot. As highlighted earlier, the deployment of BS 11000 can be selective across the organization by function, location or type of activities, but the assessors will need to understand what they are required to assess.

In the early stages of introducing any new standard there will be elements that some organizations may not be able to support in any one given pilot relationship. The challenge then is how to provide reliable assessment, if that is a driver. The approach that has been adopted in some cases is the evidence map, shown in Figure 17.2. This provides a matrix of evidence across a number of relationships, which may be at varying stages of development, but demonstrates the organization's understanding and implementation capability.

Relationship	Awareness	Knowledge	Internal assessment	Partner selection	Working together	Value creation	Staying together	Exit strategy
One	▓	▓						
Two			▓		▓			
Three					▓	▓	▓	
Four			▓					

Figure 17.2 – Evidence map

Obtain executive approval and implementation budget

Organizations will need to assign adequate and appropriate resources to successfully deploy any change programme. They will be engaging internal resources, perhaps with partner/customer support, and in some cases also requiring high levels of external support.

PART 2: How?

Prepare outline process review and evidence

This is the most intensive aspect of implementation. There needs to be an outline review of existing processes and necessary changes, collation of past evidence and creation of additional processes, if necessary. BS 11000 requires the creation of an RMP for this purpose. This can take many forms but outlines are included in the standard. Existing processes should be signposted, not duplicated, but the RMP can also act as a repository for any new requirements specific to collaborative programmes.

Formalize scope with assessor

At this stage the team should be in a position to meet with the assigned assessor and agree a programme for the assessment. In some cases organizations may consider a pre-assessment in order to validate the approach being taken and identify any significant gaps that may need to be addressed.

Implement detailed process review

Experience shows that in almost all cases – even in the most collaborative of organizations – some development will be necessary to meet the requirements of the standard. At this stage an action plan should be established which will further help to refine the assessment planning.

Implement action plan

This phase can only be established on an organization-by-organization basis, based on how much work needs to be done. Some organizations may decide to draw in external specialist support; others will have their own dedicated team.

Internal audit review

It is recommended that organizations establish an internal audit review to ensure that all requirements have been addressed and that sufficient evidence is in place to meet the requirements of the standard. Such audits will be a required aspect of the ongoing operations to the standard in any event, so it is a sound platform for the future.

Stage 1 assessment

The stage 1 assessment by BSI is a detailed process review where the assessor will seek to identify any process gaps and be satisfied that robust processes, procedures and systems are in place. This stage frequently reveals minor issues that may require attention

Implement necessary updates

Where gaps may have been identified, these need to be addressed and incorporated into the RMP.

Prepare evidence

Under normal circumstances there will be a three month window between stage 1 and stage 2. This allows organizations to ensure that all issues have been addressed and that there is sufficient evidence in place that the processes are being followed.

Stage 2 assessment

The second stage of the assessment is focused on assessing the actual operational practices and their adherence to the organization's operational processes, the RMP and evidence of performance to the standard. The scope may differ depending on the range of activities, locations and people involved. It will, however, be relatively detailed and in many cases it will select random aspects of the process across the organization. It is important, therefore, that at the operational level all personnel understand the background to the standard and where their role fits in the process.

Babcock International – case study

In the face of the global credit crunch and the various knock-on effects following it, those who are prevailing are facing difficult decisions head-on. At times like these it has perhaps never been more important to take an open and honest approach, and break down the traditional customer–supplier barriers. Developing the ability to work in partnership is not only an enabler to an organization, but also helps it to build for the future.

Babcock is collaborative by its nature, so the BS 11000 accreditation process was more about finding and managing information than about changing processes. The most common expression heard when gathering evidence for the accreditation was, 'Oh, you mean this!' Babcock will use this experience to build future relationships.

PART 2: How?

Babcock's relationship with its key customer has developed over the life of the contracts, from the initial bidding, mobilization, steady state running and exit planning. There have been numerous examples throughout many contracts where both parties have needed to be open and honest with each other.

It was interesting that, when Babcock's quality assurance team analysed the standard and assessed how we could adapt our processes, it seemed that Babcock was meeting most of the requirements. All that remained was to make a number of minor additions to our set of corporate level procedures, additions to meeting agendas and the creation of a relationship management plan. Audits and management reviews for the collaboration were included in our normal management system schedules.

For several years we have been encouraging our customers to support joint business plans for their contracts and, where possible, co-location of staff. A good example of this relationship working was when, in response to our customer's concern regarding funding levels, Babcock developed an innovative and flexible approach to facilities management that prioritized budgets and focused on the most critical assets. This approach provided a commercial model, embraced by our customer, and developed into a programme that could be rolled out nationally throughout the UK. On some contracts this sort of innovation saved just under 2 per cent. It was due to the strong relationship between our customer and Babcock that this scheme was such a success.

Working towards accreditation was very much a learning experience for the team. It was enlightening to see how much of what we did was considered collaborative. Another aspect that was particularly important was getting the scope of the accreditation right. When the scope was adjusted to suit the structure of Babcock and the way it works, it was easier to see that multiple parts of the business were working collaboratively. This meant the accreditation could cover the work being done by teams working on bidding contracts right through to those working towards exiting contracts. This way of writing the scope allowed an all-inclusive approach, which has meant that every contract that Babcock delivers can be accredited as long as those operating the contract follow corporate procedures.

There are two things that stood out the most during the process of getting accreditation. First, there was the fact that a lot of what Babcock does is already collaborative; and secondly, the flexibility of the standard allows for the scope of the accreditation to be adjusted to fit with your company. To achieve the most from the accreditation it is important to understand not just how your organization fits with the standard, but how you can fit the standard to the way your organization operates.

John Rowe, Process and Systems Manager – Infrastructure
Babcock International Group

Receive certification

All being well, the assessment will be successful and the certificate will be issued. This is the start of the journey; the processes must be rigorously maintained, as there will be annual reviews. And, where desirable, further deployment of the process from the initial blueprint RMP can be incorporated by agreement with BSI. It is the rigour of the standard and assessment process that ensures organizations effectively maintain their operational processes, based on the value that was initially identified, and benefit from a consistent and validated approach to collaboration.

Conclusion

It needs be reiterated that certification to the standard should be seen as an output of good collaboration and not the objective. While it is recognized that some customers may mandate standards and compliance, in the case of BS 11000 this would be a contradiction in terms of collaboration. Certification should be viewed as an independent validation of performance capability; this has the internal benefit that once organizations are certified they are prompted to maintain their standards of performance through annual reassessments, keeping operators on their toes.

PART 2: How?

Checklist

For those organizations that feel independent certification could be of benefit in establishing market recognition and to create a basis for maintaining internal compliance, then the checklist given in Table 17.1 may help to establish initial focus for development.

Table 17.1 – Implementation checklist

	Activity	Actions/comments	Done
1	Identify potential for the organization	Obtain standard and support publications	
2	Undertake an initial gap review	Check level of compliance	
3	Establish executive support	Make sure the executive sponsor is behind the development	
4	Brief the executive management team	Get the key players bought in	
5	Identify initial pilot	Keep the focus as tight as possible initially	
6	Appoint pilot project manager	Make sure the project manager understands the requirements	
7	Identify key players in pilot	Engage internal champions	
8	Undertake detailed gap analysis	Consider using specialist external support	
9	Evaluate cost and impacts of pilot	Review the commercial benefits and internal impacts	
10	Develop benefits analysis	Get the business case in place	
11	Define scope and cost of assessment	Contact BSI	

Chapter 17 – Implementing collaborative certification programmes

12	Obtain executive support and budget	Establish that the necessary resources can be made available	
13	Prepare outline process review	Undertake a initial process review to identify magnitude of changes	
14	Formalize assessment programme	Contact BSI	
15	Implement detailed process review	Assess all business processes to identify necessary changes	
16	Establish action plan	Implement an action plan to ensure all requirements are addressed	
17	Implement internal audit	Carry out an audit to ensure the processes are in place	
18	Proceed with stage 1 assessment	Contact BSI	
19	Implement process changes/updates	Implement any necessary updates to business processes	
20	Prepare detailed evidence	Collect evidence to ensure support for stage 2 assessment	
21	Proceed with stage 2 assessment	Contact BSI	
22	Receive certificate	This is the start of the collaborative journey; consider expanding scope	

PART 3: Where?

Chapter 18 – Customer engagement

> Part 3 looks at a number of specific applications, starting with the customer – since without them there is no business. This chapter begins the 'where' journey with customers and customer engagement. We should recognize that we are all both customer and supplier. As customers seek to improve their own objectives and develop more effective solutions and efficiencies, this cascades through the supply or value chain. Collaborative approaches can be used in either direction to improve the relationships to meet these challenges; this, however, requires operational and cultural change on either side of the relationship.

The potential to exploit collaborative models has many benefits, but a key factor is that these approaches have to recognize the two-way process that must be created. Historically the concept of partnering was significantly devalued by customers. The perception was that customers were using the partnering messages as a ruse to draw in their suppliers and then exploit them, while often the supplier approach was seen as simply trying to secure some form of exclusivity and freeze out competition. Neither approach worked well; many people developed a view that these relationships were untenable – even uncompetitive – and perhaps so cosy that commercial benefit was eroded. If there is no recognition of mutual benefit, risk and reward there can be little (if any) real advantage to be gained from the superficial adoption of a collaborative message. Terms such as partnering, collaboration or alliances can often lead to greater confusion and not meet expectations, resulting in failure, where a more traditional approach would have been adequate to drive the desired outcomes. The two golden rules ought to be:

- one: don't go into collaboration purely to exploit the other party;
- two: don't transfer a problem through collaboration simply to 'pass the buck'.

PART 3: Where?

'Push' or 'pull' for collaboration

There are many reasons why a customer might promote and seek collaborative relationships. The most obvious is to exploit skills and capabilities that they don't have. More recently there has been the need for innovation to reduce operating costs, or to bring together more progressive approaches from industry. It is also the case that as demand increases, customers look towards more complex operating models and ranges of capability that can only be harnessed through combinations of providers. Where historically they may have traded individually, now they recognize the need to take a broader perspective of the value chain. Whatever the driver, the customer makes a 'pull' call on the market, which is then challenged with responses. Too often the customer's invitation sparks a reactive approach from the market, which is based on largely presenting the best possible positioning; this frequently does not challenge the validity of the request (the customer is always right even if we feel they may not be). The 'push' comes from those providers who either want to combat competition or seek advantage by offering an enhanced approach that may be beneficial to the customer. In either case of 'push' or 'pull', the robustness of the approach or the recognition of the complexity it involves is often ignored for short-term gain. It is in this arena that BS 11000 can provide a framework that will help to structure the approaches, highlight the challenges and ideally introduce more sustainable propositions.

The 'intelligent customer'

The concept of the 'intelligent customer' is not new, but when entering the world of collaborative programmes the traditional strengths of purchasing power may not be enough to deliver the required results. The idea that a supplier may not want your collaborative business because they feel exposed to traditional pressures seldom seems to resonate. But if there is a real desire to pursue this type of model, then a neutral standard that works for all can be a valuable catalyst. From discussions with organizations around the implementation adoption of the standard, it often becomes clear that historically 'push' or 'pull' has been fraught with risk on both sides. Customers fail to recognize that their pressure on the market to use collaboration is opening a line of engagement that they are not ready for, or that suppliers have ignored the risks simply to be compliant.

The first thing to consider as a customer, when inviting offers based on collaboration, is that the smart supplier will be initially prejudging the customer's intent and capability to support such a change in what may have been a traditional adversarial business model. While suppliers may be outwardly responding to the collaborative call, the underlying response will be based on traditional thinking and raise the question, 'Do

Chapter 18 – Customer engagement

they really mean what they are asking for?' On the other side of the equation, when seeking to evaluate the traditional supply base against an alternative business model, it is crucial to ensure that the capabilities and processes are in place to be effective. This is particularly important in (say) public bodies, where the constraints and demands of procurement rules may leave organizations exposed when assessing and selecting partners against collaborative principles, rather than solely technical or commercial elements.

Strategic development

For some organizations the adoption of collaborative models is seen as a 'paradigm shift', which needs to be effectively communicated and supported in order to open more effective dialogue. The values, benefits and challenges need to be acknowledged. Adopting a structured approach immediately signals a change, but this has to be seen in action to establish the credibility of the customer. It is a brave salesperson who turns down possible business; but, in this environment of collaboration and its potential to lead to interdependence and vulnerability, declining to play can be the most sensible step. Some business may only be worth having under a change of engagement rules. There are other pressures for the supply chain, where (for example) demands by customers to reduce costs simply result in ever-increasing pressure on the supply chain, which may negate the value of the business. In this case the promoting of an alternative business model could be mutually beneficial to both customer and supplier.

The value proposition

The key to any change in business must be creation of value; in the collaborative environment there needs to be an acceptance that this value is mutually beneficial, though not necessarily in equal parts. If organizations, whether buying or selling, are going to ask others to step outside traditional well-established operating models, then WIIFM (what's in it for me?) must be appreciated.

Customers need to demonstrate what they expect to achieve and what their partners (no longer suppliers) can expect to gain. Where customers are being asked to consider a more integrated approach they need to see where the value will come from and – perhaps equally important to both sides – where the risk will reside when either side is asked to drop their conventional protectionist approaches (see Figure 18.1). We live in a world that has become very litigation-focused, so changing the rules of engagement has to be based on a balanced approach.

PART 3: Where?

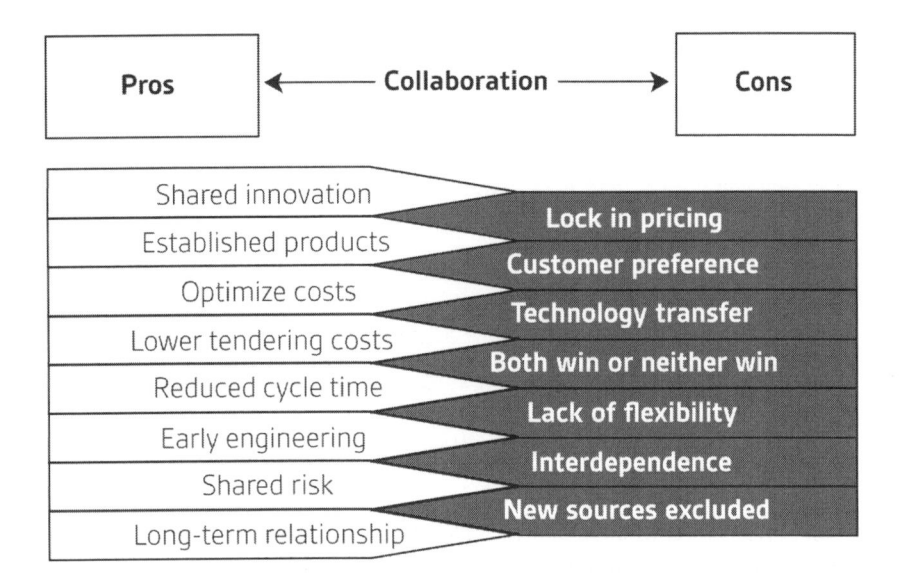

Pros ← Collaboration → **Cons**

Pros	Cons
Shared innovation	Lock in pricing
Established products	Customer preference
Optimize costs	Technology transfer
Lower tendering costs	Both win or neither win
Reduced cycle time	Lack of flexibility
Early engineering	Interdependence
Shared risk	New sources excluded
Long-term relationship	

Figure 18.1 – Advantages and disadvantages of collaboration

Marketing collaboration

It is easy to promote the concept that collaborative working is a good thing, and it is generally intuitively acknowledged while there is no commitment to be signed. However, when we move from concept to implementation, then a wide range of issues emerge. In adopting a structured method, organizations can develop sustainable approaches and open up a constructive dialogue. This should drive the parties towards a satisfactory conclusion – or it may, on occasion, cause one or all parties to decide that it is not viable after all.

Balfour Beatty – case study

Balfour Beatty as a Group is now a global, multidimensional business with both the desire and capability to expand our vision. Increasingly, our views and experience are sought after all around the globe. We see it as our responsibility to share our deep resources of knowledge to help shape the future proactively.

Chapter 18 – Customer engagement

Balfour Beatty is a market leader in articulating, developing, operating, owning and maintaining strategic assets that are the lifeblood to a society. The Group has gained a reputation for developing best practice that is at the heart of its success story. Central to this narrative has been a new style of working based on openness, trust and honesty. We have shared this approach amongst ourselves and with our clients and their customers, stakeholders and our suppliers.

Balfour Beatty's safety programme, 'Zero Harm' also has collaborative working as an essential enabler and relies on the approach – we can only achieve our ambitious targets through working together with others. We recognized that where focus and effort has been put into these relationships, all parties have enjoyed the process and have seen the virtue and business benefits in joining together in the Zero Harm journey. Our senior management has always been deeply committed to finding new approaches to create value over the whole life cycle of an asset, to eliminate waste, and to improve the safety of construction.

Our work in the Balfour Beatty Alliance Exchange has been central to recognizing this store of knowledge and brings it to the surface for us to explore its full potential. Collaborative working is at the heart of our strategic vision. We recognized that the introduction of BS 11000 provides an opportunity for us and our customers to obtain recognition for our joint development of exploiting the benefits of collaborative working. Most importantly, this new standard provides a structured approach to enable the transfer of best practice across sectors, programmes and projects. BS 11000 also gives us a 'universally' recognized structure and the catalyst to develop the next stage of our work in the Alliance Exchange.

Mark Sewell,
Head of collaborative business relationships
Balfour Beatty Group

Sound collaboration starts by increasing openness and transparency, which is not something that traditional business management is based on. We generally start from a position of mistrust and share only the minimum we need to in order to exploit the position later, or simply to protect our position. If organizations aim to harness collaboration then this is the first major consideration; whether buying or selling, once you have stepped across the Rubicon there may not be a way back to business as usual.

The transition from 'steady state' to a less well-defined position is not one anybody takes easily; where this may involve some degree of exposure it is not surprising that many are reluctant to consider even small steps. This particularly has implications where such a change can involve the future roles of those personnel on either side; the term 'turkeys voting for Christmas' can easily apply. So, from a customer perspective, those charged with developing the approach may be less than enthusiastic; and from the supplier side, selling to someone who could become vulnerable is no easy task. Understanding these dynamics is crucial. For collaboration to work effectively the concept of 'who does best does' has to be the ultimate goal.

The next key element involves creating a clear vision from which to develop the approach. In most cases the cost aspects can be easily defined, but it is less simple to establish the risk profile that integration carries. Clearly, part of the risk encompasses the capability of the organizations to adapt and have the experience and skills to see it through. After at least a century of business development based on command and control, these skills are not commonplace. This is why one of the unique features of BS 11000 is its focus on cultures and behaviours in support of process change, which underpins every requirement of the standard. While many organizations cite case studies praising the successes of working in alliances and collaborative ventures, few can demonstrate how these were achieved; and even fewer are prepared to share their experiences of when it went wrong. If organizations are going to promote collaboration or seek collaborative propositions, then they need demonstrable evidence of capability and structure that will provide confidence for others to follow.

Key relationship management

Most organizations have what is a commonly recognized as a key account management function; often this is captured under business development. However, not many have incorporated supplier relationship management programmes and sadly most of these are focused on a limited profile of performance measures and compliance. In this brave new environment of networks, alliances and collaborative programmes even fewer have relationship management as a recognized function. Relationships are crucial to all business, but where collaborative working practices are involved then managing relationships becomes a critical success factor. Some forward-looking organizations have embraced this idea; those that have integrated collaborative best practice into the key account or strategic supplier programmes can show the benefits. If organizations are to bring innovation, risk management and value to their partners, they need to be reaching beyond traditional transactional relationships and adopt next-generation thinking. It is important to understand the type of relationships and, in some cases, recognize that there may be a variety even with one organization. This issue is addressed in more detail in Chapter 21 'Collaborative contracting'; what is important is that the parties understand the rules of engagement.

Joint development

Where the benefits of collaborative approaches have been assessed and validated, the development of the approach will be joint. This may seem obvious, but frequently initiatives are driven by customers without recognizing the implications for potential partners. The opposite can also be true, when organizations pursue a collaborative approach where the customer has not been fully engaged. It is equally common for organizations that have more traditional trading models in place to launch collaborative approaches without working through the implications and setting the expectations and objectives. The result is that what may have been a sound business relationship becomes confused and even fractured. By developing an alternative model jointly, organizations and their partners can assess the practical approaches and benefits without initial commitment and only proceed to implementation if appropriate.

Exit strategies

Collaborative models can change the relationship interaction and introduce progressively higher levels of interdependence. It is a valuable exercise to individually and jointly consider the implications if the relationship was to fail, or perhaps become no longer valid because of changes in market requirements. The development of an exit strategy will help firstly to define the levels of interdependence and then the rules for controlled disengagement.

Conclusion

Customers are essential to any organization and alternative business models can, without doubt, bring benefits to all parties. The challenge is to ensure that such approaches are mutually beneficial and are developed to underpin these benefits. Where customers see collaborative models as potentially advantageous, then they need to consider the implications for their partners and the profile they project, since this will influence the response and commitment they get from the market. The innovative supplier, on the other hand, needs to consider the aptitude and ability of the customer to engage in an integrated manner where the value proposition can be identified.

PART 3: Where?

Key messages

When developing collaborative business models the customer perspective is crucial. To help focus, the key messages given in Table 18.1 may provide the catalyst for business development.

Table 18.1 – Key messages for business development, marketing and sales

BS 11000 Business development/marketing/sales		
	Focus point	**Rationale**
1	Alternative business models	Collaborative approaches broaden the capability of organizations to respond to (pull) or propose (push) more complex propositions to meet the demands of the market or specific customer challenges
2	Customer profiling	Marketing collaborative approaches rests both on internal capability and the willingness of customers to respond positively to these approaches
3	Customer confidence	Where a collaborative model is being requested or offered the standard provides an independently validated approach. This can be a market differentiation, providing confidence beyond a sales positioning
4	Solution development	The integration of collaborative thinking enables organizations to add to their own capability and resources to expand the scope of any proposition or required solution by incorporating third parties to establish a seamless delivery solution
5	Delivery partners	Identifying and selecting additional partners to meet business demands requires organizations to seek partners with compatible visions and values and to develop joint objectives that support the customer requirement
6	Risk management	Adoption of alternative business models introduces the perception of risk for a customer and potential internal risks. The standard outlines a structured approach to building and sustaining these models through joint risk management

7	**Business case development**	Gaining support for an integrated solution against a more traditional operating model can increase internal constraints. In this situation the standard's processes and requirements ensure that organizations take due account of the key factors in developing the business case
8	**Speed to market**	Complex relationships can take time to develop; through the adoption of BS 11000 organizations can have a common language and understanding to speed implementation
9	**Creative negotiations**	Moving from a traditional relationship to one that is more integrated changes the dynamics for negotiations. Adoption of the standard enables all parties to address their issues in a more open and transparent way
10	**Collaborative contracts**	In the modern world the foundation of business is captured in formal contracts, which can on occasions be divisive. Incorporating the standard is an alternative platform to ensure equitable benefits and underpin the required behaviours to achieve success

Chapter 19 – Supply chain

> In this chapter we look at assessing the potential benefits from incorporating collaborative approaches, where appropriate, to extend the reach of supply chain management to focus on sustainable value. The supply chain is a major aspect of most business operations and in today's market it is not uncommon to find that the external spend represents between 60 per cent to 80 per cent of operating cost. This is both a significant opportunity and a major potential risk.

We have become accustomed to terms such as 'supplier relationship management' (SRM), 'strategic sourcing' or 'category management', all of which will contribute to managing high spends. Perhaps less obvious is the recognition that many of these relationships are mission critical and create interdependency that needs special care. Identifying providers that fit this agenda and developing a more integrated approach through the medium of BS 11000 will underpin the objectives, opportunities and risk management.

Cost is always a significant issue; it is usually an important aspect of the evaluation process alongside traditional aspects of quality and delivery. However, these alone should not be the only criteria when considering any contracting arrangement that has to be balanced against aspects of performance and overall risk. Risk is a crucial factor for any business; in developing a strategy, the exposure to potential risk is a key aspect that can be classified in many ways from simple security of supply to the mission-critical nature of the requirement for overall success.

Complexity in the modern marketplace is a broad-ranging strategic aspect of procurement, which may cover a variety of issues resulting from the interaction between contracting parties and – significantly – their performance over time. Interdependence is the most difficult aspect of modern business models where the performance of the parties is by necessity interwoven. This may result from joint development of products and solutions based on sharing of information and resources beyond traditional contracts, to the creation of joint solutions and propositions where interdependence is crucial, where the outcome can only be delivered through the joint activities of the parties.

NATS (National Air Traffic Services) – case study

NATS sought to pursue accreditation to BS 11000 from the very early stages of its development. It made a conscious and deliberate decision to invest in the concept of a collaborative working standard because of the value it believes this will add to its business. It was supply chain management in NATS that initially recognized its potential. This is a strategic business function, which controls over 95 per cent of external spend. It takes the lead role in managing NATS' strategic supplier relationships, determining supply chain/supplier strategies through working closely with internal stakeholders.

NATS decided to adopt the standard to manage its supplier partner relationships, building on existing collaborative processes. It brought additional real benefits because it:

- established an overarching governing structure to manage collaborative relationships;
- ensured processes were put in place to manage future collaborative relationships as well as the development of suppliers within its supplier base into partner suppliers;
- enabled benchmarking of the work that it is doing with its collaborative suppliers to ensure continuous improvement;
- established a common framework for working with partners.

Based on NATS' successful application of BS 11000 when working with partner suppliers, NATS is introducing it into relationships with major customers. Through adopting a collaborative framework with individual customers, a strong message is established of a committed relationship that can generate mutual benefit. This is of particular relevance, with an increasing need to work differently in the Air Traffic Management Industry with many types of organizations, driven by the aspirations of Single European Sky and its predicted impact on changing the future business environment. In view of this NATS is making sure it is at the very leading edge of thinking and best practice in business relationship development.

NATS is also keen to demonstrate how BS 11000 can support its 'innovating for growth' strategy through successfully demonstrating the benefits of its collaborative capabilities and practices when bidding for external business opportunities – as well as exploring opportunities to work with other organizations, particularly overseas where it can exploit new markets. Not only does it differentiate NATS from other air navigation service providers, but because of the continuously evolving, long-term and complex nature of ventures synonymous with the ATM business it is crucial in ensuring better value for their customers.

Adrian Miller,
Supply Chain Manager, NATS

For most organizations, operating cost is largely spent through its supply chain. With high levels of external spend, it is little wonder that there has been a marked increase of focus both in the private and public sectors to optimize these costs. This leads to many initiatives to improve procurement through enhancing skills, improving processes and harnessing technology. In many cases these initiatives have delivered significant results, possibly because they focused on operations that had a degree of inefficiency. Developing a strategy for sustainable efficiency requires organizations to look beyond the traditional 'cut and thrust' of purchasing power. The concept of the glass floor (see Figure 19.1) suggests that in many organizations the initial focus on purchasing was directed towards improving processes and skills.

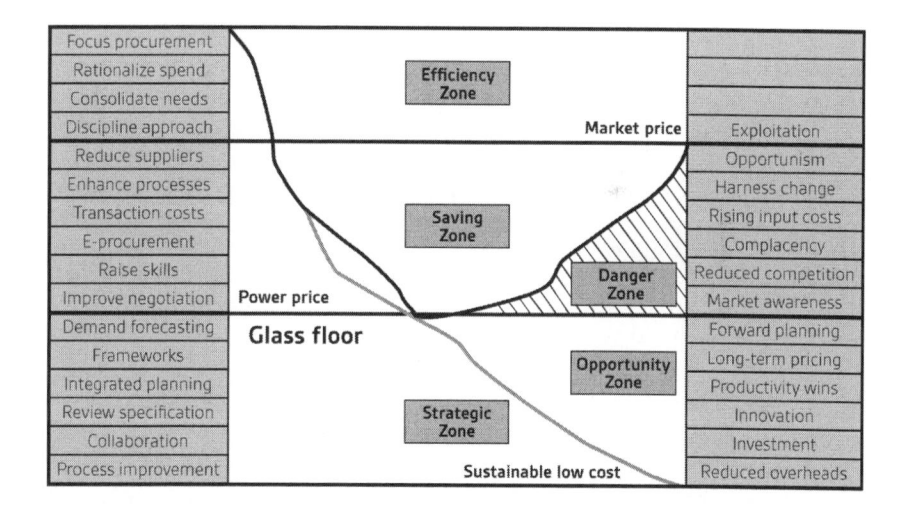

Figure 19.1 – The glass floor

Creating an awareness of the issues and focusing attention on harnessing the value of the supply chain to address efficiency is often a challenge in organizations where expenditure is solely benchmarked on price. Understanding the spend profile and rationalizing spend helps organizations start to direct attention where it will deliver most value. Consolidation of requirements, whether through standardization or aggregation, creates potential leverage in the market. Then, increasing the rigour of the process and implementing a disciplined approach starts to bring greater efficiency to their spending; this creates the efficiency zone shown in Figure 19.1, which should bring a more realistic market price. The next stage is to look at harmonizing the approach and raising the capability to exploit the market. Often the early wins come from reducing the supply base, enabling greater focus on the key issues and consolidating spend – thus increasing leverage. As organizations start to generate greater focus they soon recognize the need to improve their operating processes, which leads on to tackling transaction costs. This is aimed at cost reduction and also frees up resources to direct efforts towards delivering savings. The implementation of technology and e-procurement can eliminate much of the low-value high-volume activity. The more difficult element of this stage in creating the saving zone is the recognition that skills need to be improved or replaced, in particular those of negotiation skills.

At this point the organization reaches a stable state, but also it becomes the 'crunch point'. As the methods and capability increase, so the market will react and reposition itself. Those who have enjoyed a favourable position as suppliers and recognize the changes in approach will adopt alternative approaches. Market awareness becomes the enemy of sustainable savings. Reduced competition through consolidation can lead to challenges. Rising input costs that had previously been absorbed through high margins start to bite. On the other side of the fence, the savings achieved may induce complacency and lead to opportunism by suppliers, leading to the danger zone where organizations need to consider their next moves. It is at this stage in the development cycle that organizations need to consider the implications of the glass floor. If they do nothing, then the investment and the savings achieved will slowly be eroded. Looking beyond the conventional stages, organizations need to consider what to do next and how working together can sustain savings – and perhaps enhance them.

There are two complementary influences that can be brought to bear. On the buy side, supply chain management needs to become more strategic in its thinking. Improving the longer-term demands enables organizations to rationalize the potential for framework agreements, which can be valuable to both buyer and supplier in predicting requirements and reducing costs. Integrated planning allows more transparency and less opportunity for short-term exploitation. Process improvement can develop through understanding the joint impact on cost and performance. Through collaboration, specifications and requirements can be harmonized to eliminate specialty pricing. Establishing the strategic zone provides an enticing opportunity for the supplier to be more creative and innovative in bringing value to the table.

Chapter 19 – Supply chain

The more sophisticated supplier will probably see this as an opportunity zone, where by harnessing forward planning they can optimize production demands and present longer-term pricing models that provide stability. This in turn helps to focus future investment and, through collaboration, introduce innovation, process improvement and reduced overheads, all of which can increase their competitive edge. Clearly, going beyond the glass floor is not appropriate for all procurement; but targeted correctly it can introduce greater stability for key markets and offers more sustainable savings.

> **MOD (Ministry of Defence) – case study**
>
> The Defence Information Infrastructure (DII) Group is the first programme in MOD to achieve BS 11000 certification and we believe that this is recognition of our continual commitment to collaborative working. The Strategic Defence and Security Review requires MOD to seek to meet defence outputs with fewer people and DII Group believed that a more collaborative way of working could deliver significant value when implemented and managed correctly. The question was how to embed and sustain collaborative working in the DII programme and how we would know we had achieved this.
>
> Collaborative working is about developing two-way, mutually beneficial relationships that deliver greater levels of innovation and competitive advantage than could be achieved by operating independently. It improves cost management, use of resources and risk management to increase business value and unlock innovation.
>
> The DII Combined Operating Model was established to exploit collaborative working principles and put in place an operating framework that would enable improved delivery of DII business outputs and better position DII to support the future Defence Core Network Services programme. It also provided a stable framework to minimize disruption from anticipated reorganizations and enable seamless succession planning.
>
> BS 11000 provided a mechanism to measure the effectiveness of collaborative working and validate the Combined Operating Model, giving MOD an external measurement vehicle to sustain their collaborative business relationship.
>
> Mike Rogers
> MOD Partnering Support Group

Partnering and collaboration has become part of the supply chain armoury in the search to maintain competitiveness and develop alternative business models. This approach may take many different forms, from outsourcing of internal support activities through to external integration of business processes. There are many examples where the collaborative approach has shown significant benefit to organizations, but there are also many potential pitfalls that arise from greater interdependence. These challenges may reflect performance or reputation issues, which need to be addressed as part of any overall strategy.

Collaboration promotes integration of the value chain, placing the focus on the wider delivery structure by removing non-value added activities and sharing skills, resources and knowledge to improve business processes. Partnering may be more helpfully illustrated by replacing the 'chain' metaphor with a 'bridge', where focus is drawn to the interdependent strength of the interfaces instead of the individual strength of the component links themselves. Bridging the value chain supports and accelerates the complex flow of ideas, ingenuity, resources and expertise that interconnect designers, producers and consumers. Bridges ultimately connect all segments of the chain to one another, making all parties in some way responsible for the efficiency and competitiveness of the whole. This network of interdependence forms the foundation of strategic programmes and overall performance is enhanced by integrating supply partners.

At every stage of the strategy development process it is important to maintain a perspective on the risk and potential value of a particular business relationship. In many cases, while a less confrontational relationship will add value, developing a formal collaborative arrangement may not be justified. Collaborative ventures take time and effort and must be able to demonstrate a value contribution that fits with the overall business profile and targeted objectives. In the same way the risks need to be evaluated and a balanced view taken that reflects these same objectives. Effective relationships bring many potential benefits, but these will, conversely, generate a number of limitations on the traditional way of working with either customers or suppliers.

Supply chain risk

Organizations should consider the supply chain as a major potential area of risk, in terms of every aspect of the business profile from profitability to long-term reputation. Failure by any major supply component will be viewed by customers as a failure in the selling organization. The whole process of risk management has, in general, traditionally focused on passing risk down the control chain, through tight contracts and penalties for poor performance. What is often ignored in this profile is the ability of the supplier alone to influence the outcome, or the impact of penalties to truly reflect the overall impact of poor performance. Thus, balancing of customer risk and supplier risk should be a crucial part of creating an optimized risk strategy.

The supply chain is the most underrated facet of the business landscape; the potential that it can introduce to improve performance and reduce cost is significant. However, the greater the level of exploitation the higher the risk potential, thus, high on the risk management agenda must be the development of strategic procurement approaches. Key elements such as complexity, criticality and hazard evaluations are normal parts of most selection processes, but wider issues such as customer acceptability can be a major deciding factor. The issue of risk is not simply a question for the buyer; it has a major impact on the profile of the supplier. How a supplier is perceived in the market is a critical part of their marketing profile and a key element of how they present themselves to customers.

Conclusion

The adoption of collaborative concepts into strategic supply programmes provides an alternative perspective on the traditional trading relationship. Beyond the commercial benefits that are usually the prime focus for pursuing collaboration to find or improve competitive edge, it offers a sound and mutual platform on which to support and develop new ideas, manage risk and help to underpin sustainability targets.

Poor relationships between organizations and their supply chains are perhaps the major contributor in the failure to address many aspects of globalization. The characteristics of any successful business are the common factors in building effective relationships. Collaboration can move this integration even further towards success, underpinned by developing trust, through mutual performance, and it is through this trust that more effective optimization and development can take place. This in turn will identify opportunities for cost and time efficiencies, while at the same time creating the framework and background to develop more effectively the roles and responsibilities, which will largely define the success of the partnership.

Collaboration addresses short and long-term integration, so it must take consideration for the wider implications of social interaction at the business level. The mutual focus on the future will inevitably lead to organizations having greater knowledge of each other, and more fully appreciating the benefits that can be derived from joint development rather than short-term exploitation. The BS 11000 framework provides a robust and neutral platform on which to explore the potential benefits of collaboration to support the move through the glass floor toward sustainable procurement.

PART 3: Where?

Key messages

The increased focus on strategic sourcing and supply chains offers many opportunities to exploit the potential of collaborative models. The key issues given in Table 19.1 can help to promote considerations for collaborative working.

Table 19.1 – Key messages for strategic supply chain

BS 11000 strategic supply chain		
	Focus point	**Rationale**
1	**Business objectives**	Effective supply chain optimization has become a critical aspect of overall business performance. Collaborative relationships reach beyond the traditional perspective of price, quality and delivery but must be integral to the goals of the organization to consider alternative approaches and direct efforts to those relationships which will contribute maximum value
2	**Benefits**	While price will always remain a key factor in supply chain management, adoption of the standard establishes a robust framework to evaluate more inclusive approaches in assessing innovative solutions to meet business goals
3	**Risk**	Reliance on the supply chain to support business drivers increases the risks and vulnerability of operations; thus these strategic relationships become an integral aspect of business risk while at the same time introducing some additional risks
4	**Collaborative profile**	In seeking to develop alternative business models, organizations frequently assume the marketplace is willing to collaborate or considers the customer has a collaborative ethos
5	**Partner evaluation**	The process of choosing the appropriate collaborative partner can frequently ignore the culture that will be a crucial ingredient for success. Basing evaluation and selection on

		pure perception raises issues of auditability, whether private or public sector
6	**Contracting**	The reliance on contracts to enforce performance and behaviours is seldom successful. The integration of the standard ensures there is a structured approach which can be developed by the parties without compromising the integrity of the contract and its inherent liabilities
7	**Management**	The control of complex supply chains is most frequently directed through a master/servant relationship, which constrains effective engagement and limits mutual development of added value
8	**Interdependency**	Supply chain vulnerability increases where key aspects of performance are externally delivered and is further complicated where integrated models are adopted that harness joint capability and ownership
9	**Performance**	In any business venture delivering the required outcomes is crucial, which can be damaged by protectionism and 'blame culture' diverting resources. A robust collaborative approach ensures that transparency and joint responsibility are established
10	**Innovation**	Sharing knowledge and capability allows organizations to harness value across the relationship and potentially extend the contribution to overall success

Chapter 20 – Outsourcing

> Outsourcing has become a major area of business focus over the past decade. It has demonstrated the valuable potential to enhance competitive edge, but has also highlighted the many challenges that organizations face when seeking to capitalize on the potential of transferring internal activities and resources to a third party organization. In this chapter we examine the key role of relationships in this environment and the 'outside in' theory.

Outsourcing creates a whole new spectrum of challenges and risks, whether it is for internal support services, the development of external manufacturing or the creation of extended enterprise business models. These external organizations are moving inside another organization's imaginary boundaries or firewalls to become part of the overall delivery process. However, their remote location often means that they are not physically absorbing the ethos or culture of the host customer. In some cases they may be operating with a completely different set of conflicting values. The process of integrating external organizations into a cohesive business process places increased demands on the trading relationships and those charged with managing them. The *outside* is coming *inside* but is frequently evaluated on the basis of traditional command-and-control thinking. The rush to exploit the potential of outsourcing opportunities must be balanced with a robust process that ensures a holistic approach is created, which considers the wider implications of this strategy.

The progressive move from a command-and-control structure to one of interdependence, however, highlights the need to develop a more collaborative approach. The deployment of collaborative approaches can help to underpin effective outsourcing strategies, enabling organizations to capitalize on the benefits and create future opportunities.

PART 3: Where?

EMCOR Group (UK) – case study

EMCOR UK is the first facilities management (FM) provider to achieve BS 11000 certification, recognizing EMCOR's track record in developing long-term client relationships. EMCOR's clients have always benefited from its collaborative approach, but since April 2010 an independently assessed framework has been in place that effectively ensures the knowledge, skills, processes and resources to meet mutually defined objectives are in place. BS 11000 sets out a framework that will enable companies like EMCOR to apply good practice principles to its own way of working, and has wide applications on how to manage valuable business relationships within the supply chain.

At EMCOR UK we focus on the concept of 'collaborative working' as we feel this better sums up the practical relationship between independent businesses working together. Collaborative working implies that organizations are not 'joined at the hip', but that they share mutual goals on specific programmes. I am firmly of the view that any business relationship needs shared outcomes that should be agreed formally, so that all those involved know exactly what is expected of the other and that assumptions are not made about motivations that may be wrong. In doing so, collaborative organizations get to think in more detail about what they want to achieve together.

Many organizations and the companies that serve them are simply locked into the transactional approach and cannot see past it. This is exacerbated when many FM service providers are seen to be too far down the 'food chain', when actually their knowledge and expertise could make a real difference if a more collaborative approach was considered. This is simple common sense and recognition of the value of FM to an organization.

The Lean Learning Academy implemented by our aerospace client encourages maximum focus on the aligned goals and the dismissal of those issues that are irrelevant to achieving them. The result can provide innovative but practical solutions to problems or the grasping of opportunities that present themselves when everyone on the team knows exactly what they are contributing to and why. In practical terms this has amounted to cost savings in excess of £500K per annum and faster job completion.

Christopher Kehoe,
Divisional Director, EMCOR UK

Exploiting any outsourcing initiative is commonly focused on the promise of significant cost savings. While this is clearly possible, the ability of

Chapter 20 – Outsourcing

organizations to capitalize on the opportunities depends very much on how the programme is evaluated, and – more importantly – developed and implemented. Outsourcing will have an impact on the whole organization, either directly or indirectly, and it is likely to meet resistance. It also has to be developed within the wider market environment. Creating an effective programme must be based on fully understanding the internal capabilities and drivers; at the same time any programme must incorporate recognition of integrating a risk management approach within its development. Defining clear objectives will help to assess aspects of knowledge transfer and the wider implications of meeting the sustainability agenda.

The development of an outsourcing programme should be reviewed first from a strategic perspective, and then with an evaluation plan set in place that will enable various aspects of the business to be reviewed and assessed, to ensure that every aspect and impact has been taken into account. The importance of relationships in this business environment is fundamental; yet while there is often acknowledgement of the principle, frequently relationship management is low on development programmes. This is perplexing, particularly when you consider the growth of outsourcing and offshoring, where the interfaces between organizations are always a point of vulnerability and risk. Often the assumption is made that managing relationships is just a normal part of business life and thus low on the 'needs development' profile. This dilemma prompts consideration about how organizations look at themselves and the marketplace as a whole, and how this may affect the way the impact of relationships is perceived. Many traditional organizations have developed under a command-and-control structure that looked from the inside out to the marketplace and were controlled through arm's-length contracts with either customers or suppliers. This approach assumed that they would operate within known rules and behaviours; it is relatively easy to manage relationships and behaviours as a factor of location.

The 'outside in' theory poses the view that when assessing the importance and value of relationships we should be evaluating from another perspective. If organizations looked at their operations from the perspective of 'outside in' then the realization is that managing relationships is a more complex and crucial ingredient for these diverse business models. It highlights the need to bring into play a much wider range of considerations than the traditional price, quality and delivery mix. It also brings into question whether the traditional approaches of contracting can effectively be applied in this environment.

The traditional tried and tested operating model (see Figure 20.1) for supply chains – and perhaps the basis of most organizational approaches – has been developed around manufacturing concepts: we view the marketplace from a perspective of how it fits with our operations. In this context organizations acquire materials or components, move these into

PART 3: Where?

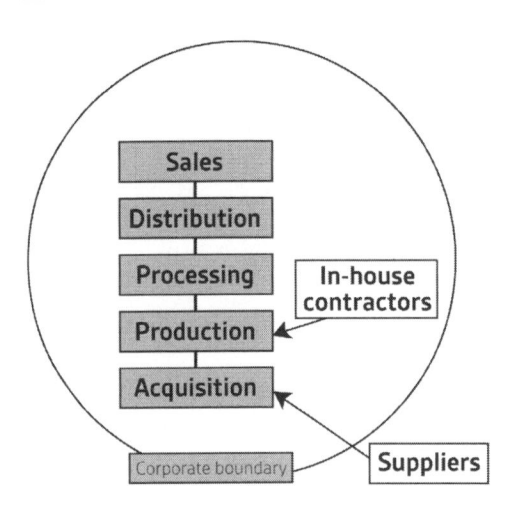

- Price
- Quality
- Delivery
- Management

Figure 20.1 – The traditional trading model

a production programme where they are processed, then possibly distribute to the point of sale. In this model the key is to ensure that we achieve the most competitive price and the right level of quality, and our products are available when needed. The only challenge is to orchestrate the balance between these three key drivers. The model becomes slightly more complex when decisions are made to have certain elements of the processing undertaken by external specialists. This often occurs where organizations have a periodic requirement that does not justify a full-time internal capability. In these cases the integration of the external capability is largely achieved through effective management at a local level (see Figure 20.2). This ensures that those third party providers operate within the internal structures and governance. The external parties will often, to greater or lesser extent, also absorb the ethos and culture of the organization.

As organizations look for greater efficiency and strive to focus on their core capabilities while reducing costly internal infrastructures, the next step is to consider external contractors to undertake all or part of the processing, and often distribution too (see Figure 20.3). Progression to this model leads to a greater emphasis on the scope and rigour of contracts. In many cases these relationships or contracts aim to transfer risk and responsibility to the highest possible extent, relying on the contract to allocate liability in the event of a breakdown. Clearly, at this point the relationship has become fragmented, where on each side of the contract wall the parties are working to protect their position while exploiting their relative positions as much as possible in terms of performance. While many organizations seek to impose their principles and values through contracts this is seldom fully effective.

Chapter 20 – Outsourcing

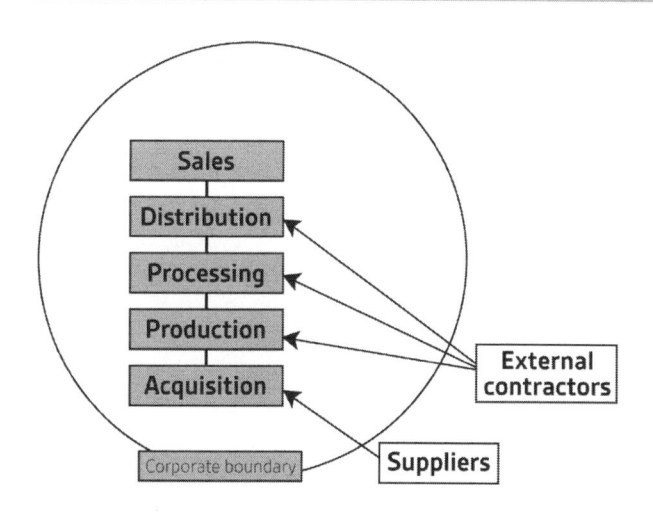

- Price
- Quality
- Delivery
- Management
- Contracts

Figure 20.2 – Incorporating external contractors

- Price
- Quality
- Delivery
- Management
- Contracts
- Performance
- Integration
- Culture
- Ethos
- Commitment
- CSR
- Interdependence
- Trust

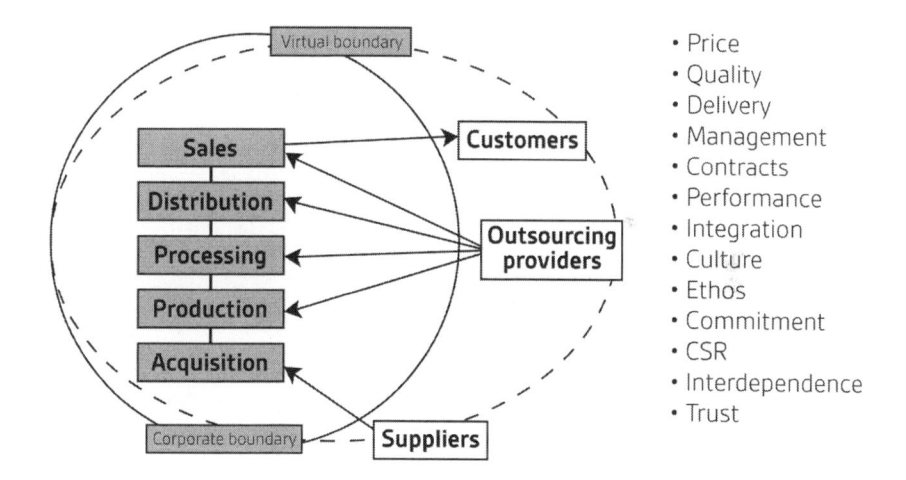

Figure 20.3 – Moving to outsourcing

Perhaps the most vulnerable stage is where organizations seek to reduce cost by outsourcing large areas of operational process activity. These external providers become an integral part of the overall delivery model but remain completely independent companies. At this point the contract can only provide the financial and performance framework; it is unlikely to be able to influence integrated performance or – equally important – aspects such as maintaining visions and values, culture, ethos and commitment. There is plenty of evidence that it is the culture and values of an organization that really drive excellent performance, not regulations and measures.

At this point the relationship and profile of the provider, who may be directly interfacing with customers, becomes a critical factor. How they represent the organization and perform is a direct reflection on the prime company and its reputation. When viewing the model from the outside in it becomes clear that traditional thinking based around a simple self-contained production environment is no longer sufficient to ensure the success of an integrated operation. The 'outside' comes inside the firewall and needs to be assessed, developed and directed with far greater focus on the ability of external providers to blend in and support the host organization's goals and values.

Effective performance is created through integration of both internal and external suppliers. Awareness of the holistic impacts of management must extend beyond the functional boundaries of purchasing organizations in order to ensure that opportunities are fully exploited. Building on the strengths of the organization, it is critical to establish the level of knowledge and skills that exist to ensure that suitable training can be developed to provide an effective platform to move to outsourcing with confidence. The supply chain has developed over the later part of the last century and moves into the 21st century with many innovative approaches; however, these must be balanced against true need and risk management processes. Often what is needed is best practice approaches coupled with the ability to spot the strategic opportunities. However, in many cases organizations ignore their own capabilities and focus solely on the potential outsourcing provider, which is a recipe for disaster because internal constraints will almost certainly emerge to dilute performance.

When an organization has structured its internal perspective it needs to evaluate and select partners. The nature of the provider's organization is crucial to overall success in developing value for money propositions. The relationships (vertically and horizontally) in the value chain are a key factor in exploiting the value development process. Organizations should (and frequently need to) learn from each other; thus, ensuring that the potential partner has a compatible ethos and culture is an important contributor to optimizing value. The nature of an arrangement will be developed based on the objectives and goals from each side of the relationship. How organizations expect they will be working together will help to define the nature of the contracting relationship, the style of integration and the level of interfaces; this will have a significant impact on the development of risk management approaches. The key to effective outsourcing is ensuring a clear definition of scope and services to be provided, which can then be assessed to create an overall approach and establish SLAs.

Chapter 20 – Outsourcing

The balance of power in any relationship shifts over the period of the association; in an outsourcing context this shift may be critical to overall delivery performance for the buyer. Staying together, whether over short duration contracts or long-term supply arrangements, requires that both parties maintain an effective working relationship. Dispute resolution is seldom simply a question of depending on the terms of contract. Effective management depends upon the leadership abilities of the key players to understand and respond effectively to issues that could undermine the delivery process. Having a clear focus on the exit strategy provides both partners with a clear perspective of their individual positions; it will also certainly help to provide a clear background, which will allow the relationship to mature more effectively.

Building on this foundation of collaboration, it is important not to forget the fundamentals of any good contracting relationship; ideally these can be agreed with a focus on success and not the traditional concepts of contracting for inevitable failure and legal conflict. We don't have to change the fundamentals; we simply have to address them to ensure that they facilitate success. Scope and standards are clearly important, along with frequency of performance contract reviews and a clear understanding of total cost. What will complement the arrangement is a focus on communication, cross-training where necessary, skills assessments, and well-developed and visible processes. Certainly quality must be maintained and performance linked to effective and meaningful measurement, which drives improvement – not conflict. Perhaps most important of all is the need to understand how change will be managed within the relationship. This is frequently lost in the euphoria of building a proactive approach, but will likely become a major burden in the future.

The focus for an outsourcing programme may often be obvious to those closest to the problem, but is frequently lost in the wider context of the organization. The first part of the strategic focus is to present these targets within the context of a wider profile, which helps to focus the validity of the approach. This helps to demonstrate that selection has been done effectively, ensuring a buy-in across the organization that will lead to success. The simplest of assessments is often enough to put the focus in the right place for the organization as a whole, but it may also demonstrate that initial thinking requires further evaluation. The second critical stage is to assess the potential impact of outsourcing, where the true impact of external integration starts to change the organization's traditional profile. It will certainly raise many questions around existing resources and approaches, intellectual property and – most importantly – the retention of skills within the organization. This is where the crunch comes for most organizations within the context of integrating corporate strategy and organizational development, as outsourcing will inevitably lead to internal changes at every level. Understanding why outsourcing is being considered means defining the rationale for taking it forward. Reasons why outsourcing is being considered include:

- cost and competitive edge;
- effort and optimization of resources;
- product or service availability;
- sustainability and ethical performance;
- risk – both performance and market;
- complexity;
- performance improvement;
- customer benefit.

Creating an outsourcing strategy should be approached in a holistic manner. Developing a programme that blends the attributes of diverse organizations must begin with recognition that each may have significantly different approaches and demands. This may be more clearly apparent in the context of global trading, but should not be ignored even in the more localized and traditional markets. In a conventional trading relationship the ability to build such challenges into a uniform approach can be very difficult and often the contracting rules can be counterproductive.

The multidimensional nature of the global landscape creates an environment that inherently generates an ever-increasing profile of risk and opportunity. The search to exploit these opportunities of the global market, and the volatility of the many factors that can change the platform of a business deal, means that there must be a focus on managing the risk. The pressures of regulation and environmental liabilities, together with the wider and more indirect ramifications of global trading, are factors that every organization must recognize. The political and cultural challenges of working outside the comfort zone of traditional business networks are complex; developing a structured approach is critical. The implications for organizations are far-reaching and necessitate an increasing focus on risk mitigation and management to ensure successful ventures. The attraction of low-cost sourcing and manufacturing is certainly a potential opportunity for all organizations, but the implications and risks should not be underestimated.

Conclusion

The challenge is for organizations to adopt a more flexible perspective that enables maximum exploitation of the potential but retains effective management of the processes and performance. Outsourcing has become an accepted methodology to capture competitive advantage, but this extended enterprise approach brings its own level of risk through interdependence and reputational risk. The need to ensure that external providers share a common focus on the business visions and values is crucial to long-term sustainability and maintaining a perspective on corporate social responsibility.

Today the paramount challenge for any business is to create value for its shareholders, while meeting the demands of an increasingly competitive marketplace. The complexity and volatility of this business environment creates a landscape that requires constant flexibility of approach and resource investment. Building an integrated business relationship between two or more organizations involves an increasing number of players from each side; focusing on the critical path issues will help to maintain momentum. Company success is influenced by both internal and external factors; outsourcing has impacts across an organization and beyond, yet too frequently corporate strategy is not adequately integrated, evaluated, communicated, absorbed and risk-assessed. In addition, partner selection is driven by cost rather than compatibility. The foundation of BS 11000 provides a structured approach to addressing these challenges through building more effective outsourcing relationships.

PART 3: Where?

Key messages

In developing an outsourcing programme it is important to consider how the relationships are developed and sustained. Table 20.1 provides key messages about the BS 11000 approach to outsourcing.

Table 20.1 – Key messages for outsourcing

BS 11000 outsourcing		
	Focus point	**Rationale**
1	Integrated delivery	The integration of the standard provides a platform on which to evaluate and develop these collaborative models on a more rigorous basis
2	Alternative business models	Outsourcing has become a major efficiency tool in the business armoury; however, in many cases the decisions and effectiveness often fail to consider the compatibility of organizations to undertake key aspects of the current business processes
3	Customer profiling	Marketing outsourcing capability is largely dependent on capability and the willingness of customers to respond positively to these approaches
4	Customer confidence	Where a collaborative model is being offered the standard provides an independently validated approach; in some cases this can be a market differentiation but in any event provides confidence that collaboration is in the mindset of the organization
5	Solution development	Outsourcing solutions can often require organizations to expand their own capability and resources to the scope of any proposition by incorporating third parties to establish a seamless delivery solution
6	Delivery partners	Identifying and selecting partners to meet business demand requires organizations to seek other organizations with compatible visions and values and to develop joint objectives that support the customer requirement

7	**Risk management**	The adoption of outsourcing models introduces the perception of increased risk for a customer and potential internal risks. A structured approach to building and sustaining these models through joint risk management enables more effective management of risks
8	**Creative negotiations**	Moving from a traditional relationship to one that is more integrated changes the dynamics for negotiations. Adoption of the standard model process as a starting pointing enables all parties to address their issues in a more open and transparent way, based on joint objectives and desired outcomes
9	**Collaborative contracts**	In the modern world the foundation of business is captured in formal contracts; however, these can on occasion be divisive. This is why the standard introduces an alternative platform to ensure equitable benefits, based on risk and reward, which underpins the behaviours necessary to achieve successful outcomes
10	**Termination and transition**	The most vulnerable aspect of outsourcing programmes is the eventual termination of the contract and transition to other providers. The exit strategy is a key aspect of relationship management, which can be both an evaluation criterion and a means to ensure business continuity

Chapter 21 – Collaborative contracting

> In the modern marketplace reliance on contracts has become normal practice. There is often a perception that collaborative working is not compatible with most model contracts, which may lead to poor behaviours. While this may be true in some areas, it is important to ensure that where collaborative working is established as a route to deliver outcomes the contract supports these arrangements. This chapter explains how BS 11000 can provide a model with which to build more effective contracting arrangements.

Today most business activity needs the structured support of a contract to underpin what it hopes to achieve. In developing a contracting approach it is important to define the individual responsibilities and then to place these obligations with the correct party. In the initial stages of developing a collaborative strategy the temptation is to set objectives that are too wide-reaching and have varying chances of being achieved.

When considering the appropriate contracting model it is important to distinguish between a collaborative arrangement and contractual deliverables. The former of these is often the route taken by organizations and is outside the contract. Frequently this may be a simple arrangement within which organizations adopt a more open way of dealing with each other; the downside of this is that as a non-contractual requirement it often fails to deliver the full potential. However, by incorporating the principles of the standard the parties can blend both contract and relationship.

Contracting for failure

In cases where the parties recognize the commercial or technical benefits from a closer commitment over time there is a commercial consideration being taken, which reflects how the parties may contract with each other. Any contract that incorporates risk and reward elements needs careful consideration by both parties to ensure there is sound understanding of the potential outcomes, because contracts are only valuable in a legal sense when parties fail to meet their individual obligations. The reality of any contract is that it should provide the platform on which organizations can perform; how organizations expect they will be

PART 3: Where?

working together will help to define the nature of the contract and level of interfaces. The general trend, unfortunately, is to 'contract for failure' so we tend to see most elements as negative. *Collaborative Change*[12] by Humphries and Gibb draws together a wide range of professional and academic views that complement this subject. The focus for any contract should be to ensure that it delivers what is required and when. This is the same in a collaborative relationship, but many traditional contracts are developed without the parties identifying what is really crucial to each of them.

Most contracts are focused as effective legal tools and in configuring a contract it is the potential impact of failure that may raise questions around existing relationships, approaches, intellectual property and risk. The crunch point for most organizations is the challenge of integrating corporate strategy with organizational development and contracts that are solution-based. There are multiplicities of contracting options, many of which may suit the needs of the organization and do not require the effort of developing a collaborative approach; so it is often worthwhile starting with the most appropriate traditional contracting model and building on this to incorporate the wider issues that have been identified as potential collaborative benefits. This approach provides a solid basis for the parties to work from and can often be the first test about the parties' commitment for collaboration.

Lockheed Martin – case study

Lockheed Martin has long recognized that in order to deliver a successful programme the parties involved have to work together. Programme objectives are more likely to be successfully achieved if all parties involved are focused on those end goals, encouraging positive behaviours and removing roadblocks to the ability to work together.

The type of long-term, large scale, complex programmes that form the core of Lockheed Martin's business often demand a different type of working relationship from the traditional 'arm's length' contracting models of the past. The parties involved need to work collaboratively over the long term to successfully deliver challenging programme objectives. The BS 11000 standard has provided Lockheed Martin with a framework for implementing and objectively measuring the benefits of collaborative working. Using the standard to evaluate past activities, Lockheed Martin has been able to identify repeatable collaborative working good practice, as well as areas that could benefit from increased focus.

---

[12] *Collaborative Change: Creating High Performance Partnerships and Alliances*, Humphries A and Gibbs R, CreateSpace, 2010.

Chapter 21 – Collaborative contracting

Our approach to working with suppliers and customers has always included many of the collaborative working concepts articulated in BS 11000. This meant that the business case to justify inclusion of the standard into our policy and process baseline was relatively easy to define. With accreditation gained, our focus is now on continuous improvement of our collaborative engagement that will allow us, our suppliers and our customers to achieve success on increasingly demanding programmes in the future.

Mark Cooper, Managing Director,
Lockheed Martin UK IS&GS Civil

If the desire for collaboration is strong, then the traditional contractual debates will be a catalyst for change. Where the concept is weak these exchanges will highlight the true focus of the organizations. More importantly, in the cases where collaboration can really add value to both parties the process of evaluating a conventional model helps to focus the potential for long-term benefits. The more that organizations are prepared to engage in this process in depth, the greater the probability they will uncover potential value. Most organizations today have established contracting procedures, incorporating necessary safeguards, but in many cases these have been incorporated into the operating structures and will be extremely difficult to change. The process of challenging these procedures in developing a more open relationship with partners is a valuable test of the organization's ability to actually operate within the more integrated nature of collaboration.

Unfortunately, it is often the case that an ingrained culture creates so much tension that organizations give up trying to exploit the potential of collaboration; while operators may see the potential, the resistance of corporate process, lawyers and auditors means these opportunities for benefit are not pursued. It is important to differentiate between the way in which organizations want to collaborate and the need to establish workable legal frameworks that support these objectives. A legally binding agreement needs to define tasks, allocate responsibilities, and state the consequences in the event of specific circumstances, recognizing the implications of regulatory demands such as the European procurement directives; but with careful consideration these issues can be developed to be inclusive and complementary. It is also important to avoid creating a legal partnership. The standards framework can be a useful tool to evaluate both the objectives and issues that will ultimately be reflected in the contract, by understanding what really drives the contracting arrangements and giving focus to what helps success rather than legal conflict. Working through the culture, organizational structure, disposition of resources, skills and operating processes concentrates attention towards the success factors and ultimate objectives incorporating:

- clarity of purpose;
- contract structure;
- term or duration;
- risk and reward;
- knowledge sharing;
- obligations;
- liabilities;
- costing;
- confidentiality;
- commercial management and incentives.

A crucial part of any contract is to ensure that the selection process meets the requirements of the organization. The focus for collaboration reaches beyond the traditional evaluations of price, delivery and quality, so the process should incorporate the key elements of selection that reach beyond conventional contracting.

Scope and objectives

Contracts require an agreed conclusion point that is time-based on completion and identifies both objectives and scope (see Table 21.1). Collaborative relationships are generally more valuable the longer they operate; ensuring there are renewal points helps to maintain continuity while considering key circumstances where it may be inappropriate to continue (such as change of ownership) and raise the focus on exit strategy. When creating a contracting approach it is important to formally recognize the governance structure that will be jointly operated by the collaboration, which will include defining points of contact, authorities and dispute resolution processes.

Chapter 21 – Collaborative contracting

Table 21.1 – Collaborative contract scope and objectives

Scope	Objectives
Standards	Knowledge sharing
Delivery	Value creation
Price structure	Risk sharing
Communications	Reward sharing
Training	Cost reduction
Performance targets	Cycle time
Business processes	Investment profiles
Quality requirements	Sustainable development
Service levels	Visibility
Change management	Innovation
Documentation	Planning
Regulations	Resource sharing
Incentives	Team building
Confidentiality	Continuous improvement
Payment	Organization
Terms	Dispute resolution
Liabilities	Exit strategy
Risk	Customer satisfaction

Organizations need agreements to ensure there is a documented platform, which can vary due to many different factors. The problem with all these agreements is that while organizations all have experience with the tangible side of contract drafting it is more difficult when trying to address the aims and aspirations of collaboration. This is where the lawyers often get excited, as these concepts can be vague in contracting terms. For example, how do you enforce (if you need to) terms such as 'the parties will endeavour to reduce cost' or 'cooperation and good faith'. You can set targets, but who decides the strength of the effort that has been applied if the targets are not achieved?

We may have some sympathy with the lawyers' viewpoint; their role is to protect their client. Statements of principle such as 'working together in a spirit of trust and cooperation', 'using innovative engineering techniques', 'striving for continuous improvement' or 'being committed to achieving effective interfaces' all offer a valid style of working but are extremely hard to build into quantifiable measures.

Perhaps the most difficult concept to incorporate is an exit strategy. It is similar to the debate on prenuptial agreements – for if the commitment is there, then why plan to fail, which may undermine the principles of collaboration and create the easy way out? There are good reasons why an exit strategy is needed. The parties have shareholders, and possibly parent companies, whose long-term plans may change, affecting the agreement; takeovers may place the agreement in the hands of competitors or ownership that restricts the contract's operability; worse, there may be an irrevocable breakdown of the relationship. Nobody knows for sure, but the result could mean that the arrangement has to be dismantled and provision must be included to cover the downstream effects of such a break-up.

All of this seems very formal within the context of collaboration, cooperation and mutuality, but if collaboration is to work effectively, then the ground rules need to be clear at the start. One aspect of BS 11000 is the introduction of the RMP. This may have been established at the strategy stage; it can be jointly developed as the foundation for relationship management in future and can (when appropriate) become an annex to the contract, enabling the parties to define how they will jointly manage performance as opposed to contractual deliverables.

Litigation

The trend of litigation has done little to help the focus on developing effective collaborative contracts. Across a broad range of industries, including the public sector, it seems we are moving closer to managing our business through the legal systems. This is not to suggest that a clear contract agreement is not important; however, it does raise the question as to whether the amount of effort put in to address failure is actually detracting from the principal aims of both buyer and seller: success. For example, in public–private partnerships it seems that the strategic aims are frequently lost in a drive to shift risk and cost, often inappropriately. At the same time the challenges of accountability in the public sector do place high levels of stress on having a 'watertight' contract. As a result, during the evaluation and negotiation stages the pressure is on to maintain a defensive position; this subsequently acquires a partnering label, with the expectation that the past pressure will evaporate.

Experience in the private sector similarly offers little encouragement, even when there is more latitude for innovative approaches. The buyer is 'king' and too frequently this leads to over-aggressive contracts that have little chance of producing anything other than conflict. Perhaps the win/win should focus on making sure that both parties are satisfied with the contract so that it is not constantly used as a weapon to beat the other party. For example, the dependence on SLAs can be a way of measuring performance, but too often SLA problems are not recognized as indicators of a process problem but as a contract failure, with the resulting attitudes prevailing.

Developing an effective contracting and delivery approach is not something that emerges out of a negotiation, rather, it should be considered well in advance. If a collaborative relationship is what is most likely to deliver best value, then it must be considered from the outset. This does not mean that sound contracts are not required or acceptable, but the way in which the relationship is contracted will influence the way it is performed. Focusing on success means that in many cases we should change the way in which we approach contracts, and not the contracts themselves, which should be more proactive and less destructive. The focus on joint outcomes will be likely to set a structure that delivers the desired results, while centring on the potential for failure will most likely result in a self-fulfilling prophesy.

Collaborative negotiations and contracts

Negotiations are an integral part of business life and have been for thousands of years. These are areas where collaborative leaders must take a strong position to avoid them becoming potential points of failure. The traditional use of power negotiations may not always be the best approach, and when looking at a future collaborative relationship the negotiations should be part of the relationship-building process. Value is accumulated through many different avenues; understanding these impacts is a key part of negotiation strategy and process and a critical factor in overall success. Understanding the type and nature of the relationship desired in the future should feature in developing a negotiation approach to deliver prospective benefits. While many people may talk about the win–win approach, it is seldom a key driver and frequently not a consideration for many negotiations.

Selecting a collaborative partner can have many ramifications in the marketplace, both from competitors and customers. The culture of an organization is often a challenge. In a global market this becomes even more complex; when considering a collaborative approach it is important

PART 3: Where?

to ensure this is fully understood and recognized by potential partners. Risk will always be high on the agenda, but to exploit the potential of collaboration, risk should be jointly managed by those best placed to handle it and should not simply be transferred – while recognizing the potential for collaboration to introduce new risk elements into the equation. The world of business has evolved towards greater dependence on contracts and litigation; while clearly there needs to be an effective legal framework, it is important to recognize that successful outcomes will seldom come through the courts. Contract management is about delivering successful programmes, which open up a much wider arena for consideration about what the role of contract management becomes and what part it will play in how we raise our game to deliver success.

Interdependence →

Joint ventures
Public/private partnerships
Partnerships and alliances
Development contracts
Framework contracts
Service contracts
Equipment contracts
Commodity supply contracts

Cost **Risk**

Collaborative value curve

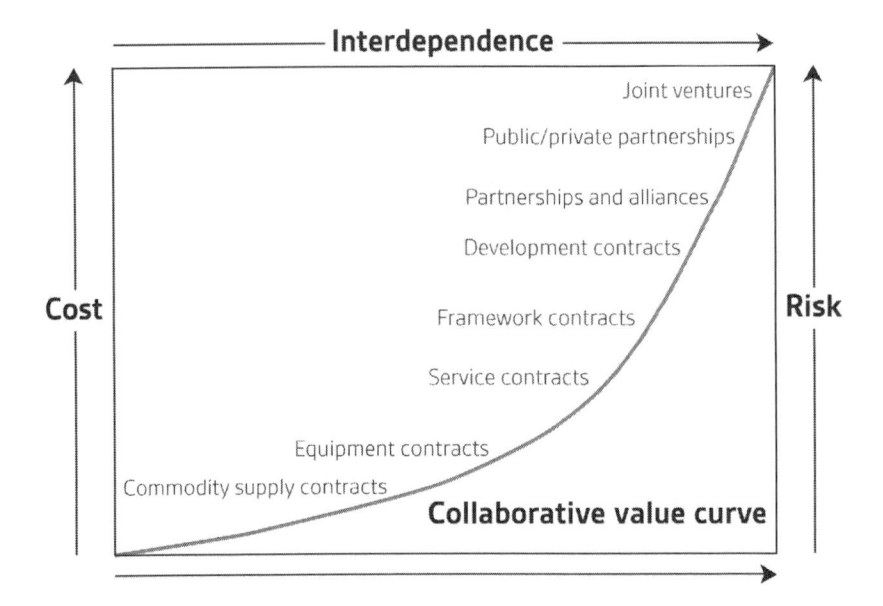

Figure 21.1 – Contracting curve

Contracting models

There is often a view within organizations that contracting should be either traditional or partnership; this clinical division frequently leads to driving contracting models in one direction or the other (see Figure 21.1). The result is that potential contracts become over-complex, such as alliances, or the benefits of collaboration are ignored in favour of business as usual. When adopting alternative business models organizations should recognize that there is a spectrum of engagement models where collaborative working could be a benefit. Which option is chosen, clearly depends on the desired degree of integration and the potential value that it may deliver. Table 21.2 may help to focus on the value proposition against Figure 21.1, which outlines the progression from transactional contracts to collaborative joint ventures.

Conclusion

All commercial operations are based on balancing risk; this is particularly true when looking at contract management. The contract process is too often led by compliance, not commitment. Organizations are good at defining what they want from others, but perhaps less willing to assess their own capability to meet the demands of collaboration. A collaborative relationship is a two-way process and to achieve the desired goals it requires commitment on all sides. This is not just about processes, procedures, systems and contracts (the 'hard process issues'). It is a question of the people drivers (the 'soft issues') such as leadership, skills and motivation. These will govern the behaviours and approaches at the working level by understanding the internal enablers that build trust between the parties, based on mutual benefit and equitable reward, while managing and reducing risk. The process should be centred on removing activities that do not add value from within the relationship.

PART 3: Where?

Key messages

There is a wide variety of contracting models. As outlined earlier, not all will fall into the profile of collaborative working, though in many cases collaboration could become a facilitator to create additional value initially or over time. The outlines given in Table 21.2 are offered for consideration.

Table 21.2 – Assessing contract types

Transactional supply chain: standard products and commodities	
Characteristics	Relatively low value with a focus on market-available products
Benefits	Easy to evaluate and repeatable requirements
Opportunity/risk	Low risk and multiple sources of supply
Contract types	Standard purchase contract
Evaluation	Competitive approach based on price, quality and delivery
Collaborative working	Limited need to invest resources in collaborative development
Equipment supply contracts: commercial off the shelf (COTS) products	
Characteristics	Technical requirement with higher values but no design requirement
Benefits	Captures standard proven products

Opportunity/risk	Limited risk, except for long-term support
Contract types	Standard supply contract
Evaluation	Simplified evaluation against technical suitability, matching specified requirement and commercial drivers
Collaborative working	Possible benefit in limited cases where there is potential for repeat requirements where extended agreements may provide some cost savings
Service contracts: facilities management, standard services	
Characteristics	Localized defined service requirements
Benefits	Simplified management against SLAs
Opportunity/risk	Low risk but subject to limited flexibility for scope changes. Frequently complicated by TUPE[13] requirements
Contract types	Model type service contract
Evaluation	Capability, cost and performance evaluation

[13] TUPE: Transfer of Undertakings (Protection of Employment) Regulations, which protect UK employees' terms and conditions of employment when a business is transferred from one owner to another.

PART 3: Where?

Collaborative working	Probable benefit at a local level to ensure the continuation of appropriate service levels and acceptance of service provider
Framework contracts: longer-term engagements for equipment, support or services	
Characteristics	Higher value for more complex requirements. May require a degree of product enhancement or solution development
Benefits	Likely to be for extended time periods and require a flexibility of output and/or performance needs. Valuable in reducing repeat procurement costs through structured call-off arrangements and for establishing economies of scale over time
Opportunity/risk	Higher risk given less definition but provides a basis for a flexible approach
Contract types	Time-limited performance-based contract with effective change management mechanisms and schedule of rates/costs
Evaluation	Requires structured approach to establish variations and model for monitoring change and value for money
Collaborative working	Clear benefit in most cases to establish medium- to long-term provision and drive innovation through joint approaches

Chapter 21 – Collaborative contracting

Collaborative development contracts: integrated engagements for equipment/support/services/training	
Characteristics	High value developments requiring a collaborative approach to development based on outputs that cannot be fully defined in advance. Solution-based where value for money needs to be jointly developed and agreed
Benefits	Provides a basis for innovative development, shared knowledge towards a definable product or service without long-term investment
Opportunity/risk	Degree of joint risk in terms of performance measures. Could become the basis of the longer-term partnering model to be adopted. Often complicated by skills and staff transfers including TUPE
Contract types	Cost-plus or target contract covering agreed expenditure against jointly agreed milestone deliverables
Evaluation	Requires structured approach to establish value for money with defined cost models. The evaluation needs to reflect the collaborative capabilities of the parties to work jointly towards outcomes
Collaborative working	Highly desirable to create the appropriate level of integrated relationship that will underpin consistent performance and support innovation and flexibility
Partnerships and alliances: joint programmes incorporating multiple partners or prime contractors/consortia	

215

Characteristics	High value requirements where the relationships are combining complementary skills and resources, configured to meet market opportunities which neither party could achieve alone
Benefits	Highly flexible model that provides a sound platform for innovative approaches. Skills rather than investment-focused to establish a viable alternative to mergers and acquisitions. Partnering model can be deployed for longer-term integrated working
Opportunity/risk	Relatively low investment but high potential for commercial success. The sustainability of the relationship is a critical success factor. May involve joint and several liability
Contract types	Multiple complex models developed from complex supply or industry contract models
Evaluation	High level of dependency on establishing the strength of collaborative capability together with technical and commercial skills.
Collaborative working	Sustainable collaborative working is a fundamental aspect of developing a mutually beneficial relationship
Public–private partnerships: joint developments with long-term development/investment	
Characteristics	High value with the need for investment and return on investment (ROI) over time by partners. Focused on long-term commitment to generate private sector funding capability. Focused on complex solution requirements

Chapter 21 – Collaborative contracting

Benefits	Provides a platform for long-term investment by either or both parties. It can provide a flexible platform of joint technical solutions, service or training development and construction developments based on jointly agreed value for money model and joint ownership
Opportunity/risk	Valuable model to harness private sector finance but needs structured focus on long-term investment. Frequently less flexible based on funding models. Effectiveness dependent on high level of collaborative working to achieve desired outcomes and maintain value for money
Contract types	Highly complex models which are often backed by government guarantees to support long-term investment and financing arrangements
Evaluation	A complex evaluation balance between financial structure and funding model, delivery requirements versus capability and the ability to work in a partnering environment, which is frequently negotiated out of balance
Collaborative working	Collaborative working must be integrated as a key aspect of these types of relationships to ensure service performance and optimization of financial and performance requirements overtime

Joint venture/consortia: long-term joint investment ventures for integrated solutions and sales

Characteristics	Potentially high value strategic relationship requiring joint investment, often through special purpose vehicle (SPV). Mostly created where operational requirements necessitate multiple capabilities

217

Benefits	Provides a composite/integrated solution. Through SPV creates a single entity for contracting and funding investment. Suitable for supporting long-term contracts and/or market development opportunities
Opportunity/risk	Brings together complementary skills/resources to create unique capability. Frequently a self-funding initiative based on market potential. Highly dependent on the robustness of the relationships between initiating parties
Contract types	Frequently governed by complex contracting models with joint and several liabilities a key theme. The SPV model creates a legal entity with structured ownership and liabilities. May involve complex TUPE
Evaluation	Evaluation generally focused on the robustness of commercial model and capability of the delivery organizations. The integration of the parties needs to be equally assessed ensuring a sustainable proposition
Collaborative working	These models require collaborative working to be a fundamental aspect of the consortium or SPV to ensure integrity of performance and, where appropriate, collaborative customer relationships

Chapter 22 – Alliance modelling

> The concept of alliances has been part of the business arena for a number of years but has in more recent times become a key feature in many industries. Alliances can be a powerful commercial approach, but each has its own unique requirements and requires considerable effort to be successful. It is important to ensure that development of the strategy takes into account a broad range of inputs. The challenge, however, has been that a multiplicity of approaches have been implemented and many of these can leave significant gaps in the development process. In this chapter we describe the processes of alliance modelling.

Alliances may be created for many different reasons; to ensure a satisfactory outcome it is crucial to have a structured approach to developing the right model. It is important to test the validity of the alliance concept against the objectives, capabilities and resources of the organizations involved, together with the risks and benefits. The alliance approach may appear an attractive option and frequently one that is adopted as being the trend of the moment. To be successful an alliance must have firm foundations that consider the implications for the customer and the alliance partners. Taking an alliance to market is not simply a sales strategy; it affects the relationships between the organizations involved, the customers they serve and often functional groups within the organizations charged with delivering the proposition, frequently through a virtual organization.

The 18th century economist Adam Smith's vision of perfect competition and perfect knowledge[14] may in part be emerging from the rapid expansion of globalization and technology. Throughout history the business models have changed to reflect the development of the marketplace. This new environment is changing the way that companies compete in future and share market information; ownership of the complete process is moving towards the creation of smaller, specialized, focused units. Innovation in technology provides the platform for even

---

[14] *An Inquiry into the Nature and Causes of the Wealth of Nations*, generally referred to by its shortened title *The Wealth of Nations*, 1776.

PART 3: Where?

more radical repositioning, with the need to consider organizational development in the fluid environment of outsourcing and collaborative partnerships.

Virtual organizations

The virtual organization is not something that can simply be bolted on to an existing organization; it requires the development of new types of thinking and perhaps new management approaches. Alternative contractual models may be needed, with a greater emphasis on building individualized propositions to meet a more varied and demanding customer base. These need to be sustainable and the adoption of BS 11000 can provide the framework on which to build robust alliances.

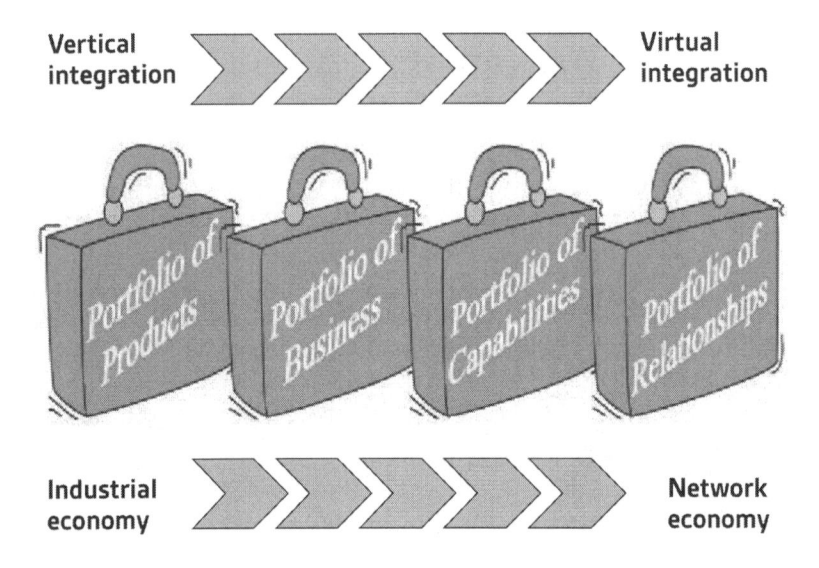

Figure 22.1 – Moving to virtual integration

We can expect to see the creation of virtual organizations that can share the infrastructure development, while retaining their individual customer base. These clusters of complementary skills need not be location-driven and therefore can respond more readily to wider markets. Meeting these aspirations and drivers – while retaining control of the business processes and organizational output, together with the expectations of shareholders – will create a dilemma for many organizations and considerable competitive advantage for others. There has been a progressive move towards a network economy (see Figure 22.1) that has its roots in the exploitation of alliance relationships. In this world,

Chapter 22 – Alliance modelling

dependence on trust becomes even more of a valuable commodity in the exploitation of the potential benefits of alliance operations and streamlining of processes. This is not simply about greater openness in the external relationships; it is a major factor when considering the harnessing of internal networks.

Supermarket banks or gas companies selling insurance are examples of developing the extended enterprise. In these cases the objective is to combine the specialized skills of one organization and exploit it through the customer base of a partner. The concept can, however, be deployed in many aspects of business development – creating alternative outlets, linking skills into alternative solutions or combining skills to address new markets, or used to bring new combined products or solutions to market.

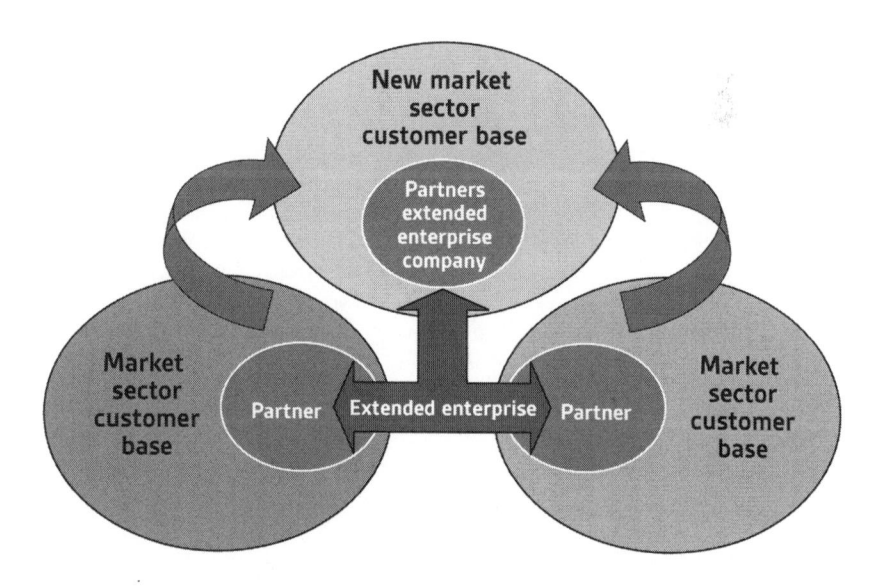

Figure 22.2 – The extended enterprise

In many cases the extended enterprise approach (see Figure 22.2) is being adopted simply to build delivery processes that are based on complementary capabilities rather than investment and ownership. The future offers the prospect of organizations being more constrained in their investment and needing to maintain greater flexibility. For some organizations, the solution to these pressures may be solved through mergers but others are considering the concept of virtual integration to address specific needs from R&D to market delivery. The mutual interests of the parties establishing working relationships are more flexible than traditional master/servant contracting; and the process of the relationship development focuses on outputs and targets rather than positioning of contracting liabilities.

The principal driver behind most alliance approaches is innovation, because the benefit of external stimulus is that the traditional constraints of 'the way we do it around here' are challenged by other organizations. External partners can often bring ideas from other industries, which can be adopted or adapted to stretch the current business profile and offerings. Another driver is the focus of the customer looking for solutions to existing problems, or searching for the catalyst to seek new opportunities for themselves. In certain cases the push comes from a need to meet the challenge of competitor innovation or simply to expand the resources and knowledge available to develop new products.

By combining the skills, knowledge and resources of disparate organizations it is possible to look beyond what we know today and challenge the thinking of the future, bringing innovation to a situation that may occur in future. Alliances should not simply be focused on exploiting sales of traditional products or even combinations of products. Market focus is clearly a prerequisite but short-term market share is likely to be a starting point for exploiting the full potential and reaping the potential benefits of a more collaborative approach. The danger in adopting an alliance model that is purely sales-oriented is that by its very nature it has a limited life cycle and will quickly meet the same development pressures as the traditional business model. Understanding the driver for an alliance is a crucial factor in the process of modelling the right approach – or indeed, deciding if an alliance is the correct path. It is likely that the drivers for the alliance partners (see Figure 22.3) may be different, which is not necessarily a constraint, providing these are fully understood and catered for within the structure that is adopted.

Market demand	New market
Market protection	Product development

Figure 22.3 – Alliance drivers

Establishing the drivers for an alliance

In considering an alliance approach, organizations must have clearly reconciled why they are adopting such models and question whether they could achieve the same results without creating an alliance. There need to be defined objectives in line with the overall business drivers;

these must be supported by the corporate business plan, with a focus on which sector of the business will deploy the alliance, or whether it is to be a company-wide programme for a specific product or service offering with a clearly defined return on investment.

Pera Training – case study

At the time Pera Training was considering formally implementing BS 11000 into our business we were presented with an opportunity to work with a premier marque automotive manufacturer who required up to 1,500 new staff to be recruited and trained as Intermediate Apprenticeships in Business Improvement Techniques. Timescales meant that the only effective way to deliver against this particular client's needs would be to collaborate. So we took the opportunity to implement and gain BS 11000 certification during the first half of 2011.

Pera Training led a consortium with TR 2000 (good apprenticeship track record) and Industry Forum (part of the Society of Motor Manufacturers and Traders – SMMT). The combined resources of the three businesses enabled the large programme to be delivered. By using the eight-stage approach of BS 11000 we optimized the working relationship. Regular consortium meetings coupled with appropriate updates to the risk register gave a framework for successful delivery of the programme. By the nature of the delivery, productivity improvement value creation has been a focal point and has yielded a high level of customer satisfaction. Also an important step was the articulation of an exit strategy for the partners. This manifested itself as a transparent review of future opportunities for the partners to work together.

Finally, the outputs from the consortium meetings and risk register have been incorporated into the senior management reviews within Pera Training. Hence the outputs from this large programme at a key strategic customer are distilled into information that is used at the highest level of decision making within Pera Training.

Anne-Marie Smith
Marketing Director, Pera Training

The customer perspective

When developing alternative approaches with alliances, organizations need to take full account of the holistic business environment. Many innovations or inventions do not make it to market because the concept may be brilliant but the customer value had not been validated. There are three basic ways to change the business profile: re-engineer the business, change the customer's perception of value or find new

PART 3: Where?

customers. In each case it is the value to the customer, not the idea, that will drive it forward. Establishing customer value is not simply about cost reduction; it has to be focused on the market drivers, for while cost is never far from the customer's agenda it may not always be the primary concern; so developing a profile of the customer's needs is important, to focus where best value can be created and alternatives exploited. Building an alliance proposition means establishing the right combination of partners to deliver the promise. How will the customer benefit or was the concept suggested by them? Does the alliance address a current need or is it intended to provide extended opportunity? Is the customer already engaged with others who provide products or services through alliances? It is important to consider the customer's principal risks in an alliance proposition. The key to this will likely be vulnerability from a breakdown in the alliance, which is where a validated collaborative approach through BS 11000 can offset concerns.

Establishing the value proposition

Innovative thinking is often constrained by awareness of existing limitations, particularly within organizations; often new ideas are not pursued because of a known lack of resources or perceived lack of management support. The potential within the concept of alliances is that for the right idea there are no resource or skill limitations, since linking with the appropriate partners will mean that additional attributes can be incorporated – providing there is a mutually beneficial commercial deal to be made.

Value creation is about innovation and realization of what may have been known by all, but not recognized because of organizational barriers. This process of seeking out competitive edge can be through collaboration and identifying a value proposition that has a unique selling point based on benefits – for example, cost, time, process, optimized resources, technology or performance. The greatest opportunity that can be derived from the integrated organization is in the area of value engineering. In many organizations true optimization is seldom achieved. This may be due to the structure and style of the operation, because of the specialized nature of individual production units, or worse – the isolation of external specialized providers. This limits the scope for evaluating the overall process, where predefinition of requirements sets the trend long before the practitioners get involved.

Targeting the alliance

The application of an alliance can be far-reaching in both the private and public sectors, as well as where these cross over. Alliances may cover a broad range of networks, both internal and external. It is crucial to

Chapter 22 – Alliance modelling

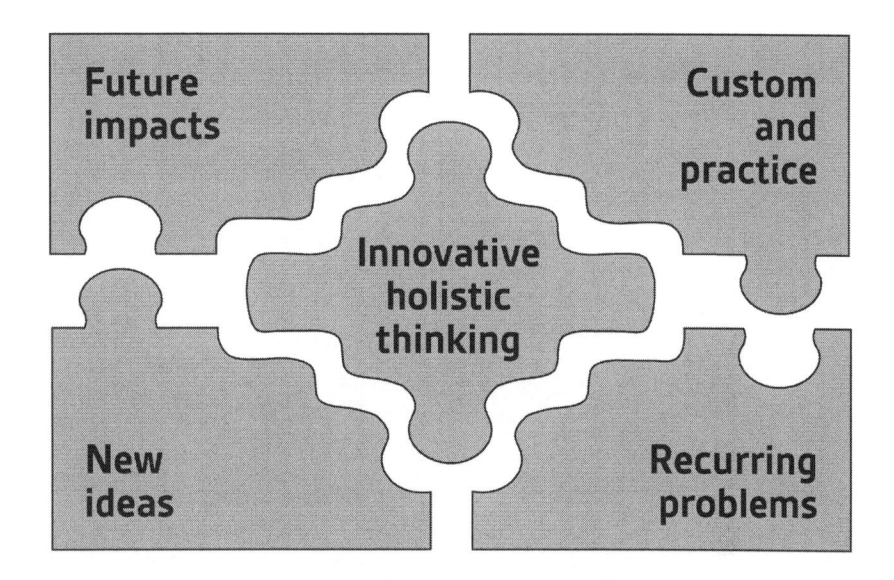

Figure 22.4 – Innovation drivers

understand the dynamics of these relationships and to consider short-, medium- and long-term perspectives by planning the immediate goals – but also developing the approach for future objectives (see Figure 22.4). It is equally important to consider the internal networks that may be involved, particularly when considering alliances with global customers or partners, where local issues may become a factor in creating success.

Business environment

The business world has always adapted to the demands of the market and customers. The current diversity of opportunity and risk prompts organizations to look at the alliance approach, particularly where the traditional merger and acquisition routes are constrained. The volatility and need for flexibility, together with a fast response to change, means that customers want their providers to be more local in real terms. These demands and challenges can only be met by a networked community. Creating an alliance operation can provide many of the answers to these ever-increasing challenges, as it allows organizations to link their strengths globally without the encumbrances of high levels of investment. There can be a combination of global reach, cultural understanding and connections without having to develop a wholly owned entity that may take years to deliver returns. There are clearly strategic benefits, but these must be balanced against the market, together with short-term training and knowledge transfer needs. In developing an approach it is crucial to understand the marketplace within which the alliance will operate and the market growth potential, opening up additional market opportunities or addressing identified gaps in the market.

Internal capability

Developing a strategic alliance must take account of the organizational structure that provides the framework for interaction. The concept of the corporate 'silo' is not a new one but remains perhaps the biggest obstacle to collaboration, innovation and change. Internal processes may superficially connect divisions or functional groups within an organization, but frequently these formal interactions conceal constraints to knowledge flow, where issues such as performance measurement, incentives and responsibilities can restrict the free flow of communication. These constraints can be more difficult to counter internally than with external operations, which have clarity of focus within a collaborative arrangement. Analysing the need for cross-flows of knowledge helps to identify the key changes and programmes that may have to be introduced, to ensure that knowledge transfer and innovation is embedded in the operation rather than forced through by edict. It is important to recognize the potential for 'silos within silos'; when considering these complications, it is clear that when separate organizations seek to develop alliances these internal silos may constrain knowledge flows across organizational boundaries, thus affecting integrated processes and damaging customer confidence.

Potential partners (existing or new)

It is becoming more common to see competitors working closely together in specific ventures. Collaborative integration has become a challenge for most business operations, often linking multiple entities within the value chain; in many cases the process of integrating internally can be even more challenging than with the external relationships. The application of collaborative frameworks across the value chain can help in both horizontal and vertical relationships to create value. Consider what the ideal partner looks like to match the proposition: can they be drawn from existing relationships or should new partners be considered?

Risk management

The appreciation and understanding of risk (and thus effective risk management) is something that has to be a fundamental ingredient in the development of an alliance, along with the training and deployment of an alliance team. The greater the distance between team members, the harder it is to capitalize on the natural flow of information between

Chapter 22 – Alliance modelling

players. Across the office many problems get solved or strategies are evolved without formal processes needing to be in place; in the virtual world the traditional risks remain but are compounded by the diversity of locations, organizations and cultures. It may be the actions of a partner that precipitate non-compliance or expose liabilities. The creation of joint risk management teams (JRMTs) within the team is crucial, since often risk is seen as a single person's responsibility and thus dilutes the focus. Within an alliance that is geographically separated there is a need to have a risk centre to ensure exchange of information to aid the overall management focus.

Knowledge fusion

One of the key benefits that come from integrating organizations is derived from sharing knowledge that combines the attributes and skills of the partners; but it is also the main area of concern for those moving into this arena. In many ways the unofficial sharing of knowledge has been taking place since businesses started inter-trading or skilled personnel moved between the various companies. There is much debate around the whole issue of intellectual property, which is often founded on perception rather than real exclusivity, and the danger of giving up the 'family jewels' in favour of short-term gain. While it would be wrong to minimize the need to protect core knowledge, there should be a realistic perspective when evaluating the potential benefits. Most knowledge will ultimately 'creep' into the public domain over time, either through the mobility of personnel or through reverse-engineering of processes, so it is worthwhile undertaking a reality check before making security a 'show-stopper' in alternative developments.

Corporate social responsibility

Every business operation has to recognize that one of the major challenges for the 21st century is the growing pressure towards meeting the goals of sustainability; there is also the increasing focus on social responsibility – how organizations not only manage and regulate their own performance, but also their interfaces with other organizations. For the business world the complications of these many-faceted aspirations create a minefield of political pressure and social risk, extending beyond the obvious issues of environmental pollution and occasional bad publicity. Most organizations are sensitive to their social and environmental impacts; integration can allow organizations to share information and optimize processes to capitalize on benefits and contribute to the long-term environmental challenges. If there is a corporate CSR strategy in place, it should be shared with partners.

PART 3: Where?

Managing integration

For suppliers, customer relationships have a trading value and should be the backbone of sustainable business. Relationships in business are vital and, while not usually a negotiable commodity, they are ultimately more important than many pure technologists would accept. The true nature of business is more about the integrated nature of dealings up and down the value chain. Technology may be the catalyst but it is only part of the equation (see Figure 22.5).

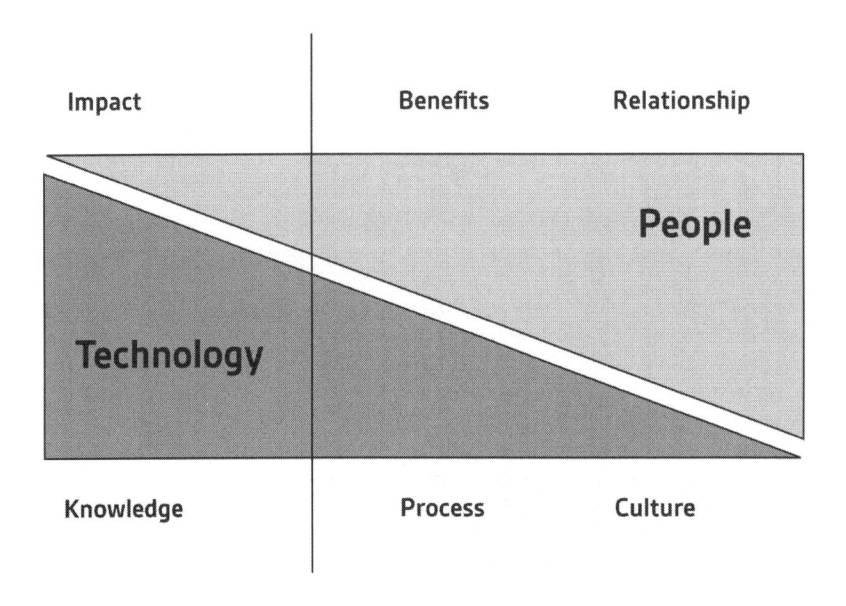

Figure 22.5 – Technology versus people

Global technology links are now feasible for any group of companies, large or small. Many international organizations already use this concept internally to provide a virtual office environment across frontiers. The wider implication and potential is for complementary organizations to integrate through the same technology; this has to be balanced against clearly defined roles and responsibilities for the alliance partners, recognizing national or cultural differences. To drive the right behaviours there should be alignment of payment plans, incentives and individual reward programmes, supported by agreed joint management and reporting structures, and agreed approaches to assessment of personnel experience and development needs.

Chapter 22 – Alliance modelling

Organizational and cultural challenges

The past six decades have produced alternative organizational initiatives and each of these has brought with it changes in corporate structures. If the contributors of resources to alliances accept to some extent a degree of control loss, then different forms of governance and control can be created for whatever period is necessary in the manner that most suits the market pressures. To achieve innovative solutions and recognizing their short-term interdependence, organizations may form specialist groups that are solely driven by the market objectives – which may eventually encompass this virtual concept as mainstream, either fully or in part. The virtual team can be structured without creating the need to completely reconfigure the current business model. It can have its own processes and rules and simply has to comply with the overall governance agreed between the partners.

Developing an alliance team

The role of leadership is far more complex today. Not only does it have to meet the normal demands of team building and motivation; it has to be achieved against the variable background of time, power, distance and cultural diversity. Alliance teaming will not just happen; it will need effective leadership, executive support, innovative thinking and training to exploit the skills and resources that will underpin the value of the alliance, together with a focus on creating the environment that allows the relationships to flourish – that will be a core element of success. The identity of an alliance needs a brand; the key individuals identified under an alliance board and joint management team will need to have agreed reporting lines, supported by performance and relationship measurements. It is equally important to have the benefits of the alliance communicated to the organizations at large.

Risk, reward and investment

The **BRITE** ideas approach (benefits, realism, investment, training and economics) was introduced to ensure that alliance groups tempered their imagination by reflecting the realities of the business world. Ideas should be allowed to run wild, especially in development workshops, since tomorrow's profits come from today's crazy ideas. It presents a framework against which each innovative thought can be checked to rationalize its value and potential ease of implementation. It will also ensure that as progress is made the foundation of a solid business case can be presented.

- **Benefits** should be quantifiable and measurable
- **Realism** ensures there is a reality check on both practicality and risk
- **Investment** should outline issues of time, resources and money

- **Training** is an important factor that is often ignored when suggesting change
- **Economics** underpins every challenge and first analysis should support validation.

Exit strategy

There must be a robust process for developing a valid and effective integrated alliance relationship, which has its foundation in the business planning process of the potential partners. The alliance development builds through the established stages of business planning to ensure that the proposed approach is compatible with, and supports, the overall aims of the alliance partners right through to how they will effectively disengage.

Conclusion

Alliance business models may well open channels to extended, flexible and networked value chains, creating competitive value propositions that expand and contract to meet changing demands and specific customer needs. Underpinning these alliances will be commercial arrangements that will exploit the joint capabilities of networked clusters. Alliance enterprises need to be founded on the core principles of BS 11000 to develop a sound, stable and sustainable model and will depend on a social structure that is very different from the traditional boundary-based business culture. Interdependence needs to be recognized and exploited, rather than perhaps a factor that many organizations reluctantly manage.

Key messages

The successful adoption of alliances, partnerships and consortia depends on the ability of the parties to work in an integrated way that delivers confidence and performance to the market. Table 22.1 provides key messages about alliances, partnerships and consortia.

Table 22.1 – Key messages for alliances, partnerships and consortia

BS 11000 alliances, partnerships and consortia		
	Focus point	Rationale
1	Alternative business models	Collaborative approaches broaden the capability of organizations to respond to (pull) or propose (push) more complex propositions to meet the demands of the market or specific customer challenges
2	Partner selection	Choosing the appropriate collaborative partner can frequently ignore the culture that will be a crucial ingredient for success; basing selection solely on technical and financial strengths raises issues of whether the partners can effectively operate as one entity
3	Business case development	Gaining support for an integrated solution against a more traditional operating model can increase internal constraints within each partner's home organization
4	Customer confidence	Where an alliance model is being offered, customer confidence that collaboration is integrated and robust is crucial

5	Integration	Effective governance is a crucial requirement when considering an alliance proposition to ensure joint management and delivery through combined processes and systems
6	Resource optimization	Where multiple partners are involved it is essential to ensure that resources, roles and responsibilities are effectively defined and allocated to create the most efficient operating model
7	Risk management	The adoption of alternative business models introduces the perception of risk for a customer and potential internal risks for the parties
8	Speed to market	Complex relationships can take time to develop; through BS 11000 organizations have the opportunity to adopt a common understanding and move more quickly to optimized implementation
9	Interdependency	Integrated models create a high degree of interdependency, which needs to be fully understood and managed effectively through a mutually responsible approach that harnesses joint capability and ownership
10	Performance	In any business venture delivering the required outcomes is crucial; but the venture can often be damaged by protectionism and blame culture, which diverts resources. A robust collaborative approach ensures that transparency and joint responsibility are established

Chapter 23 – Collaborative maturity

> How we see our own organization and how others see it can be very different, which can significantly influence the responses we generate or get back. Collaborative maturity is the focus of this chapter. The importance of understanding both the internal maturity and the projected profile for collaboration needs to be seriously considered, to ensure that when transmitting a collaborative message it will create a reaction based on your profile in the market.

For any organization to be successful it must first understand its own requirements and capabilities before trying to develop them with an external organization. In most cases, the failure of external relationships can be directly rooted in a failure to understand or develop an internal route map. This lack of clarity leads to confusion and misdirection, which in turn will result in the failure of those outside the organization to appreciate the implications of their own actions. In a collaborative relationship the benefits arise from exploiting the interfaces between organizations and the ability of disparate groups to focus on common objectives and implement a joint programme.

The concept of partnering and collaboration has reached a level of maturity within many organizations in the business community, together with the recognition that relationship management forms a crucial part of the business network. However, the adoption of collaboration can be constrained by a number of factors that create obstacles to implementation. This situation is observed both in the public and private sectors and arises through a number of common parameters, such as traditional thinking and processes, levels of understanding and experience, legal frameworks, accounting and auditing concerns and regulation.

Collaboration between organizations provides a valuable environment to evolve from today's commercial needs in response to the future likely impacts. In this environment the development of a more tangible benchmark platform for development of collaborative initiatives should be a crucial part of any long-term strategy. The application of a maturity assessment will provide a baseline and consistent benchmark to

PART 3: Where?

understand both the internal development needs and the profile being projected towards potential partners – whether customers, suppliers or alliance partners.

BT Global Services – case study

The £ multimillion collaborative partnership between the City of Edinburgh Council and BT began in 2001 when BT became the Council's strategic partner and supplier of ICT services. In 2008 the contract, initially for 10 years, was extended for a further 5 years until 2016.

With cost savings and efficiencies at the top of the agenda, the City of Edinburgh Council was considering outsourcing more of its services. However, due to its long-standing partnership with BT, the Council recognized that the adoption of a recognized industry standard for collaborative working would benefit both parties. The endorsement would allow BT to demonstrate to other customers both its commitment to partnerships and its standing in the marketplace, and the City of Edinburgh Council would be able to build upon an existing and robust ICT platform.

'Our strategy focuses on three key areas – customer service delivery, cost transformation and investing for the future. These three areas are the building blocks for making BT a better business. The better we serve our customers, the less time and money we spend on fixing faults and by transforming our costs we create new opportunities for investment in our future.' To achieve this BT has successfully demonstrated it meets best practice in terms of collaborative business relationships, following rigorous assessment of its 11-year ICT partnership; and it was the first ICT company to gain certification to BS 11000. It is also the first time the standard has been awarded to a local authority partnership.

The collaborative work started in 2006, which determined how well the parties are aligned across a spectrum of issues. With most of the operational requirements already in place, from the first gap analysis to receiving the certificate only took around four months, thanks to the foundations that had been laid.

The Smart City Partnership provides a springboard for innovation and new business opportunities as well as more efficient services, which save BT and its partners time and money. Complying with the standard helps both BT and the Council in terms of credibility and brand reputation, as it demonstrates best practice collaborative working. Collaborative working will enable the partners to identify and manage joint risks better and improved processes will aid the induction of new staff on either side of the partnership.

Bridget Taylor,
Director of Strategy and Engagement
BT Global Services

It is imperative that organizations invest the time to embed collaborative approaches in their business processes and the ethos of the organization. The impacts on any business relationship extend throughout an organization, so in evaluating a potential partner or presenting your organization as one that embraces collaboration it is important to assess and validate the approach. Creating an effective strategy must be based on a firm foundation of capabilities and sound assessment of the arena that will be encountered. Implementing a repeatable maturity assessment process will provide a quantitative phased review, within which organizations can evaluate and develop a systematic approach to complementing their capabilities, and provide validation to prospective partners. It is often difficult to assess the underlying collaborative culture of organizations and to create a repeatable measure that can be deployed throughout the life of a relationship. The implementation of an extended enterprise introduces a number of additional factors to the whole process of partner selection, based on the degree of interdependence. In a collaborative environment the partner is integrated into the overall process and therefore the selection criteria must be extended to evaluate the strengths and weaknesses, as well as the risks this relationship may create. BS 11000-1 incorporates a maturity matrix relative to the standard, which is further amplified in BS 11000-2 guidance published in 2011. These aim to allow organizations to reflect on their level of alignment with the standard.

Maturity assessment

Most assessment processes for external organizations are generally focused on the ability of maintaining a degree of arm's-length contracting. In a collaborative relationship the partner must not only meet the performance criteria; they must also be able to adapt to suit the demands and stresses of being an integral part of the business process. There has to be a recognition that the internal profile of the initiating partner must integrate with their partners to support the collaboration challenges. The attributes of an organization that are normally evaluated (such as capability, resources, skills and quality programmes) remain a key element of the assessment, together with the commercial conditions that form the basics of a contract. However, these issues are only the starting point from which to build up a profile that can be benchmarked against a more integrated relationship. Organizations may have the attributes to deliver a sound proposition,

PART 3: Where?

and they may well have established a performance record that supports their ability to meet the required performance. Often, however, they have not progressed in developing the appropriate culture that would enable them to fit into the business process of another organization. The ability to adapt and present a flexible profile is crucial when considering bringing them into direct contact with internal or external customers.

The more subjective evaluation rests on trying to identify the attitude of the partner. This does not mean the corporate image – it means understanding their internal culture. In many cases the choice may be dictated by historical experience, conflicts with competitor programmes or specialized knowledge. The first ventures into the collaborative approach may be built around organizations that already have a long-term relationship in place. The danger with this is that past practice rolls over into the new relationship, without adding value or validating the competitive responsiveness of the potential partner.

A major factor in the analysis of the ethos of organizations is to ensure that they have the potential to build processes across the corporate divides; these key attributes must form part of the strategic profile that is developed and mapped against prospective partners. The aim of adopting a maturity assessment is to establish a consistent, identifiable and measurable approach that recognizes the benefits of developing collaborative relationships, while appreciating that every organization is unique, and is only a part of the wider strategic drivers for these organizations. It should be based on establishing a benchmark of best practice, which can be recognized throughout the trading community, whether public or private, and will provide value to overseas organizations seeking to trade with or provide services to organizations. Outward-looking organizations are willing to collaborate and will be proactively engaging customers, suppliers and stakeholders, while forward-looking organizations will be constantly challenging their position and products to improve business performance and will seek external stimulus.

The principal aim of any assessment is to provide an effective framework. The MAP (maturity assessment programme) approach (see Figure 23.1) was developed with the aim that it will complement the existing activities of organization(s) and the appreciation of the application to improve market profile. MAP provides a benchmark for any organization that is involved in or seeking to develop a collaborative relationship, with the objective of building confidence and a common understanding of the principles. The triple 'A' model provides a clear indication of an organization that has fully integrated collaborative relationship approaches in to its operating model.

Chapter 23 – Collaborative maturity

	Attributes	Ability	Attitude
A	Operational processes are well defined and integrate collaborative approaches	There is a high level of experience at all levels focused on effective collaboration	There is clear corporate commitment and leadership that cascades throughout the operations
B	There is limited application of shared processes and performance indicators	There are individuals at various levels that have demonstrable skills in collaboration	There is evidence of successful individual collaborative programmes in effect
C	There are robust internal processes and performance indicators	There is appreciation of collaborative approaches but a lack of skills	There is appreciation at the operating level of the value of effective relationships
D	Operates with a traditional contract and procedural based approach	No appreciation of a practical approach to the value of relationships	Only operates a robust and effective arm's-length contracting approach

Figure 23.1 – Maturity assessment

The profiles included at the end of this chapter capture the key elements of a company's characteristics that would reflect organizations that have collaboration embedded in the culture of their operations. The maturity assessment approach provides a basis for highlighting the underlying ethos of an organization and its willingness to work collaboratively. In developing either internal collaborative capability or assessing partners' maturity, it is necessary to evaluate the operational platform, which can be part of an implementation or selection process.

Attributes (the organization's operational platform)

Bringing two or more organizations together requires that they have established processes under which they can develop and integrate their approach. Unless collaborative approaches are integrated into the organization's business plans and objectives they will be constrained by internal barriers. The main areas of attributes that need to be in place are as follows.

- Recognition of customer needs, requirements and concerns: it is crucial to ensure that partners understand the common drivers.
- Supply chain management: this is a crucial aspect of business performance and an area that can be jointly exploited to enhance performance. Collaborative working requires not only internal integration of planning, but also the ability to blend planning requirements across organizational boundaries. Interdependence puts collaborative partners at risk if there is not a common focus on delivering quality; such programmes also provide assurance that internal processes are rigorously followed.
- People development: the challenges of collaborative working are many, but the prime cause of failure will be down to people. Organizations that focus on the skills and capabilities of the staff will have skills development programmes in place. As collaborative working is introduced, it will probably result in some changes of role, so it is important that organizations have a clear perspective of their starting point.
- Risk management: this is both an opportunity and a challenge for collaborative working; thus an organizational focus on risk is crucial. Introducing collaborative approaches requires organizations to understand the dynamics – both cultural and regulatory – of the markets within which they operate.

Abilities (the organization's capability and experience in collaboration)

Collaborative working can challenge many of the established working practices and thus need to be robustly supported from the executive level. The main areas relating to abilities are as follows.

- Communication: changing the way organizations operate can be disruptive, and thus it is important that those directly or indirectly involved are informed of the value of collaboration through effective internal communication. Customers will be the recipients of collaborative programmes and it is important that organizations have effective interaction to articulate the benefits and opportunities.
- Skills development: this is crucial when implementing any organizational change and organizations that have robust assessment

and training models reflect a strong focus on skills, capabilities and behaviours. How organizations treat their suppliers is a strong indicator of the nature and culture of the operations.
- Continuous improvement: collaborative working must be focused on adding value and organizations that promote continuous improvement reflect a capability to adopt change more readily.
- Knowledge sharing: collaborative working is based on sharing knowledge and information. Organizations that are insular in their approach to external bodies will tend to be reluctant to embrace the benefits of alternative business models. Integrated business models will inevitably lead to operational changes of processes, roles and responsibilities; those organizations that are hesitant to change will be hard to integrate.
- Behaviours: these are a key aspect of collaborative programmes and managing relationships is often ignored; those that recognize the benefits are ahead of the curve.

Attitude (the organization's ethos and culture)

Collaborative working creates interdependence and thus those that participate need to have a clear focus on their own visions and values in selecting partners. The key areas around attitude are as follows.

- Challenging the status quo: collaborative working will challenge the status quo in many organizations and management needs to be accessible to those who need coaching and mentoring. Organizations that are actively aware of their impact on the world around them will by nature be outward-looking and thus receptive to working collaboratively.
- Targeting resources for maximum value: understanding the optimum focus for the business allows organizations to target resources towards those operations that deliver maximum value.
- Communicating with stakeholders: organizations that actively engage their stakeholders have the confidence to communicate effectively and openly and will thus find collaborative engagement more comfortable.
- Future value creation: this should always be the driver for any relationship and those organizations that promote continuous innovation will be broadly open to working collaboratively.
- Value chain: integration through collaboration has to be focused on mutual benefit and optimization of resources; therefore a recognized approach to value chain principles reflects an organization that understands the core benefit of collaborative working.

Conclusion

Collaboration may not be new, but the historical approaches have frequently failed to recognize that the complex relationships between organizations and their people seldom happen by absorption alone. Building the internal platforms that will support success and drive through the organizational changes, it may be necessary to establish the level of maturity that exists and then monitor this to gauge the level of improvement required. When evaluating and selecting the right partners to work in the collaborative programme, the same degree of rigour is required both initially and over time to ensure the blending of organizations, resources and capability to deliver success. The MAP model and the Maturity Matrix provide a basis that can be used in these situations, to gauge the underlying ethos of organizations and their integration of the life cycle model, to improve performance and (where appropriate) help to focus implementation of BS 11000. Where organizations are working together, these same models can become equally useful for measuring ongoing joint development.

Chapter 23 – Collaborative maturity

Table 23.1 – MAP questions

Creating a collaborative profile

1. Mark each element A (high) – D (low) based on your organization's approach and effectiveness
2. Against each of the three aspects Attributes/Ability/Attitude total the number A's, B's, C's and D's
3. Taking the highest number in each case insert the appropriate letter in the box below (note if equal use lower letter)

ATTRIBUTES					ABILITY					ATTITUDE				
Established business processes in place	A	B	C	D	Effective and open leadership	A	B	C	D	Corporate visions and values publicly visible	A	B	C	D
Business plan includes collaborative approaches	A	B	C	D	Robust and effective internal communication	A	B	C	D	Open and visible management	A	B	C	D
Customer management programme in place	A	B	C	D	Effective customer relationships' approach	A	B	C	D	Corporate strategy includes collaboration	A	B	C	D
Supplier management programme in place	A	B	C	D	Strong focus on internal training needs	A	B	C	D	Business excellence benchmarking in operation	A	B	C	D

241

PART 3: Where?

Integrated planning process in place	A B C D	Effective supplier relationships	A B C D	Defined sustainability programme in place	A B C D
ISO or equivalent quality programme in place	A B C D	Operational partnering programmes ongoing	A B C D	Operational strategic account management	A B C D
Key performance indicators in place	A B C D	Continuous improvement programmes in action	A B C D	Strong communications with external stakeholders	A B C D
Staff training programme in place	A B C D	Ongoing regular external interface activities	A B C D	Complaint and dispute management process	A B C D
Partnering programme in place	A B C D	Change management programmes in operation	A B C D	Customer partnering programme in operation	A B C D
Clearly defined roles and responsibilies in place	A B C D	Relationship management training in effect	A B C D	Supplier partnering programme in operation	A B C D
Risk management programme in place	A B C D	Internal/external business review programmes	A B C D	Innovation programmes in operation	A B C D

242

Chapter 23 – Collaborative maturity

Sound market knowledge and expertise					Clear focus on R&D and future product delivery					Value chain focus across the organization				
A	B	C	D		A	B	C	D		A	B	C	D	
Total					Total					Total				

Attributes	Ability	Attitude

Current collaborative profile

243

PART 3: Where?

Chapter 24 – Mergers and acquisitions

> Mergers and acquisitions (M&A) are arguably the quickest ways to grow a company; equally, however, they can also be a high-risk strategy, as discussed in this chapter. Organizations often neglect to consider the potential issues beyond financial stability, technical acquisition or extended market reach. What is apparent is that most mergers fail to deliver on their promise. One of the major issues identified through research into this area of business activity is the failure to recognize the potential issues of bringing together two organizations with incompatible cultures. In this context the integration is similar to that of an external partnership and thus many (if not all) of the aspects of BS 11000 lend themselves to this environment.

There are a variety of reasons why organizations use acquisitions and mergers to develop their operations, but strategic imperatives can often cloud the issues and the challenges that may define the success or failure of such ventures. Traditionally there will most likely be a significant effort directed towards due diligence, which historically focuses on financial aspects, validation of liabilities and assessments of goodwill. What is commonly assumed (particularly in times of austerity) is that many opportunities arise out of economic pressures – which may or may not be good value. In developing M&A strategies it is clearly important to understand the drivers, then structure the approach accordingly. Experience, however, does point to a key aspect of success being the integration of organizations that may previously have even been competitors. In this chapter the author would specifically like to acknowledge the research work done by Rachel Kessler, *Mergers and Acquisitions: a study on collaborative working;*[15] there are many works in this area, but this study was specifically developed around BS 11000 concepts.

The prospect of acquisition can be outwardly very attractive; subject to the commercial investment model, the capturing of assets, resources and markets creates the possibility of immediate growth and market collateral. However, in most cases it is associated with a high degree of risk relating to the parties' ability to harness these benefits and

---

[15] A paper prepared for the Institute for Collaborative Working (ICW) March 2011: www.instituteforcollaborativeworking.com/intern_reports.html

harmonize the operating models to capitalize on the potential. It has frequently been seen that the financial markets offer their own opinions and valuations on the potential M&A propositions, which often present a significantly different perspective from those that internally drove the strategy forward. An option which is less frequently used as a precursor to the full acquisition or merger direction would be the adoption of an interim model based on developing collaborative models. These alternative business models have the potential to deliver many (if not all) of the benefits of linking two organizations – but with a less risky investment strategy.

Generally the term 'acquisition' can be applied to those transactions where primarily one party is seeking to acquire the assets of another, for strategic or market development objectives – a 'takeover'. An example could be the move by Kraft to acquire Cadbury to break in to the UK chocolate market. In most cases these will be seen as hostile takeovers, where the prime mover is principally interested in assets rather than synergies. Mergers, on the other hand, can be about vertically absorbing capabilities into another organization or a mutual merging of two organizations to develop and enhance market position, which will be beneficial to both parties by exploiting synergies. These would typically be in related industries or manufacturing fields where assets can be jointly harnessed. For example, in the 1999 merger of Glaxo Wellcome and SmithKline Beecham, both companies ceased to exist when they merged, and a new company, GlaxoSmithKline, was created. There is also another option: this is the acquisition of consumer networks which can be exploited by parallel selling – for example, the UK telecommunications providers T-Mobile and Orange merged to share their network.

In each case there is one factor that is common: this is the ability of the organizations to create an effective integration of assets, resources, people and culture. One of the most classic examples in recent times was the merger between Time Warner and AOL which was heralded as perhaps the most significant merger of the 20th century. Both organizations were extremely successful; it was positioned as a merger of equals. Given the media reach and internet coverage, the combined organizations were potentially seen as outstanding. There were, without doubt, some strong egos involved; this may have been the first sign that merging could have its difficulties. There were also significantly differing views, both internally and externally, on the nature and culture of the two organizations – AOL being entrepreneurial, West Coast and less sophisticated than Time Warner, which was established East Coast and intellectual. The pressures of these conflicts eventually led to the reversal of the merger and significant financial losses all round.

The message is clear: what perhaps looked like a good and sound financial proposition imploded, not because of the market, but because of the inherent internal stresses that the diverse cultures and egos

Chapter 24 – Mergers and acquisitions

created. If we look to an alternative value position, then combined capability between these two giants could have been forged through collaboration and partnership. In this model the appropriate synergies could have been harnessed and integration would have been on an 'as required' and structured basis, rather than a full-blown merger. Individual identities could have been maintained while exploiting resources, skills and market reach as appropriate. External pressures would have been reduced, further enabling the organizations to progressively develop cross-capability. This case is certainly one of the most high profile, but does highlight the potential dangers of mergers; it suggests that broader consideration is given to downstream integration before taking these major steps.

Drivers

The reasons for approaching M&A are many. Like any relationship development, they need to be fully understood and assessed before setting objectives, which may cloud decision making – even at the highest levels of organizations. Where public companies are concerned, they cannot simply decide to announce a hostile takeover or propose a merger without invoking a considerable amount of regulatory compliance, impacts of customer confidence and (for that matter) the performance impacts and implications of talent loss. So, understanding the rationale and setting the parameters are crucial. Examples of these drivers are shown in Table 24.1.

Table 24.1 – Drivers for mergers and acquisitions

Growth	Product development	Diversification
Market share Market reach Economies of scale Asset optimization Resource reduction Customer access Increased capability	Technology acquisition Joint new product R&D IPR Skills and experience Product harmonization Integrated solutions Competition dilution	Customer exploitation Parallel marketing Cross-fertilization of ideas Service support Parallel capabilities

What is interesting is that, when considered outside scenarios of corporate ego, most (if not all) of these objectives can be achieved through an appropriate collaborative relationship without the complex legal and regulatory minefield of M&A. This might be without the full realization of commercial benefits, but certainly there would be a high degree of value and substantially less risk. However, whatever the option of collaborative models, the strategy to be deployed must be clearly focused on the key outcomes. For example, where the driver is capture of assets, then acquisition is the most likely course where the resources are less of a consideration. But where resources are a key consideration, then an effective merger that retains those capabilities is more appropriate. In all cases, the implications of any action that is initiated must also be considerations in the likely success of the merger – recognizing that in numerous studies such success is reported to be perhaps as low as 20 per cent.

Benefits

The benefits of merging any two organizations can be equally varied and will reflect the strategic drivers, if executed effectively. In today's market, economies of scale and cost reduction are likely to be major considerations. Acquiring skilled resources that are already in place can provide a rapid growth in capability and reach. Similarly, the combining of buying power and harmonization of sourcing can be an early win. Reductions in resources can be beneficial, but this generally takes time to implement and can on occasions be fraught with obstacles. However, experience would also suggest that identifying and gaining practical access to these potential savings can be very much dependent on the willingness of those within the organization to share information. Clearly, ownership and direction can be established; but, depending on the nature of the approach, it may take time to harmonize and realize these benefits. The more acrimonious the venture, the more time needs to be allowed to harness the potential.

Clearly, the biggest value within any organization is its human resources, skills, knowledge and capability. The potential benefits or perceived risk at an individual level can be a major factor in the success of any merger. There is seldom a merger of equals, even when corporately declared; there is likely to be one party more dominant than the other. This creates the perception of biases being developed and the potential for key players to seek safer ground. Access into new markets can open up significant growth potential; but again, since these markets may have been developed over time, there will be valuable relationships and reputations established that will need to be refocused to a greater or lesser degree. It can be particularly difficult when the merger involves previous competitors. Old loyalties can be a key factor that governs early returns. The benefits from technology harmonization, integration and future development may be vast, but amortizing these will take time.

Chapter 24 – Mergers and acquisitions

Where the driver is purely acquisition, this may be less time-consuming – but it does depend on the ability to acclimatize and integrate these technologies. This is often implemented by personnel who do not see or share the bigger picture or who fear for their own long-term stability. Asset-stripping may be seen as a short-term benefit from M&A, but frequently these strategies falter when it comes to dismantling operations where individuals have a personal vested interest. This is particularly true in western industrial areas where social, legal and regulatory controls can introduce a wide range of obstacles.

Risk

When a merger strategy is being initiated there will be consideration about the risks involved. This tends be on two levels: firstly, the risks associated with declaring intent, and then the implications of establishing a market position. Acquisitions and mergers can be costly, not just in terms of the purchase price, but also in consideration of the market perceptions of investors, regulators, customer confidence and personnel, all of which can (and probably will) have an impact on current performance. The longer the acquisition battle (if there is one), the more difficult the value proposition is to sustain. Time, therefore, is the key to successful merger strategies, but this also has to pre-empt the stakeholder implications. Perhaps the biggest risk comes from uncertainty at the trading level, where customers become unsettled by the impacts of transition – and perhaps even more, that key personnel seek to protect their own positions by 'jumping ship' for a more stable option. While it may be externally possible to validate technology benefits and take a commercial perspective on visible assets such as property and equipment, it is less easy to fully appreciate the complexities of personnel assets. Key designers and executives may be visible, but in many organizations the full dependence on key personnel at many levels may be shielded by the outward perception of an organization. Many will be familiar with the sub-strata within organizations that compensate for operational weaknesses. Lose these and the operational machine starts to creak.

Tangible assets can be relocated or sold off, as can non-core parts of the business. People, on the other hand, can be a significant dilemma. Rationalization of two businesses is never a comfortable environment. The vulnerability of assets is frequently not their market value but their performance, which can decline rapidly in the face of change. Thus the planning and due diligence processes need to look beyond the obvious appraisals and seek to prioritize the post-merger plans. Too often the premise for a merger is supported by offloading non-key assets; but the post-merger activity is centred on optimizing the key assets, leaving the rest to progressively be dispersed – which is most likely to lead to a reduced asset value. What is clear is that in the merger and acquisition arena, relationships on all levels become a crucial ingredient for success.

Not the least of these is the potential blending of organizations, where retaining key capabilities and targeting jointly towards new or expanded markets is a key success factor.

Cultures

This raises the question of evaluating the cultures of organizations and the potential to integrate these into a newly defined composite operational model. As was highlighted earlier in the Time Warner–AOL case, to most onlookers the dangers were obvious and many people questioned the validity of the merger. The business strategy may have been strong, and certainly the financial potential was significant, but its realization was in question from the outset. Where organizations seek to harness the human assets of another, then the ability of those organizations to blend together becomes a critical success factor. Experience in the development of alliances, collaborations and partnerships has exposed this over a number of years. Too often the concept of partnership is driven by senior individuals, and the approach is activated or imposed without considering how it will work in practice. This is clearly one aspect of M&A where the nature of relationships, spurred on by the culture of the organizations, is crucial to delivering the benefits.

Identification of the cultural fit should be high on the due diligence agenda; in some cases it may be a pointer towards the type of operating model to be adopted after the merger. For example, if we look in retrospect at the Time Warner–AOL case, if the cultural misfit had been fully recognized and the financial benefits remained robust, then the adoption of more segmented or arm's-length integration could have survived the in-fighting that was in part the cause of its demise. The question of culture, as outlined in earlier chapters, is complex; where the merger of multinational organizations is being considered it cannot be ignored. Some readers will have experienced what may be referred to as a 'perennial culture', where despite the passage of time traditional loyalties and operating approaches remain, regardless of the implementation of new names, systems and processes. The persisting culture and identification remains an underlying thread that can survive even multiple mergers and takeovers. Where this is related to semi-autonomous operating units it may be less debilitating, but in the case of acquisitions where integration is a key to success it can easily become a cause of failure.

Integration

The reputation of one company, as seen by those being acquired, can set in motion a wave of negativity that may take years to overcome. In earlier chapters the issue of integration has been explored; where this is being managed within semi-independent but formal collaborative models, between willing parties, it can be managed. In the case of mergers, the aim must surely be to bring together the best of each to build a more sustainable and effective business operation. Traditionally within the world of mergers the focus has been to urgently address the outward profile of the newly combined company. This makes sense in terms of customer retention; establishing new names over the door, high-profile marketing and public relations activity help to provide short-term confidence. Internally, however, a new name on their overalls is seldom going to create the new loyalties required to exploit the expanded potential. In some cases these public demonstrations of unity only compound the issue. In Chapter 3 the concept of osmosis and process addressed the need to look at both people and process; and Chapter 4 focused on the nature of culture. For integration to be successful, organizations need to clearly define the new world and relate this to the individuals involved. There will need to be persuasive communications about the rationale, objectives and values that a merger can bring and how these will affect those involved; this is because the less people know, experience suggests, the more they will invent – generally negatively, which in turn will be reflected in their performance.

Customers

The issue of customer confidence has already been raised but it is worth considering how any merger will be viewed externally. The financial markets may offer their views, but at the end of the day the value proposition depends on acceptance by customers and the realization of value through the combined entity. From experience, that in turn will depend not on publicity, but on the daily interfaces and performance of the newly formed organizations – the people who are the touch-point for customers and the outward reflection of internal capability.

Conclusion

There may be many valid reasons for M&A, but statistically most are deemed failures. It is clear that relationships with all the stakeholders are a key ingredient in success. It is also clear that for many people the importance of the relationships is subsumed by financial models; the relationships' factor is seldom high on the agenda. It prompts the first question, which is: 'Before launching a merger, should organizations consider the benefits of developing a collaborative partnership to deliver the desired objectives and drivers?' These alternative business models can be less costly to create or unravel, if necessary, and they are perhaps less prone to creating the relationship tensions that can undermine even the most viable of merger strategies.

PART 3: Where?

If M&A remain the most obvious way forward, then organizations need to consider a more robust approach to understanding the cultures of the entities involved and adopting a structured framework that can more effectively support the integration and focus for the future. It was this concept that prompted the review of mergers against the framework of BS 11000. In doing so, perhaps some mergers would not progress, as success would be doubtful; some may decide to adopt alternative collaborative business models – and those that did so would find it easier to target strategies using best practice relationship management approaches.

Chapter 24 – Mergers and acquisitions

Key messages

Table 24.2 provides some key messages for consideration when contemplating M&A.

Table 24.2 – Key messages about mergers and acquisitions

BS 11000 mergers and acquisitions	
Focus point	**Rationale**
Business objectives	Understanding the business objectives when developing an M&A approach is crucial. Collaborative approaches broaden the capability of organizations to respond to (pull) or propose (push) more complex propositions to meet the demands of the market or specific customer challenges, without the need to take a high-risk strategy of M&A
Target evaluation	Evaluating a target for M&A can frequently ignore the culture that will be a crucial ingredient for success. Basing selection solely on technical and financial strengths raises issues of whether the target organization can be effectively integrated as one entity
Cultural integration	The established culture of any organization can create significant constraints to the effective integration of an M&A target. In many respects this challenge is comparable with building a collaborative alliance; it can be equally applied to the blending of disparate organizations
Joint business planning	Effective governance is a crucial requirement when considering an M&A proposition, to ensure joint management and delivery through combined processes and systems. It is equally important to ensure transparency and joint ownership in future
Implementation	Integrating two organizations creates interdependency and uncertainty, which needs to be fully understood and managed effectively to develop a mutually responsible approach that harnesses capability and ownership jointly

PART 3: Where?

Customer confidence	BS 11000 provides an independently validated approach which can be used to clearly benchmark the collaborative culture being deployed, providing added confidence for the customer through the transition
Innovation	Sharing knowledge and capability allows organizations to harness value across the relationship and potentially extend the contribution to overall success
Resource optimization	Many M&A programmes result in confusion, concern and often resource rationalization, which will affect effectiveness and performance. Establishing clarity of objectives, joint management and defined roles and responsibilities provides transparency through change programmes
Risk management	Adoption of BS 11000 complements programmes to ensure there is a focus on people and cultures, to enhance integration building and sustaining relationships – both internal and external
Performance	In any M&A process delivering the required outcomes is crucial. It can often be damaged by protectionism and blame culture, which diverts resources. A robust collaborative approach ensures that transparency and joint responsibility are established

Chapter 25 – SME collaborative clusters

> In this chapter we focus on the potential benefits for SMEs. Collaborative working is often viewed as the prerogative of large organizations; however, the concepts of collaborative clusters can be equally deployed as a mechanism for increasing the potential opportunities for SMEs. This chapter explores the integration of businesses into virtual networks, challenging many of today's concepts, considering necessary culture change and risks that may exist against a background of accelerating change.

Enhancing the role of SMEs through collaborative clusters opens the debate for organizations large and small to consider the opportunities and benefits that may be exploited to create competitive advantage. In business, boundaries are created to manage risk and ring-fence financial exposure. Linking people as well as systems, 'follow the sun' working is now a reality. But social and political obstacles have still to be managed in the new borderless business community; in exploiting the potential of a frontier-free trading environment, existing thinking and relationships will come under pressure.

In the construction industry, projects are frequently executed by groups of independent specialists, brought together in different configurations depending on the task by their local network. Based on the customer's initial contact, different members of the network may lead on different projects. This simple model of creating networks of smaller companies enables innovative value propositions to be created that individually they could not support; it also challenges larger organizations, which have to carry more complex infrastructures. In this model interdependency is by design, not forced upon the participants, and so operates with reduced conflict. The added benefit is that as teams work together they mutually support each other and generally improve performance over time because of their close association. In the corporate world interdependence usually evolves as a result of progressive strategies and therefore functions with a lot of internal stress. This proposition is not about what individual organizations can do, but what groups can deliver together. It is not a question of providing the lowest price but of targeting total cost. Traditional supply chains have allowed the customer to manage their risks in isolation, whereas this model spreads these risks

– but also demands that the customer shares some of the partners' risks, including the perceived financial stability of the group.

Changing dynamics

A framework of relationships will already exist for most companies, being the business network within which they operate. It is an easy step for a group of independent companies to expand its area of influence by simply sharing data and information on customers. If 10 companies each have 100 customers, of which 50 per cent could use the services of the other companies (but do not do so) then each could expand its potential customer base to 500 if all share their information. Competitive edge requires a level of innovation and adaptability such as has not been seen before. This is not to suggest that these new models are exclusive; as we have seen, many that tried to ignore the basic rules of business failed. However, there is certainly a trend that recognizes an alternative.

Not every idea or innovation results from a flash of inspiration. Innovations may just be the realignment of old and forgotten practices, like a twist of a kaleidoscope, revealing a new pattern. Many fads have been heralded as the business thinking of the future. The better of these often embody traditional values and common sense, albeit with new buzzwords. These revalidations may be valuable, nonetheless, by challenging the status quo and providing a benchmark for the next few years. Developing novel approaches in the context of complementary clusters, which propose the incorporation of external partners, needs to take full account of the holistic business environment. Virtual organizations are not invention but innovation, which in some cases may cut through traditional thinking on the customer side; so developing a concept has to be focused first and foremost on the customer need. The increasing focus on social responsibility has raised the profile of how organizations manage and regulate their own performance and also their interfaces with other organizations. Sustainability is a triple platform, which looks at economic development within the three-dimensional perspectives of financial, social and environmental impact, giving sound reasons to consider the benefits of promoting clusters of smaller companies.

Developing clusters

SME communities nationally are likely to be focused closely on individual industrial sectors, tackling the normal business constraints with limited resources to consider wider exploitation. This tier of the industrial base does, however, contain a significant proportion of the wealth, based on contribution to gross domestic product (GDP), employment growth and innovation. The development of a focus that assists in stretching the reach of these organizations will support the future position against a background of increasing competitiveness in the global arena, as well as the inward flow of products and services from overseas. The concept seeks to capitalize on the diverse skills, knowledge and resources within the SME business community by creating focus and knowledgeable support and is based on traditional thinking and practice that has been part of local business community thinking for centuries. It takes the ideals of the partisan trading network and looks to exploit modern technology and business approaches through the support of key organizations, both governmental and non-governmental organizations (NGOs).

The emergence of an idea

The cluster proposition has more 'traditional' business foundations than most current business models. The horse-drawn cart was the principal method of transport until the coming of the internal combustion engine. It still is in many parts of the world. The wheelwright, blacksmith and carpenter combined their respective skills to meet their customers' requirements. The eventual sale and the reputation of each were interdependent: if the cart broke all would share the criticism. By linking specialists together an infinite number of virtual enterprises can be created with greatly reduced investment and thus improved value to the customer.

Partners are independent players

It is a common experience in large firms to find that the different divisions compete with each other although, as parts of one organization, they are totally interdependent. This competition may be between functions or product teams. In a cluster non-competitive independence allows the efforts of all to be centred on the business objective.

Each is a specialist in their field

In many organizations effort is wasted in conflict between specialists and others, to prove superiority or improve position. Building a network that recognizes each player's particular skill and contributions reduces overlaps and aids interfacing between the components.

Skills configured to requirements

Often the skill base of established organizations is either over-populated or deficient in certain aspects of their current business need. The cluster enables skills and a resource profile to be established for individual projects on an as-needed basis – allowing more focus and reduced overheads.

Revenue sharing proportional to input

A fundamental of the approach is that returns are based proportionally on the investment profile of each player.

Minimal hierarchy

Generally the bigger an organization, the greater the management effort needed to coordinate activities effectively. Communications can be complex and time-consuming, with an impact on the profitability of any venture. A network of independent partners provides clear divisions of responsibility and simplified channels of information flow. This ensures that the business objective is kept in focus.

Shared risk

All businesses must identify and manage risk. It is important in a networked environment to ensure that risk is addressed and the overall position of the group protected. Ownership of risk must be clear without evasion of responsibility.

Focus on customer satisfaction

The core of all business activity is to attract customers and then keep them. In a networked environment it is in the interests of all partners to maintain a true customer focus.

Revolution or evolution

The average customer's perception, for example of the 'nationality' of most motor cars, is now effectively a fiction, based on the manufacturer's name and heritage. Brand has overtaken origin. The old supply networks have been abandoned and local producer networks at every level have been forced to merge or close. As quality demands increase and price levels decline, the pace of global exploitation increases. Although this natural evolution is not new, the increased speed at which organizations are forced to restructure and adjust their networks is a new thing. In this environment established trading practices and relationships are broken down, opening the way for more flexible adaptations. This pressure affects SMEs more than multinationals, which can spread the risk. Some large firms have tried to support their existing suppliers by helping them to exploit low-cost advantages while maintaining the comfort zone of long-term relationships. In the longer term both small and large companies will have to establish new strategies for sustainability. The challenge now is to develop new initiatives and flexible business models that harness the opportunities presented by globalization, while being aware of the pitfalls that it may present.

Relationships

Relationships in business are vital and, while not usually negotiable, they are ultimately more important than many technologists would acknowledge in our wired world. A collaborative model is emerging now that makes better sense for the long-term future of e-business. Becoming an extended communications medium, the internet portal still handles transaction-based commerce, but also provides a more flexible e-platform for traditional, but wired, trade. So 'we have the technology'; creating virtual networks of different organizations is no more complex than creating an internal IT network. The online communities formed are direct descendents of those that have existed since trading began. But now the automated transfer of data between companies is within the reach of every company with an internet link, enabling all to exploit the full benefits of business networks.

Networking in business

The idea of collaborative clusters is driven by pressure on the marketplace, so considering alternative strategies to build a more flexible future is directly related to growth. As bigger organizations looked to improve their position by outsourcing non-core activities or consolidating (sometimes globally) their buying power. The effect is to reduce the potential for their localized networks. However, if these independent local companies could operate within some form of network, which aimed to develop benefits or openings for its partners, then new potential could be created. The driver has to be the customer, since business exists to serve their needs or perceived benefit. In the traditional model the customer collects a portfolio of suppliers and service providers; each is independent and in most cases is unaware of the others' role or activities. As these suppliers lose out to the pressures of rationalization and consolidation they have to find new ways of maintaining their business capital and position. If they can provide a wider range of services or create new alternatives to meet the customer's need, then they can re-establish their position. Thus they look to reinvent themselves, but are often hampered by their existing cost and knowledge. The alternative is to look for partners who have

PART 3: Where?

supplementary skills or services (see Figure 25.1). In simplistic terms the manufacturer, installer or maintainer could take on a larger portion of the customer's needs.

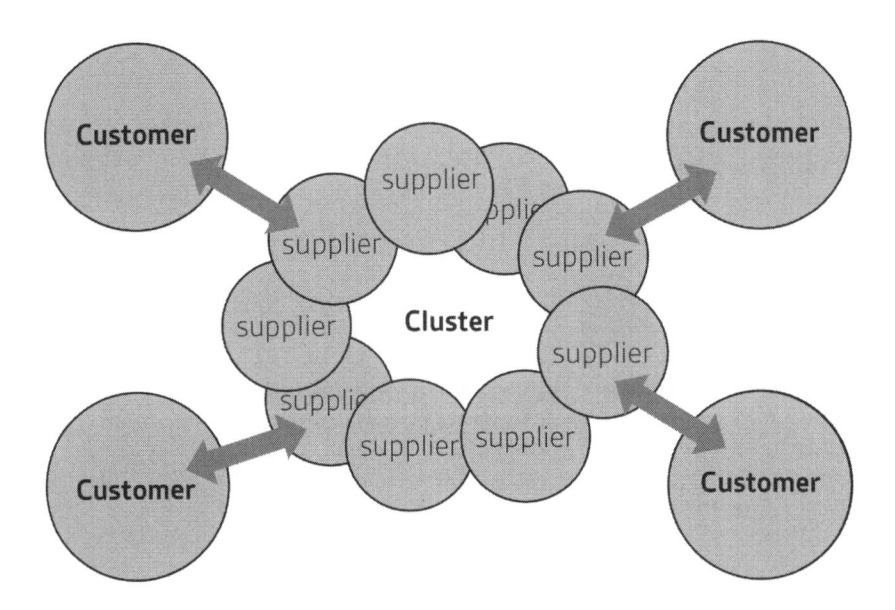

Figure 25.1 – Clusters

A composite capability introduces the dimension that each supplier has its own customer base, so the compound proposition can be extended to meet the needs of multiple customers. The cluster is not simply re-establishing an existing business relationship; it is potentially opening up new ones. The greater the number of attributes or services the cluster can offer, the wider the opportunities. The approach creates the critical mass that enables them to survive, and at the same time allows them to compete with larger organizations (see Figure 25.2).

Relationships and trust will play a major role in the building of these clusters, not only in terms of the individual suppliers, but also – more importantly – from the customer perspective. The cluster has to be credible. The progression of this development is the wider global implications: if a cluster can be successful in one arena, then why not in others? This is a challenge, since not all the players will be able to contribute in every case. For example, local manufacture may be a necessary competitive addition. This may create tension, but also could lead to a new level of thinking where product knowledge is shared and low cost supply is pulled back through to the original market. However, these clusters must recognize the traditional driver for any business

Chapter 25 – SME collaborative clusters

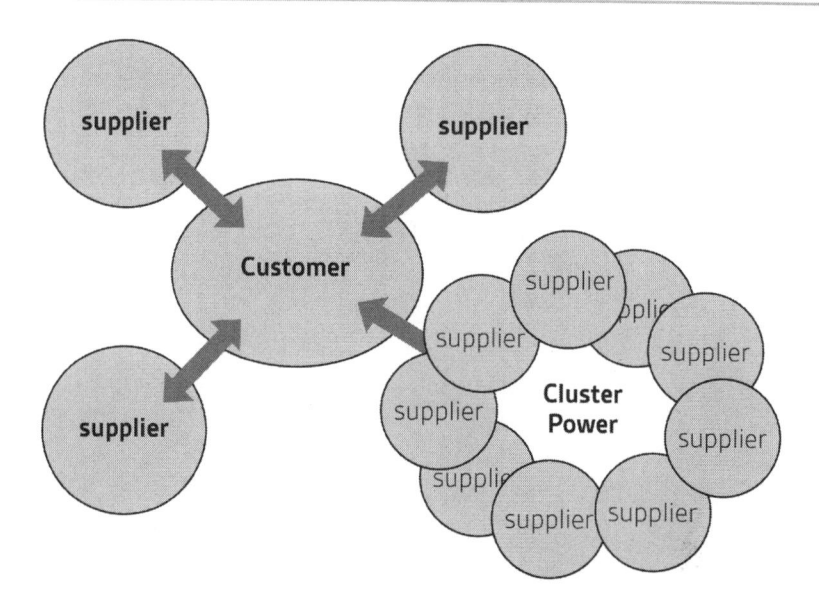

Figure 25.2 – Cluster power

venture – that of meeting the customers' expectations. Price will always remain a significant factor, but many other factors will be part of the selection criteria; it will be satisfying these elements that will underpin the viability of any virtual proposition.

Aspects of collaboration

One of the obstacles in promoting the cluster is the assumption that it should cover all trading relationships. If a partnership cannot add value, why invest for no return? Traditional trading methods and approaches fit most business cases. The more integrated the trading relationship, the higher the interdependence; thus improving the approach makes sense. This is one of the core principles established within BS 11000. Where there is a close interaction between two or more trading partners, then the opportunity to improve the business process should be exploited. The same issues and drivers need to be addressed horizontally and vertically to break down traditional independent thinking.

Innovation infrastructure

The gap between creating a business concept and seeing it adopted in the marketplace is wide. The ideas may be sound and the potential recognized but industry, financial and regulatory infrastructure may be

PART 3: Where?

lagging some way behind. *The Midas proposition*[16] was conceived to find ways of supporting or promoting the SMEs. While, however, there may be a desire to help there are many practical hurdles to be overcome. The first is customer acceptance, which will only start once there is a value proposition for them to consider. Many organizations express commitment to local communities and often (even in a global environment) will create models that support the development of local industry; but by extending this opportunity to clusters the seeds are sown for wider deployment and exploitation by those same organizations.

Conclusion

Innovation is often stifled not by concepts but by the negativity and traditionalist views held by those performing the evaluation. The emergence of the internet or wired world has brought to the fore the virtual company and looks to be setting the concept firmly in the business vocabulary. It was Professor Garelli of Lausanne University who suggested that future business would be about access to assets – not ownership – that would drive future business models.

The profile of companies and organizations operating today ranges from divisions of multinationals, through major regional businesses to extensive SME communities. This environment provides a comprehensive, culturally diverse and adaptable skill base. The challenge in most cases is that global competition and economies of scale create a business environment where frequently opportunities may be lost through limitations of resources, capabilities and scale. The challenge for the business community today is to ensure that suitable capabilities are grown within their organizations to recognize, develop and exploit the potential that clearly exists. The future offers exciting prospects for those with the vision to create the future, instead of trying to predict it.

---

[16] *The Midas Proposition* is a report published by Institute for Collaborative Working which develops the clustering approach as the business model of the future. In particular, it focuses on the potential benefits for smaller organizations developing approaches to enhance future opportunities.

Chapter 26 – Collaborating for sustainability

> It is clear that in today's business environment the conflict between economic pressure and the demand for forward-thinking business strategies to address environmental and social responsibility is challenging. This chapter aims to explore the role of collaboration in building profitable collaborative business while supporting sustainable strategies.

Corporate social responsibility (CSR) is not about transferring responsibility and risk; it should be focused on optimization to balance profitability and outcomes across the value chain. The challenge is the polarization between the 'green' agenda and the role of industry in developing a collaborative approach to integrating sustainable objectives within profitable business. When the subject of CSR is raised any discussion quickly devolves into a number of themes such as financial propriety, ethical trading and human rights. Sustainability, on the other hand, will quickly turn towards environmental impacts and global warming. More recently there has been the emergence of CR (corporate responsibility) dropping the social aspect specifically in an attempt to provide a more wide-ranging agenda, adding to the confusion as to what should be considered by businesses. Perhaps we should simply redefine CSR as 'corporate sustainable responsibility' and expand the brief: for a business to prosper, it has to be sustainable and thus must consider itself part of the wider sustainable ecosystem. The overriding acronym is less important than the concepts behind it; the key to success is about exploiting the opportunities of sustainability, rather than simply focusing on the business risk.

Sustainability is increasingly an important agenda item for executive boards and one that is exceedingly complex to manage across a wide spectrum of stakeholders. As with any long-term strategic plan, collaboration is a crucial ingredient for organizations to consider in their integration within the global market. This is not simply to react to the implications of public opinion on issues of third world exploitation; it is also about the development of sustainable business propositions. There is a difficult balance between the corporate drivers of competitiveness and shareholder value and the practical implications of ignoring the sustainability implications of investing in overseas operations (either directly or indirectly) together with the pressures of balancing the demands of regulators, customers, consumers and pressure groups.

PART 3: Where?

Building effective business relationships is a crucial factor in exploiting the potential of extended value chains and alternative business models, but also in evolving development programmes that support the long-term sustainable objectives. Collaborative approaches can provide a platform on which to create innovative solutions within a business environment that can deliver competitive advantage, while allowing organizations to jointly address the sustainable agenda to their longer-term commercial benefit alongside the wider sustainability issues.

As the business landscape becomes more complex and challenging, the relationships between organizations also take on new and varied configurations. It is generally accepted that for most organizations they are both customer and supplier in relation to different aspects of the value chain; but often organizations miss opportunities. As the market profile changes, so the complexity of these relationships increases. The pressure to improve competitive edge and develop alternative value-based solutions has introduced a greater need to ensure that organizations can work in an integrated way to maximize potential benefits. The sustainability issue has become very complex, embracing corporate governance, ethical trading, human rights, environmental impact, regulation and so on. At the same time, the pressure to improve margins, reduce costs, increase outsourcing and the like creates conflicts in meeting the sustainability agenda (see Figure 26.1).

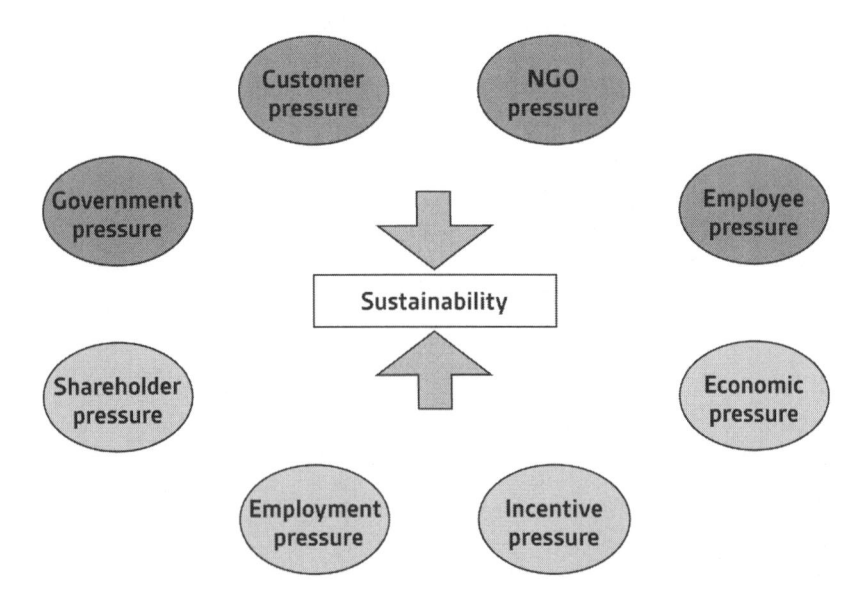

Figure 26.1 – Sustainability impacts

Chapter 26 – Collaborating for sustainability

The paradox is that many of the issues associated with the sustainability agenda are the ingredients that facilitate achieving competitive goals and are the essence of market economics. Low wages, basic working conditions, resource exploitation, reduced regulatory demands, lack of pollution control – all of these things contribute to aggravating the situation. There is growing evidence of customer pressure (and more recently consumer pressure), but is this superficial and vulnerable to the 'feel good factor' and the impacts of an economic slowdown, which increases the focus on costs/price? In many organizations there is paranoia about managing the risks of exploiting the global market, not the least of which is reputation risks. This puts increased pressure on business leaders and their operations in meeting objectives that are frequently diametrically opposed. It is not dissimilar to the challenge closer to home – to support the SME and 'diversity' businesses as a key part of the economic structure and growth, while demanding economies of scale that frequently exclude those communities. Setting rules and ethical policies that are perhaps counter to the business goals and incentives is not in itself sustainable. The problem in many cases appears to be that organizations do not have a clear perspective on CSR and sustainability and the complexity of the relationships that it covers.

Profit and CSR

As organizations put more and more of their operations out into the value chain and harness alternative business models, the risk increases. If there is really to be a sustainability ethos, this has to come from a more integrated corporate programme to balance the issues. Developing the theme that sustainable CSR is a real commercial opportunity and not simply about risk mitigation, a proactive approach to collaborating for sustainability that is focused on linking CSR to commercial benefit should look beyond the risks and start to assess the value creation that can enhance profitability. This would mean embedding the concepts into operational activities and driving a collaborative sustainability culture that contributes to the bottom line by looking for value creation, rather than simply counting the cost of risk management.

Perhaps the biggest constraint has been a prevailing view that CSR and sustainability is about doing the 'right thing', which is what many critics of the business community would say. While industry should indeed be responsible in the broader sense, its primary responsibility is to deliver value to its investors. There are many people who challenge the right of business to make a profit and promote the concept that in striving to do so industry is totally untrustworthy and devoid of any interest in sustainability. It would be foolish to ignore the fact that some high-profile organizations have seriously damaged the image of the business community but this should not distract us from the point that those in industry are stakeholders themselves in the community at large.

PART 3: Where?

- **Without** creating wealth there is no investment.
- **Without** investment there is no development.
- **Without** development there is no sustainability.
- **Without** sustainability there is no future.
- **Without** collaboration there is no possibility to advance.

Wealth creation is about delivering a return on investment that can be reinvested and can stimulate economic growth to the benefit of all. This can be a dividend for shareholders of multinationals or a weekly wage for workers in the developing world. Profit is not a bad thing in itself, but how it is generated can be; and it is this concern that has driven the CSR agenda forward, raising a broad spectrum of sustainability issues. The pressure on industry and the business community has driven (in many cases) a culture of minimal compliance, doing only what is necessary to keep ahead of the regulators and investing in media programmes to protect a sustainable image. The problem is that this culture of compliance is frequently not really addressing the key issues and is driving a gulf between the stakeholders. Regulation is always likely to be significantly behind events; superficial programmes focused on public opinion will usually be seen through and thus damage the image of business further.

Sustainability is an issue and a risk for all stakeholders in one form or another, which influences how we behave as individuals, groups or organizations. It affects the thinking behind the way we invest and trade either as customers, suppliers or consumers; based on current trends it will be far more of a marketing and sales factor in the future. Sustainability is increasingly an important consideration for investors too – there is now the Dow Jones Sustainability Index, for example. It is a highly volatile topic, which makes it crucial that organizations have a clearly defined and supportable strategy and policy in place that reflects their specific operating model. The challenge is that at every level we are different and have to make choices, whether as individuals or organizations. For the progressive company, CSR is no longer a question of simple compliance; it defines the mandate for organizations to operate and their licence from the marketplace/customer to trade. Meeting regulatory demands is only a part of the equation; regulation is itself becoming more and more complex. There is a multitude of aspects that organizations need to consider in developing a sustainability strategy and building a proactive approach.

Sustainability should not be viewed as a negative thing; it has many attributes that can, if managed effectively, contribute to operational excellence and profitability. Given a positive commitment, which can be translated into process and people development, the objectives of business sustainability can establish market differentiation. Put simply, if you reduce waste, optimize energy consumption, rationalize transport, packaging and the like you save money. When you improve working conditions you increase productivity and quality. By recycling you maximize the value of raw materials. Through investment in education, training and socio-economic development you provide a stable business platform for growth. Through effective governance and ethical behaviour you increase the trust and confidence of stakeholders, and as a result you reduce costs and enhance your sustainability profile.

For companies to take a proactive approach to sustainability they must balance economics with their broader sustainable responsibility, since they must maintain profitability in order to contribute. Developing a meaningful strategy requires a focus on the issues that are specific to each organization's business operation. The emerging business models and networks are the shape of the future; sustainability is no longer an issue for companies independently – they must collaborate.

While the business environment comes under continuous and growing competitive pressure, the manner in which business conducts itself may have significant impacts on the ultimate perceptions of the marketplace; it is seldom a level playing field. It is often easy for those outside the active business arena to demand standards of practice that are in direct conflict with the realities of the local cultures and diversity. These varied considerations must be part of the business planning profile and need to be addressed when considering integrated partnerships. When developing trading arrangements, whether in the local business landscape or in the wider global contexts, there are many factors that reach beyond the traditional trading relationships. The higher the degree of interdependence, the greater is the opportunity for many of these key issues to be overlooked in the short-term drive for commercial advantage. Sustainability should be seen as a focus to create more effective and efficient business operations that can adapt to the market for both robust commercial sustainability, as well as meeting the future with the long-term programmes that we need to benefit the wider society.

The 'green' agenda

The key challenge is not our response to individual issues such as global warming, but how to take a more holistic view. For example, one response to pressure on the carbon footprint is for us to move towards hybrid cars that offer low emissions but may have significant impacts downstream that had not been considered. At the same time, the focus on biofuels has already affected the food supply chain and may over time cause more of a challenge than benefit, if not corrected. As organizations seek to make a public stand on one initiative they potentially expose themselves to other challenges throughout their operations. Every organization is different and has varying economic, social and environmental impacts. As we focus on carbon footprints, perhaps we are missing the bigger picture and in some ways creating greater threats.

Supply chain integration has a significant role to play in this arena. How, what and where we buy can make a difference; but we need to avoid the hype and focus on what is right for the organization – that is what is important, not the current headline-grabbing messages. Sustainable business, not green, should be the backdrop to all activities that are linked directly to the business goals of the organization it serves, and tied to effective business performance to ensure that they are sustainable. There is no doubt that some companies are leading the way, such as AMEC, John Lewis and Skanska; they are building business goals that support both the commercial interests of their stakeholders and contributing to the bigger picture. If we are to achieve the changes needed, then we must create commercial drivers for sustainability and integrate them in the business operations – which means there has to be greater collaboration.

Confidence and trust

The business issues associated with sustainability are fundamentally a question of establishing trust and confidence with the stakeholders. There is no doubt that many of the high-profile cases of recent years have seriously damaged the perception of the business community and industry at large. Rogue activities of major corporations have done little to convince stakeholders that industry can be trusted. In this environment any activity that is focused on maintaining profitability is frequently met with suspicion. As we move to the complex interactions of collaborating for sustainability the problem is that as business seeks to find opportunities for trade, avenues to exploit competitive edge or simply to constrain costs, the need for trust has grown.

The emerging alternative business models of today, however, are causing a rethink about this central command-and-control model. The investment challenge and diversity of the marketplace is creating an environment where business propositions are more likely to be based on the development of alliances and networks of companies being linked together to form temporary organizations, to exploit a particular proposition or meet a demand. This is causing resurgence in thinking that is beginning to revalue the traditional importance of relationships as a key ingredient of success and a crucial factor in risk management and mitigation, which extends to the sustainability arena. The report 'Corporate Social Responsibility Communications'[17] published by the global public relations company Edelman (along with Net Impact and others) identified across 3,100 business executives that the key to

---

[17] Downloadable as a PDF from this website:
www.bcccc.net/_uploads/documents/live/EdelmanCSR08.pdf

effective CSR communications was transparency, which strongly influences stakeholder engagement and the bottom line.

Eco-efficiency

The wider implications of developing sustainable business models, within the context of extended value chains, run in parallel with external pressures on business strategy.

Long-term strategic initiatives for organizations should consider the integration of supply chains and outsourcing operations within this arena of global change. This is not simply to react to the implications of public opinion on issues of third world exploitation, but in the development of sustainable business propositions.

Every change in direction or demand places even greater pressure on the business planning process, to meet the conflicting demands of shareholders in their quest for return on investment. There is also the pressure of the customer's increasing demands for greater innovation, against a background of lower prices reflective of a global marketplace. While the political and environmentalists' agenda grows in strength, the pressures from the market to deliver ever more competitive products means extending the business enterprise to satisfy the demand. The development of sustainable programmes requires the integration of multiple business relationships focused on building long-term operations. These must recognize the global implications and the furthering of local agendas that support growing economies and add value to an organization's business profile. Sustainability should create more effective and efficient business operations and eco-efficiency by exploiting the potential benefits from cost savings and passing these to the bottom line, while simultaneously contributing to the long-term sustainable returns (see figure 26.2).

Collaboration is primarily about improving and integrating business relationships through innovative collaboration and enhancing competitive total solutions. The spin-off from these partnering activities has a direct impact in areas of efficiency improvement, which include subjects such as waste, energy etc.

In fact, sustainability, social responsibility and profitability are linked but also complementary. In terms of sustainability, the definition of 'value' may be viewed as being less commercial; but in reality if business is to prosper itself and help developing areas, then commercial concerns, market demands and profitability have to be viewed as interdependent. Whatever the aims of the business or social partnerships, the value creation process still needs to address the fundamental facets of the operations. Eco-efficiency highlights the potential to move the integration process beyond an initial one-on-one partnership and seeks

PART 3: Where?

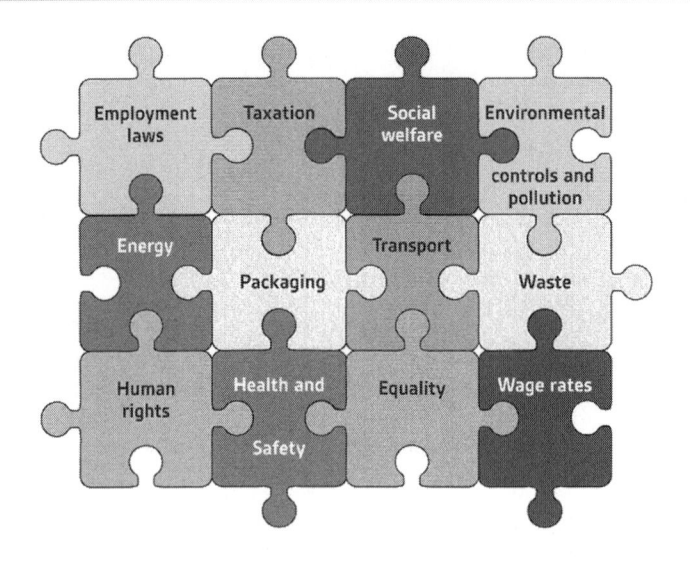

Figure 26.2 – Eco-efficiency

to move the profile into a customer-focused approach, even incorporating the customer in the delivery process. True sustainability can only be achieved within a holistic trading environment, which will be likely to take time to develop. In the meantime the benefits of closer working relationships can be exploited to commercial advantage while supporting the wider principles.

Sustainability strategy

The key to strategy and policy development should provide a platform on which corporate boards, executive management and operational personnel can evaluate sustainability in the context of their business. This can then be translated into process development, implementation, education and reporting approaches that deliver compliance and a broader perspective on benefits; more importantly, they demonstrate how the primary objectives of wealth creation opportunities can be evaluated to embed broader thinking within organizations and provide a valuable backdrop to sustainability. Embedding the right strategy is a crucial part of any business development; but when it comes to sustainability it is often delegated outside the operational teams and focused on issues of compliance. The reality is that many of the aspects of sustainability are critical to business stability; but also, if handled correctly, they can enhance potential profits. However, for this to be achieved the strategy has to be fully integrated and effectively deployed through policy, procedures and training. This constrained view is one that

Chapter 26 – Collaborating for sustainability

is progressively changing as the recognition of forward-looking companies becomes a feature of the marketplace.

Stakeholder inclusion

For any organization to operate effectively it needs to ensure that its stakeholders are in tune with the business objectives outlined below.

Governance

In recent years the failure of many high-profile corporations has damaged the reputation of the business community in general, which in turn has resulted in more and more regulatory requirements being imposed. Sound governance is crucial in all respects, from legal compliance to investment confidence.

Environment

Global warming has heightened the focus on the environmental impact to the extent that many governments are setting significant targets for many aspects; and public awareness and concern is growing, forcing corporate responsibility and performance.

Natural resources

The consumption of resources is already outstripping availability and the quest for new sources is creating pressures on the ability of organizations to grow and develop.

Human resources

A major constituent and critical success factor of any business is its labour force, whether this is directly employed or engaged through partners and suppliers. Their behaviours, approaches and commitment to the overall vision and values are crucial for success. It is also an area of CSR where unfair practices in labour exploitation may become a significant reputational risk.

Ethical trade

Trust and confidence are key constituents of any business relationship; they significantly influence the way an organization is viewed throughout the stakeholder community. A number of high-profile cases have seriously affected these catalysts for success.

Economic and social development

Trade is at the core of every community; thus the impact of business is crucial to both economic and social development, which in turn is a cornerstone of sustainability.

Operations

The globalization of business and the increasing trend towards outsourcing, alliances and collaborative partnerships creates a wide dimension for the operations of today's business; this means that the sustainability agenda requires integration at every level.

Globalization

There can be few, if any, business operations that are not directly or indirectly affected by globalization, which introduces the implications for sustainability to every operation.

Sustainable development

Business is not usually founded on a short life cycle, though is frequently driven by short-term targets. Sustainability is focused on the long term, but clearly must provide intermediate returns to survive; balancing these is the challenge for the business community and engaging the stakeholders is crucial.

Conclusion

The exploitation of collaborative relationships, while providing the basis for improving competitiveness and meeting sustainable targets, needs a clear corporate agenda that is adopted by all participating organizations to ensure a uniform approach. The effective implementation of collaborative ventures must be based on the establishment of a robust mandate from board level; the imperative increases where this relationship then seeks to take a robust position on the organization's sustainability issues down through the value chain. This is because many aspects of the overall programme may have a direct impact on investment returns.

Chapter 26 – Collaborating for sustainability

Creating a sustainable strategy must be approached in a holistic manner. The traditional linkages between organizations may well be established through arm's-length contracting positions, but the implications of the effects of failing to recognize the potential reactions to sustainable issues can flow through the trading relationship. Collaborative business models allow the parties to evaluate all aspects of the business delivery process and incorporate the needs and drivers for each, while finding opportunities to reduce costs and waste as a by-product of continuous improvement.

Sustainability is a subject that at an individual level either inspires people to be very proactive or produces apathy, in terms of it being someone else's problem. In a collaborative culture one of the key ingredients to success comes from the joint commitment to a set of common goals and objectives, but often the potential commercial benefits of adopting a sustainable approach are ignored in favour of short-range profits. All relationships are founded on personal interaction and thus it is important that in developing a business partnering structure the objectives and rewards for all players must be consistent with the overall objectives. These must be developed and deployed to ensure that all those involved in the business process appreciate their individual and joint contributions to sustainability. The future holds increasing challenges, so organizations must consider in their long-term strategies how they will meet the callenges while maintaining the business' public profiles and profitability. All levels of the value chain must be integrated to achieve overall success, but those who take the lead in the integration process will be most likely to take a significant lead in building sustainable alternative business models.

PART 3: Where?

Checklist

Table 26.1 provides a matrix that can be used as a starting point to develop a collaborative approach to sustainability.

Table 26.1 – Elements of sustainability strategy

Stakeholder inclusion	Governance	Environment	Natural resources	Human resources
Customers	Vision and values	Greenhouse gases (GHG)	Energy	Working conditions
Shareholders and investors	National standards	Pollution	Fossil fuel	Fair pay
Regulators	Legal compliance	Waste management	Renewable sourcing	Social welfare
Employees	Regulatory requirements	Contamination	Minerals exploitation	Equal opportunities
Consumers	Risk management	Packaging	Water conservation	Discrimination
Suppliers	Brand management	Transport	Recycling	Human rights
Partners	Codes of practice	Community impacts	Resource stewardship	Incentives
NGOs	Transparency	Reclamation	Managed quotas	Work–life balance
General public and media	Accountability	Carbon footprint	Ecological balance	Cultural diversity
Industry associations	Industry standards	Infrastructure impacts	Product disposal	Health and safety

Chapter 26 – Collaborating for sustainability

Ethical trade	Economic and social development	Operations	Globalization	Sustainable development
Fair trade	Economical growth	Profitability	National regulation	Innovation
Exploitation	Social impact	Productivity	Cultural integration	Material alternatives
Bribery	Education	Quality	Supply chain security	Sustainable technology
Corruption	Humanitarian aid	Change management	Market development	Future prosperity
Inducements	Sustainable growth	Continuous improvement	Political profile	Induction and training
Market dominance	Social investment	Product performance	Social challenges	Process integration
Cartels	Poverty reduction	Return on investment	Custom and practice	Product optimization
Small business support	Social welfare	Skills development	Cultural conflicts	Logistics
Religious values	Community development	Industry benchmarking	Boycotts	Food output management
Organizational behaviours	Health care provision	Knowledge management	Integration	Measurable reporting

Chapter 27 – Third sector

> In the context of collaborative working, this chapter considers the voluntary sector which has for decades provided a valuable contribution to society in terms of social development. There are many thousands of charity operations working in almost every area of society. In recent years this vast resource has become an integral part of future thinking. What becomes apparent is that to enhance their involvement they need to align horizontally with other charities, government bodies and with industry. This raises the vista of two or more very different cultures and the structures that will be needed to develop a robust relationship that supports the overall objectives.
> BS 11000 provides the platform on which these sometimes difficult relationships can be formed against the background of a common structure.

There are tens of thousands of voluntary organizations across the world, ranging from high-profile internationally recognized names to small local charities. Each provides a valuable service to their relative communities and specialist areas. The largest of these, while they are charities, can rank alongside major corporations in terms of their operating revenues and have sophisticated business models. The smaller ones can be equally competent but are often much less structured in operational terms. In this chapter acknowledgement is made of the paper produced by Douglas Rowles in July 2011 *BS 11000 and the Third Sector*,[18] which focuses on improving delivery of the work programme in conjunction with private firms.

It is interesting to note, based on anecdotal evidence, the degree to which these organizations interface with the public, with industry and to some extent with governments. Certainly those working in emergency environments have more than once demonstrated the essential role they can play. In many cases, were it not for these organizations and their speed of response, many disaster situations could be far worse. Others work less publicly but contribute extensively to support society. It is also apparent that, driven by their particular agendas, these organizations can

---

[18] This paper for ICW can be downloaded at:
www.instituteforcollaborativeworking.com/intern_reports.html

be highly collaborative, such as on the ground in a disaster area, but also very competitive when seeking to build their membership and secure donations.

Similarly, the degree to which voluntary organizations work with industry or governments can be variable; in some cases they work with these bodies and share common goals, while in others the focus is often seen as attacking industry as a way of promoting and gaining publicity for their cause. This contradiction is one that crystallizes everyone's perspective. This is not to suggest that they do not have a strong message to project as specialists in their fields, but it does pose the question as to whether a more collaborative approach could be more beneficial all round.

From an industry perspective, the obvious benefits of aligning with charitable ventures are the routes to engage with the wider social community; it should be equally recognized that by association this helps to promote their brands and products. For charities, while there may be short-term benefits in challenging industry through the press, working with industry could enable a more integrated approach to further the aims of both, acknowledging that the focus on corporate responsibility and social impacts is a clear goal for most industry leaders today. It has often been a view that the combination of the expertise and capability of the voluntary services could be very effective in enhancing industry developments to mutual benefit.

In a more practical context, the need for collaboration between voluntary organizations can be a catalyst for more focused support to those in need. For example, in discussions with Guide Dogs for the Blind, the charity's aim is to broaden the service offering to blind and partially sighted people by linking with other organizations in the field. On an industry front, clearly collaboration rather than conflict provides the opportunity to share knowledge; in some cases industry could provide more practical support rather than simply donating. The development of the third sector by government brings collaboration to the fore, where potentially voluntary organizations, industry and government departments work together to deliver services.

Cultures, goals and objectives

The challenge in these collaborative models is the potential misalignment that comes from the different backgrounds, cultures and drivers of each organization. We might consider this to be over-complication, but experience suggests that these background influences will significantly affect the way each group and the individuals involved behave. To focus these aspects, consider Table 27.1.

Chapter 27 – Third sector

Table 27.1 – Background influences of the different sectors

Organization	Culture	Drivers	Objectives
Voluntary sector	Principally not focused on commercial outcomes and mainly resourced by freely given time and effort. Often weak in terms of operating structures	Clearly focused on the visions and values of the organization with specific area of interest and driven largely by the passion of its members and donors	To improve or support the target communities and overall aims of the organization
Industry sector	Generally highly focused and structured around commercial performance, brand and stakeholders	Commercial outputs to deliver value for its shareholders within a regulated governance model	Profitability and growth while protecting or enhancing brand and reputation
Public sector	Structured and regulated environment that is responsive particularly to social care	Politically responsive and focused on accountability, generally within highly focused media-sensitive operations	Service delivery within budgets and political agendas

While some people may challenge these simplified characteristics, they do highlight the potential for conflict when considering any blending of capability and resources. This is not to suggest that they do not each have a commitment to the desires outcomes, but organically they have different routes and measures of success. As outlined earlier, even within the voluntary sector there may be scope for conflict when two or more organizations need to operate in close proximity. Yet when there is a crisis and the pressure is on it is sometimes difficult to distinguish who works for which charity.

PART 3: Where?

Commissioning services

When considering what might be seen as blended services, the impacts of not addressing the fundamental differences and background of each party can be a significant risk; so structured approaches to collaboration might provide the catalyst for success. The early signs of this tension come when governments or international organizations seek to harness the value and capability of the voluntary sector to deliver what may previously have been public sector services, or to collectively harness and coordinate on-the-ground support.

Mobilizing the third sector has long been (for example) a desire of the UK government, since it has vast resources and a skill base that is difficult for the public sector to support. The potential downside of this is that many organizations with an in-depth knowledge of a specific issue may not have the financial resources or backroom capability to undertake contracting services directly. The solution is to encourage partnering between industry (which has the machine) and the voluntary sector (which has the resources and skills). It is easy to see on the surface how this approach may provide a model, but it does not necessarily address the more fundamental challenge. On the one hand, government organizations are more and more focused on 'payment by results', which is a model that industry understands and has the capacity to support. The voluntary sector, on the other hand, is predominantly resourced by passionate enthusiasts who want the same results but who are not driven so much by key performance indicators and service level agreements. In a social environment their measure of success is the final outcome, irrespective of time and effort. So the traditional structure tends to lead to government contracting with industry, who in turn partner with the voluntary sector. Industry is driven by performance, timing and cost – which then drives the volunteers to meet deadlines and performance targets.

Thus the seeds of tension are easily identified. This linear model of commissioner to industry to local delivery partner has the potential to disenfranchise the front-line resources and could eventually undermine the longer-term potential. A more balanced tripartite collaborative model, based around the principles of BS 11000, could offer an alternative. In this model all three organizations form a collaborative structure that recognizes the differing drivers and objectives while creating a composite delivery model.

Voluntary organizations are passionate about doing their work but have to be realistic about contracting relationships. The most difficult part is establishing a level of trust between prime and subcontracts so that they can negotiate freely without fear of that trust being abused. There is clear benefit in establishing a common and robust collaborative model that supports the views of each party, which to some extent levels the playing field for all groups – especially smaller charities. As a national standard, the principles and structure of BS 11000 provide a neutral platform for these developments.

Knowledge sharing

In a broader context the subject of sharing knowledge is a key aspect of using the voluntary sector to enhance outcomes. As with any collaborative environment, the potential to benefit from shared knowledge is significant, yet (as within industry) the reluctance to do so is often driven by localized concerns and aspirations. For example, recently a retail do-it-yourself (DIY) chain's overtures to a major environmental charity were rejected. The development of sponsorship programmes and quest for donations is a frequent battlefield between charities, in some cases leading (one might suggest) to disenfranchising the public. However, there is the inspiring example set by McMillan, the UK cancer charity. If we consider the strides take by McMillan to not only share its knowledge but to embed its work in National Health Service (NHS) programmes, the combined drive for good cannot be ignored.

Resource optimization and supply chain rationalization

We can also look to industry to see why and where they collaborate to extend or share resources for mutual benefit, and wonder why the third sector is not harmonizing backroom support more widely for mutual benefit. 'Shared services' in the public sector has been clearly identified as a significant opportunity; however, in fairness, even here it is not always easy to develop a common understanding and level of trust. In the voluntary sector there must be ample scope to rationalize support services without impinging on their primary objectives. Taken a stage further, perhaps there is also an opportunity for industry organizations to provide services rather than simply signing donation cheques or releasing staff for a few days' good work. In a similar vein, we have already recognized the potential for supply chain optimization between partners; so why not within the third sector through economies of scale? The more focus there is on reducing overhead costs, the more funding there is for front-line activity. This can be as simple as office consumables right through to fleet management.

Conclusion

Collaboration is a powerful tool. It is not just for industry or government; it has the potential to bring value to almost any organization that needs to harness relationships. The challenge is always to have a platform on which to identify the individual drivers and build a level of trust that

PART 3: Where?

works to support mutual benefit. The primary constraint is that organizations need to open their minds and look beyond localized boundaries. The benefit of BS 11000, as for industry and government, is that best practice and a structured approach are embedded in a national standard that is available to all and provides the foundation to allow organizations of any size to create robust collaborative approaches.

Chapter 28 – Future of collaboration

> Having looked very much at today, it is worth looking ahead in this chapter to a future perspective where alternative business models will become a substantial aspect of the business community. Many people would suggest that these network models will in time become the predominant framework for business, providing a more flexible and agile approach to meet the convergence of industries in response to customer demands. At the same time the economic pressures on organizations will drive many organizations to reconsider their investment strategies in favour of collaboration in one form or another.

What becomes clear from a wide range of futurist perspectives is that the key word in future is interdependence. The spectre of the banking crisis is just one example of how integrated the world has become. The pressures within the European Union (EU) reflect the need to focus on mutually agreed solutions. The social and commercial implications of the Arab Spring showed how countries need to recognize the implications of their actions, both locally and globally. Emerging economies both draw from and impact on traditional trading models.

The world is changing, and at a faster rate than perhaps ever could have been envisaged. Globalization is no longer an aspiration; it is a fact of life. Economic pressures at all levels are challenging organizations large and small to re-evaluate their operations. Emerging nations are changing the face of economics. Communications technology has condensed the marketplace but it has still to conquer the cultural divide. The networked economy is rewriting traditional business thinking of ownership; it is creating alternative business models based on interdependent and complementary alliances. The supply chain is giving way to the concept of a more holistic value chain. Competition is growing, to reflect the demands of a more informed customer. Consumer choice is starting to influence the way organizations behave, both ethically and in terms of sustainable responsibility. In this turmoil one factor remains constant: relationships are a core ingredient for successful business.

Looking to the future, managers will work in an environment where cultural understanding (corporate as well as national), language and relationship skills will be as important as IT and technical skills are today.

Complex collaboration and management at a distance will be essential parts of daily life. But will we be prepared? The complexity and volatility creates a landscape that requires constant flexibility of approach and resource investment. Collaboration or partnering is not a solution in itself, but does offer an alternative perspective through integrated delivery networks. These networks will be locally and globally optimized by focusing on the boundaries between organizations, based on what each does best in a complementary process. To take advantage of this potential, we will need to evaluate the strengths and weaknesses of our organization's current capability, then develop a strategy to enhance skills, processes and operations. The impacts on competitiveness and reputation from a significant proportion of business process activities will be outside our direct control, which can leave even the most professional of organizations wanting. To harness this added value means challenging the traditional thinking and getting 'outside the box'. Management professionals should be looking to the future business models and developing programmes to support their organizations. Collaboration does not mean disregarding traditional values or skills, but it does require looking at today's challenges from a more collaborative viewpoint and capturing addition benefits.

The *Future Connections* research undertaken by PSL and supported in many other publications highlights the growth in alliances, partnerships, consortia and collaborative programmes. In this changing paradigm BS 11000 provides the basis to support early and robust engagement to build more sustainable relationships. It brings approaches together in a holistic manner, based on the principle that the management of each relationship is a process that can be applied to all types of business partnerships to improve effectiveness.

Each organization is unique; their level of knowledge will vary in relation to their level of development and the sector or application they are focused towards. The challenge for many organizations is that they are based on looking outwards but frequently fail to look at their internal capability. The adoption of collaborative approaches will mean integrating internal and external processes and will depend on the readiness of the organizations to embrace this integration. In many cases organizations may already be in a collaborative relationship or have identified potential partners through experience. However, the progression into a more integrated relationship changes the dynamics. In the case of organizations that are already working together, the relationship enhancement provides a comparison of the positioning of the two organizations and at multiple levels.

At the core of every relationship the objectives must be clearly defined. There will always be three sets, the joint objectives and those of each partner; successful relationships will be those where the partners recognize the need to support each other's objectives. The collaborative approach is focused on creating benefits for the organizations involved and for the customers they serve.

Collaborative relationships have shown that they can release potential value from within organizations. However, these programmes do require investment and effort outside the normal business interfaces; thus it is important that organizations have a clear view of what they consider to be the value they are looking for. Defining value will be different for each organization and may differ between partners. The important aspect is to ensure that these can be managed simultaneously and avoid conflict that may dilute the focus on the outcomes.

The foundation of a collaborative relationship is that risk and reward must be shared equitably between the partners. In developing value creation approaches the platform of risk profiling will help to stimulate innovation and balance investment. Value creation comes from a sharing of knowledge and knowledge creation programmes will usually run in parallel with driving innovation. While there may be a requirement to stimulate the process, the aim should be to build a process and ethos into the arrangement that seeks to promote a continuous focus on developing new value for the mutual benefit of the partners.

Conclusion

The aim of this book is to draw together concepts and approaches within the framework of BS 11000 to give readers a perspective and outline of the opportunities and potential applications of collaborative approaches to support their needs. It is hoped that the advice and guidance in this book will help to provide the foundation for future programmes by building confidence to expand the degree of interaction with partners and create longer-term relationships that are mutually beneficial to meet the challenges of the 21st century.

Further information

Gibbs, Richard and Andrew Humphries (2009). *Strategic Alliances and Marketing Partnerships: Gaining Competitive Advantage Through Collaboration and Partnering*, London: Kogan Page.

Hansen, Morten T. (2009). *Collaboration: How Leaders Avoid the Traps, Build Common Ground, and Reap Big Results*, MA: Harvard Business School Press.

Hawkins, David E. (2006). *Corporate Social Responsibility: Balancing Tomorrow's Sustainability and Today's Profitability*, London: Palgrave Macmillan.

Hawkins, David E. (2006). *The Bending Moment: Energizing Corporate Business Strategy*, London: Palgrave Macmillan.

Hawkins, David E. and Shan Rajegopal (2005). *Sun Tzu and the Project Battleground: Creating Project Strategy from 'The Art of War'*, London: Palgrave Macmillan.

Humphries, Andrew and Richard Gibbs (2010). *Collaborative Change: Creating High Performance Partnerships and Alliances*, SC: CreateSpace Independent Publishing Platform, Amazon.

Lank, Elisabeth (2005). *Collaborative Advantage: Organisations Win by Working Together*, London: Palgrave Macmillan.

Lipnack, Jessica and Jeffery Stamps (1997). *Virtual Teams: Reaching Across Space, Time and Organizations with Technology*, NY: John Wiley & Sons.

Partnership Sourcing. *Future Connections*.

Partnership Sourcing. *Vision 2010*.

Tate, William (2009). *The Search for Leadership: An Organisational Perspective*, Devon: Triarchy Press.

Tompkins, James A. (2003). *No Boundaries: Break Through to Supply Chain Excellence*, NC: Tompkins Press.

Index

A theory of human motivation, 2
Ability versus attitude, 6
Abraham Maslow, 2
Academic research, 3
Adam Smith, 22
Alliance partners, 3
AMEC, 26
Awareness initial parameters, 9
Babcock International case study, 17
Balfour Beatty case study, 18
Behaviours and policy, 2
Behaviours and trust, 15
Benefits and business case, 9
BP Andrew, 8
BS 11000 and the third sector, 27
BS 11000 implementation checklist, 17
BS 11000-1:2010, *Collaborative business relationships*, xii
BS 11000-2:2011, Guidance, 1
BS 5750, 2
BT Global Services case study, 23
Business continuity, 16
Business continuity and CSR, 10
Business environment, 3
Business objectives, 9
Capability and competence, 13
Clusters and cluster power, 25
Collaborative benefits, 7
Collaborative change, 21
Collaborative leadership, 6
Collaborative profile, 11
Commissioning services, 27
Commitment, 5
Communication, 5
Communications flow, 5
Communications plan, 13
Competencies and behaviours, 13
Compliance, 5
Confidence and trust, 26
Consortia/joint ventures, 3
Constituents of culture, 4
Consumers, 3
Contracting curve, 21
Contracting for failure, 24
Contracts and people, 5
Contractual boundaries, 8
Corporate culture, 4
Corporate social responsibility communications, 26
Costain Group case study, 8
CRAFT methodology, 8
CSR Corporate social responsibility, 26
Culture, 4
Culture crunch, 4
Customers, 3
Define value, 14
Defining expectations, 7
Developing clusters, 25
Developing relationships, 1
Dispute resolution, 5, 15
Distribution/retail, 3
Eco-efficiency, 26
Egan, 7
Elements of trust, 6
EMCOR case study, 20
Establishing common objectives, 12
Evaluating relationships, 1
Evidence map, 17
Exit strategy initial parameters, 16
Future Connections, 28
Future opportunities, 16
Generating innovation, 14
Glass floor, 19
Humphries A, 21
IACCM International Association for Contract and Commercial Management, 15
Identifying collaborative managers, 6
Impacts of behaviours, 5
Implementation steps, 17
Importance of trust, 5

Index

Indicators of trust, 5
Information management, 13
Initial exit strategy, 10
Institute for Collaborative Working, 1
Integration of cultures, 2
Internal assessment, 11
Internal constraints, 11
Internal influences, 4
ISO 9000, 2
John Lewis partnership, 26
Joint exit strategy, 15
Joint team management, 15
Joint risk management, 13
Joint management team, 13
Joint sponsorship, 13
Just in time, 8
Key messages for outsourcing, 20
Key messages for business development, 18
Key messages for supply chain, 19
Knowledge initial parameters, 10
Knowledge management, 4, 10
KPIs Key performance indicators, 15
KRAFT and Cadburys, 24
Kraljic model, 7
Kraljic P, 7
Latham, 7
Leadership and objectives, 2
Learning from experience, 14
Learning organization, 7
Lockheed Martin case study, 21
Management ethos, 6
Managing behaviours, 6
Manufacture, 3
MAP Maturity Assessment Programme, 12
Marketing collaboration, 18
Maslow's Hierarchy, 2
Maturity assessment, 23
McMillan cancer research, 27
Measuring trust, 5
Mergers and acquisitions, 3, 24
Michael Porter's five forces model, 4
Midas proposition, 25
MOD Case study, 19
Monitor and measure, 13
Nature of leadership, 6
NATS cast study, 19
Negotiation strategy, 12

Network Rail case study, 2
Networking in business, 25
'Outside in' theory, 20
Outsourcing, 3
Partner profile, 11
Partner selection initial parameters, 12
Partner selection process, 12
Pera Training case study, 22
Performance based collaboration, 7
Policies and processes, 11
Profit and CSR, 26
Public sector delivery, 3
Purchasing must become supply management, 7
R&D Research and Development, 3
Rachel Kessler, 24
Raytheon Systems case study, 8
Realizing the potential of GB Rail, 2
Relationship health check, 15
Relationship iceberg, 4
Relationship management engagement areas, 1
Relationship management plan, 8,9
Relationship risk, 3
Resource sharing and supply chain optimization, 27
Risk analysis, 3
Risk and integration, 3
Roger Harrison, 4
Sarbanes-Oxley, 5
Segregating relationships, 7, 9
Selex ES case study, 7
Services, 3
Sir Roy McNulty, 2
Skanska case study, 7, 26
Skills and competencies, 10
SLAs Service level agreements, 15
Social interaction, 5
SRM Supplier Relationship Management, 19
Stakeholder management, 3
Strategy development, 10
Style of leadership, 6
Supply chains, 3
Supply chain risk, 19
Sustainability impacts, 26
Technologies versus people, 22
Terminal 5 Heathrow, 3
The glass floor, 19

Index

The green agenda, 26
The intelligent customer, 18
The 'outside in' theory, 20
The value proposition, 18
The Wealth of Nations, 22
Time Warner and AOL, 24
Total cost of ownership, 6
TUPE Transfer of Undertakings, 21
Understanding your organization's character, 4
Value chain, 8
Value creation focus, 14
Value creation initial parameters, 14
Value creation model, 14
Value creation process, 14
Value of trust, 5
Virtual organizations, 22, 25
Vision 2010, 2
Voluntary sector, 3
WIIFM – What's in it for me, 18
Working together initial parameters, 13

If you found this book of interest, you may also want to consider:

Complaints Management
Turning negatives into positives
By Michael Hill

Complaints Management: Turning negatives into positives has been designed to help any company or organization improve the effectiveness of its customer complaint processes and systems. It adheres to the principles of the complaint management standard *BS ISO 10002:2004, Quality management – Customer satisfaction – Guidelines for complaints handling in organizations.*

The book draws on case studies from a variety of sectors, such as financial services, healthcare, not-for-profit, utilities, and the travel industry to present the reader with opportunities to reflect on good practice while realizing the underlying benefits of the standard.

The book includes quotes and statistics that can support an internal business case, as well as practical checklists for handling complaints, analysing root causes, and conducting system reviews.

The book also references the benefits that can be delivered from external dispute resolution schemes and how *BS ISO 10003:2007, Quality management – Customer satisfaction – Guidelines for dispute resolution external to organizations* delivers a standard for improving the effectiveness of such schemes.

The book is intended as a reference for anyone (individual, company or organization) considering a review of complaint management processes or seeking accreditation to BS ISO 10002:2004. Thus, it will be of interest to professionals in customer service related industries, regulators, ombudsman and adjudicators.

Also available with standards BS ISO 10002:2004 Quality management. Customer satisfaction. Guidelines for complaints handling in organizations. Guidelines for complaints handling in organizations and BS ISO 10003:2007 Quality management. Customer satisfaction. Guidelines for dispute resolution external to organizations (see below).

Price £40.00 (without standards) or £160 (with standards, member price)
£288 (with standards, non-member)
ISBN 978 0 580 71876 2 (without standards) / 978 0 580 76553 7 (with standards)

For further more details see http://shop.bsigroup.com/bip2211